D1880840

FOREIGN EXCHANGE MANAGEMENT AND AIR TICKETING

FOREIGN EXCHANGE MANAGEMENT AND AIR TICKETING

Editor

L.K. Singh

ISHA

ISHA BOOKS

DELHI - 110033

Foreign Exchange Managemnt and Air Ticketing

©L.K. Singh

ISBN: 81-8205-474-5

All rights reserved. No part of this book may be reproduced in any manner without written permission

Published in 2008 in India by
ISHA Books
B-63, 1st Floor, New Gupta Colony,
Near DDA Market,
Delhi-110009
Phone: 9212142040
ishabooks@hotmail.com

Laser Type Setting by: Global e-Text, Delhi
Printed at: Vishal Kaushik Printer, Delhi

Preface

With technological advancements leaving no sphere of life untouched, and due to the changes they have brought about, the globe has economically become a small village with some sort of balance to be stricken. This new wave has paved the way for the advent of foreign exchange management, a mechanism for maintaining the necessary balance.

The subject of the book is management of foreign exchange and it covers a wide range of areas (with specific reference to Indian context) including forex management for enterprises, foreign exchange reserves of India, forex risk management strategies, FDI in tourism industry, performance of tourism firms, principles of tourism marketing, tourism destinations and tour packages, travel bookings using the Internet, and tourism economics and demand for tourism patterns etc.

The book also has chapters dedicated to studying the laws governing foreign exchange and exchange management in India, the examples of which being Foreign Exchange Regulation Act, 1973 and Foreign Exchange Management Act, 1999.

In spite of the care taken during writing, *Foreign Exchange Management and Air Ticketing* does not pretend to be a perfect book without any mistake. The publisher in fact acknowledges the room for further improvement and any suggestion for improvement is invited from the readers.

Editor

Contents

1

Forex Management for Enterprise

Management Reporting

Bring a part of the control framework it is important to take care on the details of management reporting requirements for reporting the performance of the foreign exchange activities of an enterprise.

The following points are required to be considered:

- Frequency of reporting;
- Recipient(s) of report;
- Content of reporting submission;
- Position reports showing hedging in place at period end and mark to market value;
- Forecasts of net exposure and hedges outstanding;
- Forecasts of future exchange rate movement;
- Proposed hedging strategy for approval;
- Scenario analysis;
- Statement of compliance with control procedures.

Forecasting and Quantifying FX Currency Risk

Forecasting of FX

Among the persons who are not specializing in FX dealing, the usual mean of forecasting/understanding the trend of exchange rate is reading the various sources of research reports from bankers, FX specialists and specialized FX magazines. For others, who are more technical in nature are using economic model such as purchasing power parity to look at the long term trend. Another mean is the use of technical analysis namely using charting to forecast FX trend.

Quantifying FX currency risk

In order to ascertain our currency exposure, we deploy the use of projected balance sheet for translation exposure (only with non working capital items) and multiple operating cash flow forecast denominated in foreign currencies for transaction exposure: the value, currencies, timing of these flows to be assessed. Therefore, on the basis of the aforementioned exchange forecasts to compute the value at risk we may develop different new strategic analyses. Moreover, usually we also asses the quantity of FX currency risk based on the effect of 1% or 1 cent movement.

Operation/Management policy and procedures

There is a need for observation to the risk exposures and in fact if the FX exposure is not taken carefully it may leads undesirable financial impact. The following append show a simple checklist of what might be included as the FX Operation/ Management Policy and Procedures, which the reader can expand upon:

Currency exposure:

- We need to define the various FX exposures that the company might be confronted with like translation, transaction and economic exposure;

Methodologies to forecast currency exposure:

- might include projected balance sheet for non working item and multiple operating cash flow forecast denominated in foreign currencies;

Quantification of Currency Risk:

- Might include scenario analysis based on exchange rate forecasts,effect of 1%/1cent movement and the value at risk;

Policy framework:

- Put the statement of the group's attitude towards risk and its risk management objectives namely;
- size and nature of currency risks faced by the group;
- ability to change prices in response to fluctuating exchange rate;
- other uncontrollable non-financial risks that may be high risk averse with regard to currency exposure;

- approach taken by direct competitors.

Description of the role of treasury whether as:

- a cost centre;
- profit centre;
- value added service centre.

Explanation of how currency exposures are identified and reported:

- specify responsibility – who to forecast and who to receive reports, etc;
- the frequency of forecasting;
- time horizon and reporting periods;
- type of exposure to be forecasted;
- standard reporting format.

Description of how exposure are to be managed:

- whether subsidiaries are free to deal directly with banks, or through group treasury, or a mixture of both approaches;
- set up authorities limits and process to all hedging to be implemented;
- need to be an agreed rules for the time period in which hedges must be executed;
- need to stipulate that deals over a certain size must be quoted competitively by at least two or more banks;
- process to be followed for selecting banks that are asked to quote;
- key control processes such as segregation of duties, two ways confirmation, matching of transaction details are in place.

Specific policies as to levels of cover that must be taken and the use of particular hedging instruments:

- Specify minimum and maximum levels of cover that must be taken in respect of given categories of exposure.

Control over counterparty risk:

- Monetary limit to be applied to the maximum exposure to each counterparty;

- Procedures for monitoring compliance with the limits.

Details of management reporting requirement:

- Frequency of reporting;
- Recipients of report;
- Content of reporting submission such as position reports showing hedges in place at period end and mark to market value, forecasts of net exposure and hedges outstanding, forecasts of future exchange rate movements, proposed hedging strategy for approval, scenario analysis and statement of compliance with control procedures, etc.

The policy statement should comprise among others, the role of the Board of Directors, treasury, cash management, cash investment, borrowing, interest rate risk management risk management and foreign exchange exposure management.

Include the organisational framework

Includes the methods of Internal hedging.

Includes the type of FX hedging instrument like for example:

- FX forward contracts;
- FX future;
- Currency options;
- Option-based derivative contracts;
- Others

Includes the hedging strategy like for example:

- Type of exposure;
- Size of exposure;
- Stability of the currencies;
- Maturity period of the exposures;
- Ability to forecast exposures;
- Access to hedging instruments;
- Attitude of shareholders.

Describe the dealing procedures.

Include the Control framework which should have the following:

- Statement of treasury objectives and policies;

- Procedural manual;
- Key control mechanism like dealing mandate, counterparties limit, confirmation and reconciliation, segregation of duties and management reporting;
- Source of advice;
- Disclosure statement;
- Ethical issues.

Might include a section on performance management which includes:

- Identification of the purpose of performance management;
- At what level should measurement take place;
- What activities should be measured (transaction/translation exposure or control compliances);
- What benchmarks are appropriate;
- Is the performance measurement based quantitative re: absolute/relative terms or qualitative like accuracy of exposure forecasting, efficiency of deal execution and others.

Hedging strategy

Prior to embark on these strategies, we should have a clear idea of the following:

- The type of exposure are we exposed to;
- Size of the exposure;
- Stability of the currencies;
- Maturity period of the exposure;
- Ability to forecast exposure;
- Attitude of shareholders;
- Access to hedging instruments (Forward, FX future, currency options, option-based derivative contracts, sway and others).

Internal hedging methods

The internal hedging methods are the techniques which arises from the company. It is an integral part of company's regulatory treasury to prevent an exposed position arising in the first place. There are at least four internal hedging methods.

(1) Leading and Lagging Method,

(2) Matching Method,

(3) Netting Method,

(4) Inter-Company Foreign Exchange Contracts.

(1) *Leading and Lagging Method* : It is time adjustment process for imports and exports in order to reduce an exposure period or match a particular currency profile and to take advantage of an expected currency depreciation or appreciation. The achievements of this approach depends:

- on your relationship with your suppliers and buyers and
- the currency's strength or weakness.

Hence, leading and lagging is usually applied to intercom any transactions as there would be no conflict with third party suppliers or buyers. Relationship with Suppliers and Buyers: Relationship with the suppliers must be exceptionally good so as to be willing to grant you the extra credit period and if your company regularly leads payment because the import currency is appreciating, you should negotiate for discount for prompt payment. Interest costs incurred may be charged by one subsidiary to another where lagging has caused additional charges. Therefore, there is some costs incurred for these concessions. For this reason, such an approach is usually restricted to arrangements within the company itself. Not only these cost, there is also the administrative costs of monitoring the situation.

In case of we have involvement with third parties, they may agree to provide additional credit facilities or to clear the account more rapidly if the purchase price is allowed to reflect their additional interest and administration costs. The currency's weakness or strength also determines whether you should lead or lag. If the paying or receiving currency are equally weak or strong, there is no advantage in leading or lagging from a currency exposure viewpoint.

The advantages are as follows:

(a) facilitates the use of netting and matching systems,

(b) inexpensive in terms of running costs,

(c) this is a better method of managing group liquidity rather than using intercompany loan,

(d) it allows fine tuning for group tax management. It's allow a company to use leading and lagging to take advantage of different tax rates in different countries.

(2) *Matching Method* : The matching method deals with the intention to compensate all the foreign currency of the company to payable with the Here the intention is to offset all the company's foreign currency payables with the suitable foreign currency receivables. The net amount is then hedged. The matching method depends on a reliable cash-flow reporting systems by individual currency. In fact centralized matching requires high sophisticated on-line cash flow tracking abilities for each currency. Matching method is conducive to many international-trading organizations, as there have a lot of international trade hence the greater are the matching possibilities.

The advantages of matching are:

- Only unmatched values are hedged, hence currency flows are reduced,
- Reduced of banking charges and elimination of exchange spreads on the netted amount
- Where matching is centralized, co-ordination of the group's exposure allows greater management control including tax planning.

(3) *Netting Method* : This method is more or less analogous with the Matching Method. The only difference is that matching includes the cash flows of third parties whilst netting involves strictly the cash flows of the subsidiaries of the group. Here, the subsidiaries net their foreign currency assets and liabilities arising out of transactions with each other.

Bilateral netting which involves just two subsidiaries and for multilateral netting, it is between several subsidiaries. As multilateral netting is quite complex, it is coordinated by an internal clearing center. In this typical payment-netting program, the clearing center shall institute a pre-arranged timetable where the center will advise each subsidiaries of the net amount to pay or to receive. Often a netting system is integrated with an inter-company short-term financing system. Here, amounts owing to the netting centre by subsidiaries are transferred, say monthly to a group funding account and monitor ed accordingly. The objective of netting is to reduce the size of the exposure and hedge only the netted amount.

The netting will in reality reduce FX transactions and also reduce the float. The success of netting depends heavily on the cooperation of the participating subsidiaries. Netting is only feasible when there is a high volume of inter-company cross-border trade.

The advantages of netting are:

- Netting reduces the amount exposed to foreign currency exposure,
- Banking transfer charges are reduced. Market spreads on the part of the netted transactions are eliminated,
- Central co-ordination of the group's exposure allows greater management control, including tax planning possibilities.

(4) *Inter-Company Foreign Exchange Contracts* : It deals with the forward contracts developed between two within group companies where one company agrees to buy or sell currency to the other at a specified future date at a specified rate of exchange.

The method of working is as follows:

- Where a holding company wishes to centralize FX exposure, so it offers its subsidiaries a forward contract. This has the effect of transferring exposure to the centre and covering the subsidiary's transaction. This produces an internal hedge for the subsidiary but an open position for the parent company to hedge externally.

The advantages are as follows:

- It allows a better managed central control of exposed exchange positions,
- Local management are relieved of the burden of covering exposed positions by passing the decision to the centre who can either leave the position open or cover it on the foreign exchange market,
- If there is a clearing centre, it might act as a profit centre as it has more flexibility in negotiating the deal separately unlike those of the netting or matching series of transactions.

Forex Money Management

When putting two inexperienced personnel traders in the field, it may provide with the best high-probability set-up, and for good assessment, have each one take the opposite side of the trade. More than likely, both will wind up losing money. However, if you take two pros and have them trade in the opposite direction of each other, quite frequently both traders will wind up making money-despite the seeming contradiction of the premise. What's the difference? What is the most important factor separating the seasoned traders from the amateurs?

The answer is money management. Like dieting and working out, money management is something that most traders pay lip service to, but few practice in real life. The reason is simple: just like eating healthy and staying fit, money management can seem like a burdensome, unpleasant activity. It forces traders to constantly monitor their positions and to take necessary losses, and few people like to do that. However, as the following table shows that the loss-taking is crucial to long-term trading success.

The Big one

Majority of the traders though are familiar with the information of the above table, they tends to be ignored. Trading books are littered with stories of traders losing one, two, even five years' worth of profits in a single trade gone terribly wrong. Typically, the runaway loss is a result of sloppy money management, with no hard stops and lots of average downs into the longs and average ups into the shorts. Above all, the runaway loss is due simply to a loss of discipline.

Many traders start their trading career, either consciously or subconsciously, visualizing "The Big One" - the one trade that will make them millions and allow them to retire young and live carefree for the rest of their lives. In FX, this fantasy is further reinforced by the folklore of the markets. Who can forget the time that George Soros "broke the Bank of England" by shorting the pound and walked away with a cool $1-billion profit in a single day? But the cold hard truth for most retail traders is that, instead of experiencing the "Big Win", most traders fall victim to just one "Big Loss" that can knock them out of the game forever.

Learning tough lessons

Through discontinuing their losses traders can avoid the fate by controlling their risk. In Jack Schwager's famous book "Market Wizards" (1989), day trader and trend follower Larry Hite offers this practical advice: "Never risk more than 1% of total equity on any trade. By only risking 1%, I am indifferent to any individual trade." This is a very good approach. A trader may meets many problems as much as 20 times in a row and still have 80% of his or her equity left.

The reality is that very few traders have the discipline to practice this method consistently. Not unlike a child who learns not to touch a hot stove only after being burned once or twice, most traders can only absorb the lessons of risk discipline through the harsh experience of monetary loss. This is the most important reason why traders should use only their speculative capital when first entering the forex market. When novices ask how much money they should begin trading with, one seasoned trader says: "Choose a number that will not materially impact your life if you were to lose it completely. Now subdivide that number by five because your first few attempts at trading will most likely end up in blow out." This too is very sage advice, and it is well worth following for anyone considering trading FX.

Money Management Styles

Usually, there are two ways to practice successful money management. A trader can take many frequent small stops and try to harvest profits from the few large winning trades, or a trader can choose to go for many small squirrel-like gains and take infrequent but large stops in the hope the many small profits will outweigh the few large losses. The first method generates many minor instances of psychological pain, but it produces a few major moments of ecstasy. On the other hand, the second strategy offers many minor instances of joy, but at the expense of experiencing a few very nasty psychological hits. With this wide-stop approach, it is not unusual to lose a week or even a month's worth of profits in one or two trades.

Extensively, the methodology you select shows your personality. It is an unavoidable part in the course of discovery for each trader. One of the great benefits of the FX market is that it can accommodate both styles equally, without any additional cost to the retail trader. Since FX is a spread-based market, the cost of each transaction is the same, regardless of the size of any given trader's position.

For instance, in EUR/USD, majority of the traders would encounter a 3 pip spread equal to the cost of 3/100th of 1% of the underlying position. This cost will be uniform, in percentage terms, whether the trader wants to deal in 100-unit lots or one million-unit lots of the currency. For example, if the trader wanted to use 10,000-unit lots, the spread would amount to $3, but for the same trade using only 100-unit lots, the spread would be a mere $0.03. Contrast that with the stock market where, for example, a commission on 100 shares or 1,000 shares of a $20 stock may be fixed at $40, making the effective cost of transaction 2% in the case of 100 shares, but only 0.2% in the case of 1,000 shares. This type of variability makes it very hard for smaller traders in the equity market to scale into positions, as commissions heavily skew costs against them. Yet, FX traders have the benefit of uniform pricing and can practice any style of money management they choose without concern about variable transaction costs.

Four types of stops

Once you are ready to trade with a serious approach to money management and the proper amount of capital is allocated to your account, there are four types of stops you may consider.

(1) Equity Stop: It is the simplest term of the discontinuation. A trader usually meets problems to only a predetermined amount of his or her account on a single trade. A common metric is to risk 2% of the account on any given trade. On a hypothetical $10,000 trading account, a trader could risk $200, or about 200 points, on one mini lot (10,000 units) of EUR/USD, or only 20 points on a standard 100,000-unit lot. Aggressive traders may consider using 5% equity stops, but note that this amount is generally considered to be the upper limit of prudent money management because 10 consecutive wrong trades would draw down the account by 50%. An important criticism of the equity stop is the placing of arbitrary exit point on a trader's position. The trade is liquidated not as a result of a logical response to the price action of the marketplace, but rather to satisfy the trader's internal risk controls.

(2) Chart Stop: Technical analyses can produce thousands of feasible stops, influenced by the price action of the charts or by many technical indicator signals. Technically oriented traders like to combine these exit points with standard equity stop rules to formulate charts stops. A classic example of a chart stop is the swing high/low point.

(3) Volatility Stop: In the setting of the risk parameters, a more advanced version of the chart stop applies volatility in lieu of price action. The idea is that in a high volatility environment,

when prices traverse wide ranges, the trader needs to adapt to the present conditions and allow the position more room for risk to avoid being stopped out by intra-market noise. The opposite holds true for a low volatility environment, in which risk parameters would need to be compressed. An easy way to assess volatility is the use of Bollinger bands, which employ standard deviation to measure variance in price. In the volatility stop also allows the trader to use a scale-in approach to achieve a better "blended" price and a faster breakeven point. Note that the total risk exposure of the position should not exceed 2% of the account; therefore, it is critical that the trader use smaller lots to properly size his or her cumulative risk in the trade.

(4) Margin Stop: This method is considered to be the most independent of all money management strategies, but it can be an effective method in FX, if used judiciously. Unlike exchange-based markets, FX markets operate 24 hours a day. Therefore, FX dealers can liquidate their customer positions almost as soon as they trigger a margin call. For this reason, FX customers are rarely in danger of generating a negative balance in their account, since computers automatically close out all positions.

This kind of management of the money needs the trader to distribute his or her capital into 10 parts. In our original $10,000 example, the trader would open the account with an FX dealer but only wire $1,000 instead of $10,000, leaving the other $9,000 in his or her bank account. Most FX dealers offer 100:1 leverage, so a $1,000 deposit would allow the trader to control one standard 100,000-unit lot. However, even a 1 point move against the trader would trigger a margin call (since $1,000 is the minimum that the dealer requires). So, depending on the trader's risk tolerance, he or she may choose to trade a 50,000-unit lot position, which allows him or her room for almost 100 points (on a 50,000 lot the dealer requires $500 margin, so $1,000 – 100-point loss* 50,000 lot = $500).

Despite the consequences of how much leverage the trader assumed, this controlled parsing of his or her speculative capital would prevent the trader from blowing up his or her account in just one trade and would allow him or her to take many swings at a potentially profitable set-up without the worry or care of setting manual stops. It may be quite interesting the approach to the traders who like to practice the "have a bunch, bet a bunch" style. It is apparent that, money management in FX is as flexible and as varied as the market itself. The only universal rule is that all traders in this market must practice some form of it in order to succeed. It is not an easy to task to manage money where it shows difference between winners and losers. It was proved that if 100 traders start trading using a system with 60% winning odds, only 5 traders will be in profit at the end of the year.

In spite of the 60% winning odds 95% of traders will lose because of their poor money management. Money management is the most significant part of any trading system. Majority of the traders do not know the significance of it. It is necessary to know the idea of money management and understand the difference between it and trading decisions. Money management represents the amount of money you are going to put on one trade and the risk your going to accept for this trade. Various strategies of money management are there. They all aim at preserving your balance from high risk exposure. Firstly, you should understand the following term - Core equity

Core equity = Starting balance - Amount in open positions.

If you have a balance of 10,000$ and you enter a trade with 1,000$ then your core equity is 9,000$. If you enter another 1,000$ trade, your core equity will be 8,000$.

Because of your money management depend on this equity it is necessary to understand what's meant by core equity. We will explain here one model of money management that has proved high annual return and limited risk. The standard account that we will be discussing is 100,000$ accounts with 20:1 leverage. Anyway, you can adapt this strategy to fit smaller or bigger trading accounts.

Money Management Strategy

Your risk per a trade should never exceed 3% per trade. It's better to adjust your risk to 1% or 2%. We prefer a risk of 1% but if you are confident in your trading system then you can lever your risk up to 3%. 1% risk of a 100,000$ account = 1,000$

You should adjust your stop loss so that you never lose more than 1,000$ per a single trade. If you are a short term trader and you place your stop loss 50 pips below/above your entry point.

50 pips = 1,000$

1 pips = 20$

The size of your trade should be adjusted so that you risk 20$/pip. With 20:1 leverage, your trade size will be 200,000$.

If the trade is stopped, you will lose 1,000$ which is 1% of your balance.

This trade will require 10,000$ = 10% of your balance.

If you are a long term trader and you place your stop loss 200 pips below/above your entry point.

200 pips = 1,000$

1 pip = 5$

The size of your trade should be adjusted so that you risk 5$/pip. With 20:1 leverage, your trade size will be 50,000$. If the trade is stopped, you will lose 1,000$ which is 1% of your balance. This trade will require 2,500$ = 2.5% of your balance. It is just an illustration. Your trading balance and leverage provided by your broker may differ from this formula. The most important is to stick to the 1% risk rule. Never risk too much in one trade. It's a fatal mistake when a trader lose 2 or 3 trades in a row, then he will be confident that his next trade will be winning and he may add more money to this trade. This is how you can blow up your account in a short time. A disciplined trader should never let his emotions and greed control his decisions.

Diversification

Trading one currency pair will generate few entry signals. It would be better to diversify your trades between several currencies. If you have 100,000$ balance and you have open position with 10,000$ then your core equity is 90,000$. If you want to enter a second position then you should calculate 1% risk of your core equity not of your starting balance. It means that the second trade risk should never be more than 900$. If you want to enter a 3rd position and your core equity is 80,000$ then the risk per 3rd trade should not exceed 800$. It's important that you diversify your orders between currencies that have low correlation. For instance, If you have long EUR/USD then you should not long GBP/USD since they have high correlation.

If you have long EUR/USD and GBP/USD positions and risking 3% per trade then your risk is 6% since the trades will tend to end in same direction. In case of you prefer trading in both EUR/USD and GBP/USD and your standard position size from your money management is 10,000$ (1% risk rule) then you can trade 5,000$ EUR/USD and 5,000$ GBP/USD. In this way, you will be risking 0.5% on each position.

The Martingale and anti-martingale strategy

Both the strategies are very important to understand. Martingale rule = increasing your risk when losing. This is a strategy adopted by gamblers which claims that you should increase the size of you trades when losing. It's applied in gambling in the following way. Bet 10$, if you lose bet 20$, if you lose bet 40$, if you lose bet 80$ etc.

This strategy assumes that after 4 or 5 losing trades, your chance to win is bigger so you should add more money to recover your loss. The truth is that the odds are same in spite of your previous loss. If you have 5 losses in a row, still your odds for 6th bet 50:50. Some novice traders can make the same fatal mistake. For example, if a trader started with a balance of 10,000$ and after 4 losing trades (each is 1,000$) his balance is 6000$. The trader will think that he has higher chances of winning the 5th trade then he will increase the size of his position 4 times to recover his loss. If he loses, his balance will be 2,000$. He will never recover from 2,000$ to his starting balance 10,000$. A disciplined trader should never use such gambling method unless he wants to lose his money in a short time.

Anti-martingale rule = increase your risk when winning & decrease your risk when losing

It means that the trader should adjust the size of his positions according to his new gains or losses. Example: Trader A starts with a balance of 10,000$. His standard trade size is 1,000$. After 6 months, his balance is 15,000$. He should adjust his trade size to 1,500$. Trader B starts with 10,000$. His standard trade size is 1,000$. After 6 months his balance is 8,000$. He should adjust his trade size to 800$.

High return strategy

It is the strategy adopted by the traders who are looking for higher return and still preserving their starting balance. Based on the management systems, you should be risking 1% of your balance. If you start with 10,000$ and your trade size is 1,000$ (Risk 1%). After 1 year, your balance is 15,000$. Now you have your initial balance + 5,000$ profit. You can increase your potential profit by risking more from this profit while restricting your initial balance risk to 1%. For example, you can calculate your trade in the following pattern:

1% risk 10,000$ (initial balance)+ 5% of 5,000$ (profit)

In this way, you will have more potential for higher returns and on the same time you are still risking 1% of your initial deposit.

Money Management Principles

Trade with sufficient capital

Attempting to trade without sufficient capital is one of the most difficult mistakes that Forex traders create. The trader with limited capital not only will be a worried trader, always looking to minimize losses beyond the point of realistic trading, but he will also frequently be taken out of the trading game before he can realize any sense of success trading the method(s) or patterns.

Exercise discipline

Discipline is often used in Forex trading education. However, despite the cliché, discipline continues to be the most important behaviour one can master to become a profitable trader. Discipline is the ability to plan your work and work your plan. It's the ability to give your trade the time to develop without hastily taking yourself out of the market simply because you are uncomfortable with risk. Discipline is also the ability to continue to trade the methods and patterns even after you've suffered losses. It should be done the best one in order to achieve the best results of discipline required to be a world-class trader.

Forex Risk Manager

Majority of the people do not know the differences of professional money managers from individual efforts to speculate. Most expert agree that the key is market selection and uncorrelated portfolio management. In addition of spreading your risk and bets around adding to winners properly is also a lost art and misunderstood by 90-percent of individual speculators. We try to break the barrier with this product and also try to educate individual traders the often their limitation is not only in monetary terms but with proper methodology and mindset. Turbo Turtle, our proprietary risk management for FOREX market is based on a Percentage Volatility Model (PVM), being a variant of a standard deviation mathematical model. Volatility as a central dispersion measurement of the mean is used in many mathematical models and it is crucial to analyze the dispersion on any time series.

In the present context one of the very important to take into account when trading is to maintain stop orders adequately and find out appropriate entry and exit levels. Since supply and demand drives markets in general, it is our commitment to discover the true volatility of the market once a trend has been defined. Turbo Turtle™ utilizes algorithms to assess that volatility. With this procedure, certain trades are either denied or accepted based on a percentage in relationship to risk/reward parameters which are set in advance.

Stop

The stop level will show on the right hand side of the software panel. While it is calculated to 10-levels we typically only use the first three. Moves in Forex are large but seldom warrant 10-levels of pyramiding.

Money management

It is the target of the price for the position. The third level, it is optional if you use it or not.

Level

The level column provided for the entry of the price, i.e. the rate the currency pairs were bought or sold. The other side of the panel has three levels of Price Targets and Stops pre-calculated. The Target prices can be entered in your Forex software at the first purchase time. Notice - We recommend profit targets on the first two positions and no target on the last one.

The profit targets will limit your overall return but also lessen the drawdown for this system. Use or don't use this feature depending on your temperament and financial situation. This is the Forex software your broker provides you. (We can make suggestions of flexible software and reliable brokers.) We do not influence you what Forex broker to use. Nor we religiously tell you the buy and sell signals. We have a trend research facility and systems in place for our coaching clients.

It may also be made into available to you and/or help you devising a system on which you would base your buy and sell recommendation. Some Forex brokers use sophisticated charting packages some use Java applets only and hence will be very limited in the area or studies and charting. We do not think money management is the Holy Grail and without an edge your trading will suffer in terms of negative returns, draw downs or infrequent trades. However, the best system using no money and position management will also suffer and a good system can become a loser if you take on too much risk relative to your account and/or pyramid incorrectly.

System using method

On the software panel the first three lines are important to be noted. The first and second "Price Target" (Money Management) boxes are to be filled in as limit orders upon getting the first signal. We suggest using price targets on the first two levels. The levels are add on trades and they can also be entered into most Forex platforms as contingent orders (this is our way of pyramiding when the order is working out) Notice that some trades are not to be taken and this will depend on the currencies rate and risk per your current account size. In case of the trade signal has a risk level of larger than 2.19 you should be well advised to avoid that trade and look for a next one. This box is on the left side of the panel under the name "Percent/Risk". The ATR (Average True Range) for the day is available from most Forex platforms please consult your platform's recommendation on how to get the ATR level. You can also ask us about the platform we suggest and if you are a consulting client with Turbo Turtle. The GL/E is the 'gatekeeper' so you will not trade over the 2 percent risk. This field depends on the account size.

Important tip

In order to meet successful, it is necessary to adjust the risked percentages. In times of high volatility this percentage should be raised and in times of low volatility it should be lowered. Volatility should be distinct to currency pairs. This software however will only take the input you have already determined. If volatility reaches a certain point cease trading. It is recommended that if ATR doubles from one day to next the market is not tradable as whipsaw potential is more than normal.

Non-correlated positions in a portfolio

Many new traders and even experts cannot understand the portfolio correlation issue; of course many do not have adequate funds to even think about a portfolio. The godsend of Forex trading is the flexibility of position size and automatic unit calculation (pip). This enables the small trader to effectively trade like a hedge fund and hence create an advantage for his/hers trading strategy. As a special purchaser of Turbo Turtle Forex CD Course you can e-mail us with any questions and problems. We want to teach you and help. The system's power stems from the fact that currencies do trend and if caught a decent move you will make money. You can take small 2 percent losses if you pyramid to three levels and your last position has no pre-calculated target. Another important issue is to spread your risk wisely. Our correlation tables are proprietary and time tested. This alone is worth the price of the software. Trading tips for Forex In order to become a successful trader, you must have sufficient risk capital- the loss of some or all of which wills neither completely ruin your morale nor adversely affect your lifestyle in any way.

In the event of loss, you must be able to handle such an ordeal calmly. Your mind should be on the market, not on your finances. In order to make the proper trading decisions, you must remain calm and concentrate on the task of trading. You should never use the last remains of your finances for trading- the responsibility and the pressure would be too great, and your mind would stray towards your finances, and not towards the market situation, thus greatly increasing the possibility of mistakes.

One should not rush in the opening of a real account after only a few days of practice. Practice for as much time as is necessary for you to feel confident on your own. Don't compare yourself to other traders- just because it took someone a certain amount of time to become proficient, doesn't mean you won't need more time. Your primary goal when practicing is to develop an individual trading style or technique such that, at the very least, your next week's trade earnings are not less than the current week's, and that your monthly earnings should increase with each successive month.

After achieving these results, an account may be opened. It is mandatory to follow the rules and regulations of the market. Cut your losses as soon as possible, and hold your winning positions open as long as possible. Furthermore, do not, under any circumstances, allow loss to occur in a position which has been making profit. It is better to close it altogether without profit if the market suddenly turns in the opposite direction, rather than to allow a profit to turn into loss. That would not be smart. New traders are not recommended to trade on Sunday nights, New York EST time, because this is actually Monday morning for Asian markets, and the behaviour of currencies at this time is the least predictable.

Trading at the morning of favourably on Friday is also recommended. Generally on Friday the market brought into changes from the trend which it sets during the week, and for the novice, this may come as an unpleasant surprise. Also, on Friday, more often than not, the market has a tendency to sell off American dollars, especially when the US economy is in an uncertain situation. Try to begin trading at the same time each day. The behavior of currencies differs at different times of the day, and by concentrating on a certain time each day, you may come to understand the characteristic behaviors of currencies at this time. Begin your day by researching events, which occurred on the market while you were away from trading. Because of this, our site has a great feature, which will help: "Market News". If you get familiar with the events of the market, look at the graphs to study the movement of the currencies, starting with "tick" charts and ending with daily charts, and select a tactic which you will use for this particular day. As rewarding as self-study may be, a more thorough and proper understanding of the market might be achieved through a formal education such as the one which our One on One Coaching provides, in both classroom and correspondence formats. In any case, were commended that you trade on your demo account daily, and research charts. Profit comes to those who try. It is not difficult to learn trade on this market as learning the stock market, but it is a gradual process.

With the courage of patience and efficient approach will bring you financial developments. Mistakes and losses are an unavoidable part of trading in any market. The sooner you learn to accept losses as inevitable, the sooner you will begin to earn. You should not blame yourself, others, or the market for your losses. Your losses are in no way related to your reasoning abilities. Your task is to calmly analyze your mistakes and to not repeat them in future trades. You should not jump for joy after winning $800, nor beat your head against the wall after losing $200. The less emotions form a part of your trading, your ability to see the true market situation and to make the right decision will improve. It is vital to develop a cold-hearted lack of emotion, and to treat winnings and losses as just numbers- not money. Understand that traders don't learn from their winnings- they learn from their losses. When every loss is perceived as one step towards your next winning trade- you are on the right track. Keep a diary in which you describe the conditions that led you to make the trading decisions that you did.

It is necessary to note down the influencing events in the trend of marketing in order to open or close a position. After every trade, write down and analyze the results in your diary. If you made a profit, it is important that you understand and remember your flow of thinking, which led you to the right decision. Market events happen often and new news may replace old news, so you will eventually forget what happened unless you keep track of it yourself. It is even more important to understand why you lost.

There are really not that many mistakes those amateur traders commit, and if you can understand them all, you can learn not to repeat them. Read the opinions of others, but base your trading decisions on your own analysis of, and feel for the market, which you will eventually acquire. If your prediction matches someone else's - good. If not, that's not a problem either. However, if upon seeing a disparity, you start doubting your analysis, it would be best not to make the trade on your real account- only on the demo. If you are confident yourself in your decision, go ahead and do it one of the predictions will be correct. If your prediction is not the correct one, find the fault in your analysis Remember that if your account contains less than $3000, you should not trade using more than one lot. If you are in the $3000-$5000 range, never trade more than two lots and that if and only if it looks safe in the current market situation. If you have $10,000 in your account you may trade two lots, but never more than three.

References

1. Deloitte Touche, Profiting from opportunities.
2. Government Actuary's Department, Population projections
3. Department for Social Security Households on Below Average Incomes, A statistical Analysis 1976 - 96.
4. Blythe, Ronald. An Inherited Perspective: Landscape and the Indigenous Eye. In Hallberg Paul (ed.). *The Feeling for Nature and the Landscape of Man* (pp. 12-25). Gothenburg: Kungl. Vetenskaps- & Vitterhets-Samhallet, 1980.
5. The Influence of Landscape and Architecture on the Composition of *Vathek*; Fothergill, Brian. In Graham Kenneth W. (ed.). *Vathek and the Escape from Time: Bicentenary Revaluations* (pp. 33-47). New York: AMS, 1990.
6. "TTRA Annual Conference Focuses on Rural Tourism Development Issues," Weaver, Glenn. 1991, *Rural Development News*, Vol. 15, No. 1: pp. 8-9.
7. "Developing a Rural Tourism Plan: The Major Publications," *Economic Development Review*, Wilkerson, Mary L. 1996. Vol. 14, No. 2: p. 79.
8. "The Rural Mystique and Tourism Development: Data from Pennsylvania," Willits, Fern K. 1993. *Journal of the Community Development Society*, Vol. 24, No. 2: pp. 159-174.

2

India's Foreign Exchange Reserves - Policy, Status and Issues

Forex Reserves

Theoretically, the proper definition of Forex reserves is not found as there have been divergence of views in terms of coverage of items, ownership of assets, liquidity aspects and need for a distinction between owned and non-owned reserves Nevertheless, for policy and operational purposes, most countries have adopted the definition suggested by the International Monetary Fund; which defines reserves as external assets that are readily available to and controlled by monetary authorities for direct financing of external payments imbalances, for indirectly regulating the magnitudes of such imbalances through intervention in exchange markets to affect the currency exchange rate, and/or for other purposes.

The sophisticated approach for assessing measurement international reserves takes into account the unencumbered international reserve assets of the monetary authority; however, the foreign currency and the securities held by the public including the banks and corporate bodies are not accounted for in the definition of official holdings of international reserves. In India, the Reserve Bank of India Act 1934 contains the enabling provisions for the RBI to act as the custodian of foreign reserves, and manage reserves with defined objectives.

The powers of being the custodian of foreign reserves are enshrined, in the first instance, in the preamble of the Act. The 'reserves' refer to both foreign reserves in the form of gold assets in the Banking Department and foreign securities held by the Issue Department, and domestic reserves in the form of 'bank reserves'. The composition of foreign reserves is indicated, a minimum reserve system is set out, and the instruments and securities in which the country's reserves could be deployed are spelt out in the relevant

Sections of the RBI Act. vccIn brief, in India, what constitutes forex reserves; who is the custodian and how it should be deployed are laid out clearly in the Statute, and in an extremely conservative fashion as far as management of reserves is concerned. In substantive terms, RBI functions as the custodian and manager of forex reserves, and operates within the overall policy framework agreed upon with Government of India.

Importance of Forex Reserves

It is possible to consider three motives technically. i.e., transaction, speculative and precautionary motives for holding reserves. International trade gives rise to currency flows, which are assumed to be handled by private banks driven by the transaction motive. Similarly, speculative motive is left to individual or corporate. Central bank reserves, however, are characterized primarily as a last resort stock of foreign currency for unpredictable flows, which is consistent with precautionary motive for holding foreign assets. Precautionary motive for holding foreign currency, like the demand for money, can be positively related to wealth and the cost of covering unplanned deficit, and negatively related to the return from alternative assets.

From the perspective of policy, it is obvious that the country benefits through economies of scale by pooling the transaction reserves, while sub serving the precautionary motive of keeping official reserves as a 'war chest'. Furthermore, forex reserves are instruments to maintain or manage the exchange rate, while enabling orderly absorption of international money and capital flows. In brief, official reserves are held for precautionary and transaction motives keeping in view the aggregate of national interests, to achieve balance between demand for and supply of foreign currencies, for intervention, and to preserve confidence in the country's ability to carry out external transactions Reserve assets could be defined with respect to assets of monetary authority as the custodian, or of sovereign government as the principal.

For the funding authority, the needs for holding reserves may not deviate from the objectives of the monetary policy, while for government, the objectives of holding reserves may go beyond that of the monetary authorities. In other words, the final expression of the objective of holding reserve assets would be influenced by the reconciliation of objectives of the monetary authority as the custodian and the government as principal. There are cases, however, when reserves are used as a convenient mechanism for government purchases of goods and services, servicing foreign currency debt of government, insurance against emergencies, and in respect of a few, as a source of income.

What are the dominant policy objectives in regard to forex reserves in India? It is not an easy task to lay down objectives in a precise way, nor is it possible to order all relevant objectives by order of precedence in view of emerging situations which are described later. For the present, a list of objectives in broader terms may be encapsulated viz., (a) maintaining confidence in monetary and exchange rate policies, (b) enhancing capacity to intervene in forex markets, (c) limiting external vulnerability by maintaining foreign currency liquidity to absorb shocks during times of crisis including national disasters or emergencies; (d) providing confidence to the markets especially credit rating agencies that external obligations can always be met, thus reducing the overall costs at which fore resources are available to all the market participants, and (e) incidentally adding to the comfort of the market participants, by demonstrating the backing of domestic currency by external assets.

Formally, the objectives of the reserve management in India could be found in the RBI Act, where the relevant part of the preamble reads as 'to use the currency system to the country's advantage and with a view to securing monetary stability'. This statement may be interpreted to hold that monetary stability means internal as well as external stability; implying stable exchange rate as the overall objective of the reserve management policy. While internal stability implies that reserve management cannot be isolated from domestic macroeconomic stability and economic growth, the phrase 'to use the currency system to the country's advantage' implies that maximum gains for the country as a whole or economy in general could be derived in the process of reserve management, which not only provides for considerable flexibility to reserve management practice, but also warrants a very dynamic view of what the country needs and how best to meet the requirements.

In another sense, the financial return or trade off between financial costs and benefits of holding and maintaining reserves is not the only or the predominant objective in management of reserves. Evolution of Reserve Management Policy in India India's approach to reserve management, until the balance of payments crisis of 1991 was essentially based on the traditional approach, i.e., to maintain an appropriate level of import cover defined in terms of number of months of imports equivalent to reserves. For example, the RBI's

Annual Report1990-91 stated that the import cover of reserves shrank to 3 weeks of imports by the end of December1990, and the emphasis on import cover constituted the primary concern say, till 1993-94.

The approach to reserve management, as part of exchange rate management, and indeed external sector policy underwent a paradigm shift with the adoption of the recommendations of the High Level Committee on Balance of Payments. The Report articulated an integrated view of the issues and made specific recommendations on foreign currency reserves. The relevant extracts are: "It has traditionally been the practice to view the level of desirable reserves as a percentage of the annual imports-say reserves to meet three months imports or four months imports. Although, this approach would be inadequate when a large number of transactions and payment liabilities arise in areas other than import of commodities. Thus, liabilities may arise either for discharging short-term debt obligations or servicing of medium-term debt, both interest and principal. The Committee recommends that while determining the target level of reserve, due attention should be paid to the payment obligations in addition to the level of imports.

The Committee, recommends that the foreign exchange reserves targets be fixed in such a way that they are generally in a position to accommodate imports of three months. From the perspective of the Committee, the factors to be considered in determining the desirable level of reserves are: the need to ensure a reasonable level of confidence in the international financial and trading communities about the capacity of the country to honour its obligations and maintain trade and financial flows; the need to take care of the seasonal factors in any balance of payments transaction with reference to the possible uncertainties in the monsoon conditions of India the amount of foreign currency reserves required to counter speculative tendencies or anticipatory actions amongst players in the foreign exchange market; and the capacity to maintain the reserves so that the cost of carrying liquidity is minimal.

The establishment of market determined exchange rate as mentioned in the RBI's Annual Report, 1995-96 a change in the approach to reserve management was warranted and the emphasis on import cover had to be supplemented with the objective of smoothening out the volatility in the exchange rate, which has been reflective of the underlying market condition. Against the backdrop of currency crises in East-Asian countries, and in the light of country experiences of volatile cross-border capital flows, the Reserve Bank's Annual Report 1997-98 reiterated the need to take into consideration a host of factors, but is noteworthy for bringing to the fore the shift in the pattern of leads and lags in payments/receipts during exchange market uncertainties and emphasized that besides the size of reserves, the quality of reserves also assume importance. Reflecting this, the report mentioned that the unreliable reserve assets must be available at any point of time to the authorities for satisfying various objectives assigned to reserves.

As a part of prudent management of external liabilities, the RBI policy`is to keep forward liabilities at a relatively low level as a proportion of gross reserves and the emphasis on prudent reserve management i.e., keeping forward liabilities within manageable limits, was highlighted in the RBI's Annual Report, 1998-99. The Annual-report of the, RBI, 1999-2000 reveals that the entire approach to India's foreign exchange management reserves highlighted the changing trend of balance of payments and liquidity associated risks with various types of flows and other requirements and the introduction of the concept of liquidity risks is noteworthy. "The policy for reserve management is built upon a host of identifiable factors and other contingencies, including, inter alia, the size of the current account deficit and short term liabilities (including current repayment obligations on long term loans), the possible variability in portfolio investment, and other types of capital flows, the unanticipated pressures on the balance of payments arising out of external shocks and movements in repatriable foreign currency deposits of non-resident Indians."

When the prudent management of foreign exchange reserves is concerned in recent years, RBI's Annual Report 2000-01 elaborated on 'liquidity risk' associated with different types of flows. The Report stated that with the changing profile of capital flows, the traditional approach of assessing reserve adequacy in terms of import cover has been broadened to include a number of parameters which take into account the size, composition, and risk profiles of various types of capital flows as well as the types of external shocks to which the economy is vulnerable. The latest statement of Governor Jalan's Monetary and Credit Policy (April 29, 2002) furnishes, a new and comprehensive view on the approach to reserve management and of special significance is the statement: "a sufficiently high level of reserves is necessary to ensure that even if there is prolonged uncertainty, reserves can cover the "liquidity at risk" on all accounts over a fairly long period. Taking these considerations into account, India's foreign exchange reserves are now very comfortable." The national security environment underscores further the requirements for strong reserves.

We must continue to ensure that, leaving aside short-term variations in reserves level, the quantum of reserves in the long-run is in line with the growth of the economy, the size of risk-adjusted capital flows and national security requirements. This will provide us with greater security against unfavorable or unanticipated developments, which can occur quite suddenly." The above discussion points to evolving considerations and indeed a paradigm shift in India's approach to reserve management. The shift has occurred from a single indicator to a menu or multiple indicators approach. Furthermore, the policy of reserve management is built upon a host of factors, some of them are not quantifiable, and in any case, weights attached to each of them do change from time to time.

Level of Forex Reserves

The fundamental motives for deserving reserves results in alternative way for determining relevant level of foreign reserves. Efforts have been made by economists to present an optimising framework for maintaining appropriate level of foreign reserves and one viewpoint suggests that optimal reserves pertain to the level at which marginal social cost equals marginal social benefit. Optimal level of reserves has also been indicated as the level where marginal productivity of reserves plus interest earned on reserve assets equals the marginal productivity of real resources and this framework encompasses exchange rate stability as the predominant objective of reserve management. Because of the measurable of the underlying costs and benefits of reserves in many ways, these approaches to optimal level provide ample scope for developing a host of indicators of appropriate level of reserves.

It is possible to identify four sets of indicators to assess adequacy of reserves, and each of them do provide an insight into adequacy though none of them may by itself fully explain adequacy. First, the money based indicators including reserve to broad money or reserves to base money which provide a measure of potential for resident based capital flight from currency. An unstable demand for money or the presence of a weak banking system may indicate greater probability of such capital flights.

Money based indicators is sometimes found to be suffer from various drawbacks. In countries, where money demand is stable and confidence in domestic currency high, domestic money demand tends to be larger and reserves over money ratios, relatively small. Therefore, while a sizable money stock in relation to reserves, prima facie, suggests a large potential for capital flight out of money, it is not necessarily a good predictor of actual capital flight. Money based indicators also do not capture comprehensively the potential for domestic capital flight.

In addition to this, empirical studies find a weak relationship between money based indicator and occurrence and depth of international crises. And, trade based indicators, usually the import based indicators defined in terms of reserves in months of imports provide a simple way of scaling the level of reserves by the size and openness of the economy. It has a straightforward interpretation- a number of months a country can continue to support its current level of imports if all other inflows and outflows cease. Because of the measure focuses on current account, it is relevant for small economies, which have limited access and vulnerabilities to capital markets.

For substantially open economies with a sizable capital account, the import cover measure may not be appropriate. Thirdly, debt based indicators are of recent origin; they appeared with episodes of international crises, as several studies confirmed that reserves to short term debt by remaining maturity is a better indicator of identifying financial crises. Debt-based indicators are useful for gauging risks associated with adverse developments in international capital markets. Since short-term debt by remaining maturity provides a measure of all debt repayments to nonresidents over the coming year, it constitutes a useful measure of how quickly a country would be forced to adjust in the face of capital market distortion. Studies have shown that it could be the single most important indicator of reserve adequacy in countries with significant but uncertain access to capital markets. Fourthly, more recent approaches to reserve adequacy have suggested a combination of current-capital accounts as the meaningful measure of liquidity risks. Of particular interest, is the Guidotti Rule, which has received wide appreciation form many central bankers including Alan Greenspan, postulates that the ratio of short term debt augmented with a projected current account deficit (or another measure of expected borrowing) could serve useful an indicator of how long a country can sustain external imbalance without resorting to foreign borrowing.

Because of practice, the Guidotti Rule suggests that the countries should hold external assets sufficient to ensure that they could live without access to new foreign borrowings for up to twelve months. This shows that the usable foreign exchange reserves should exceed scheduled amortisation of foreign currency debts (assuming no rollover during the following year). Alan Greenspan suggests a 'Liquidity at Risk' Rule that takes into account the foreseeable risks that a country could face in the event of (a) near absence of a purely non-interventionist exchange rate policies and (b) cost-benefit trade-off in the quantity of reserve accumulation. Accordingly, a country's liquidity position could be calculated under a range of possible outcomes for relevant financial variables such as exchange rate, commodity prices, credit spreads, etc. While the concept of 'Liquidity at Risks' has been broadly discussed at different forum, it appears that no specific methodology has been outlined. It has been left to institutions and countries to develop their own approaches.

Level of forex reserves in India

The approach from the Indian perspective to determine the adequacy of forex reserves coming into exist for last few years, especially since the pioneering Report of the High Level Committee on Balance of Payments, culminating in Governor Jalan's exposition of the combination of global uncertainties, domestic economy and national security considerations in determining liquidity at risk and thus assessing reserve adequacy. It is appropriate to submit stylized facts in relation to some of the indicators of reserve-adequacy described here without making any particular judgment about adequacy. Generally the foreign exchange reserves comprises of three items; gold, SDRs and foreign currency assets. As on May 3, 2002, out of the US $ 55.6 billion of total reserves, foreign currency assets account the major share at US $ 52.5 billion. Gold accounts for about US $ 3 billion. In July 1991, as a part of reserve management policy, and as a means of raising resources, the RBI temporarily pledged gold to raise loans. The gold holdings thus have played a crucial role of reserve management at a time of external crisis. Since then, Gold has played passive role in reserve management. The level of foreign exchange reserves has steadily increased from US$ 5.8 billion as at end March, 1991 to US$ 54.1 billion as at end-March 2002 and further to US$ 55.6 billion as at May 3, 2002.

The traditional way of assessment of trade based indicator of reserve adequacy, i.e., the import cover (defined as the twelve times the ratio of reserves to merchandise imports) which shrank to 3 weeks of imports by the end of December 1990, has improved to about 11.5 months as at the end-March 2002. In terms of money based indicators, the proportion of net foreign exchange assets of

RBI (NFA) to currency with the public has sharply increased from 15 per cent in 1991 to 109 per cent as at end-March 2002. The proportion of NFA to broad money (M3) has substantially increased by more than six fold; from 3 per cent to 18 per cent. The debt-based indicators of reserve adequacy show remarkable improvement in the 1990s.

The proportion of short term debt (i.e., debt obligations with an original maturity up to one year) to foreign exchange reserves has substantially declined form 147 per cent as at end-March 1991 to 8 per cent as at end-March 2001. The proportion of volatile capital flows defined to include cumulative portfolio inflows and short term debt to reserves has lowered from 147 per cent in 1991 to 58.5 per cent as at end-March 2001. Being a part of the sustainable external debt position, the short term debt component has decreased from 10 per cent as at end the end of March 1991 to 3 per cent as at end-March 2001. Similarly, the size of debt service payments relative to current receipts has decreased from 35 per cent in 1991 to16 per cent in 2001.

Management of International Reserves

Recently, due to various reasons, attention to the increasing is considered to the management of international reserves. First, advent of the Euro as an alternate currency to US dollar; second, movement of many central banks out of gold; third, changes in exchange rate regimes; fourth, changing views on reserve adequacy and its role in crisis prevention; and fifth, operational use of "reserve targets" in calculating financing gaps by IMF. The attention to the subject is evidenced by increasing emphasis on transparency, accountability in various form, and more recently, the issue of IMF guidelines on the subject. Operationally, reserve management is a process that ensures that adequate official public sector foreign assets are readily available to and controlled by the authorities for meeting a defined range of objectives for a country.

Usually a reserve management entity is made responsible for the management of reserves and associated risks. Invariably, the reserve management entity is the central bank and hence the objectives of reserve management tend to be critical as they would encompass the objectives of the monetary authority and the objectives of a portfolio manager or the custodian of reserves. As a monetary authority, a central bank's primary objective is to ensure macroeconomic financial stability in general and external stability in particular. As a custodian, the central bank's main objectives are to ensure liquidity, safety and yield on deployment of reserves. In considering management of reserves, the benefits and costs of holding reserves are constantly assessed.

On the benefits, recent international financial crises have shown those holding and managing sufficient reserves and disclosing adequate information to markets helps a country to prevent external crises, especially those stemming from the capital account. The growing appreciation of the role of reserves in crises prevention and as a buffer to manage exchange market pressures has given reserve management a more central role, now than before, in national economic policies.

Maintaining high level of reserves to tide over external shocks, however, involves opportunity cost. The opportunity cost of holding reserves is the foregone investment because resources have been used to purchase reserves instead of increasing domestic capital. The marginal development of domestic capital is the opportunity cost of holding reserves and reserves management seeks to minimize the opportunity costs against the benefits that accrue from holding reserves. The objectives of reserve management vary across countries, and a recent survey of reserve management practices of select countries (IMF guidelines, 2001) provides good insights on the subject. First, most countries hold reserves to support monetary policy. While ensuring liquidity in foreign exchange market to smooth out undue short-term fluctuations in exchange markets constitutes the primary objective, some countries take a cautious approach to intervention. Smaller countries hold reserves mainly for consideration of transaction motives to meet external payment imbalances as well as a store of wealth. Precautionary motive of holding reserves to mitigate adverse external shocks is implicit in most countries' objectives though among a few, it finds explicit mention.

Few countries explicitly use international reserves as the backing for monetary base and to maintain the stability and integrity of the monetary and financial system. From a policy perspective, the objective of holding reserves to support monetary policy is common to most countries and the objective of holding reserves in regard to many emerging economies is primarily to maintain international confidence about its short-term payment obligations as well as confidence in monetary and financial polices. Secondly, most countries have informal coordination between debt management and reserve management policies. As part of informal coordination, most countries take into account external debt indicators, particularly the maturity composition of short-term and long-term debt, as part of reserve management.

Thirdly, in regard to transparency and disclosure standards, many countries adhere to the IMF's Special Data Dissemination Standards (SDDS) requirement. Most countries publish data on external debt and reserves on an annual basis in either their central bank annual reports or other reports of Government.

Fourthly, liquidity and safety (low risks) prevail upon reserve management entities in most countries as part of objective of reserve management. The yield objective is secondary to most countries in reserve management. Fifthly, most countries use benchmarks for managing currency composition of reserves though information to the public about the benchmarks for the underlying currency composition of reserves is generally not made available. Information about the underlying norms for adopting the benchmarks are, however available in a number of countries.

Management of Forex Reserves in India

The legal provisions governing management of forex reserves in India are set out in the RBI Act and Foreign Exchange Management Act, 1999 and they also govern the open market operations for ensuring orderly conditions in the forex markets, the exercise of powers as a monetary authority and the custodian in regard to management of foreign exchange assets. In practice, holdings of gold have been virtually unchanged other than occasional sales of gold by the government to the RBI.

The gold reserves are managed passively. Currently, accretion to foreign currency reserves arises mainly out of purchases by RBI from the Authorised Dealers (i.e. open market operations), and to some extent income from deployment of forex assets held in the portfolio of RBI (i.e. reserves, which are invested in appropriate instruments of select currencies).

The RBI Act stipulates the investment categories in which RBI is permitted to deploy its reserves. The aid receipts on government account also flow into reserves. The outflow arises mainly on account of sale of foreign currency to Authorised Dealers (i.e. for open market operations). There are occasions when forex is made available from reserves for identified users, as part of strategy of meeting lumpy demands on forex markets, particularly during periods of uncertainty. The net effect of purchases and sale of foreign currency is the most determining one for the level of forex reserves, and these include such sale or purchase in forward markets (which incidentally is very small in magnitude). In practice, the degree of level of reserves is essentially a result of sale and purchase transactions, the level is also one of the objectives of exchange rate policy, and the issue needs to be considered in the overall context of exchange rate management. The market determines the exchange rate, i.e. forces of demand and supply. The objectives and purposes of exchange rate management are to ensure that economic fundamentals are reflected in the external value of the rupee as evidenced in the sustainable current account deficit.

Subject to this general objective, the conduct of exchange rate policy is guided by three major purposes: first, to reduce excess volatility in exchange rates, while ensuring that the movements are orderly and calibrated; second, to help maintain an adequate level of foreign exchange reserves and third, to help eliminate market constraints with a view to the development of a healthy foreign exchange market. Basically, the policy is aimed at preventing destabilizing speculation in the market while facilitating foreign exchange transactions at market rates for all permissible purposes.

RBI makes sales and purchases of foreign currency in the forex market, basically to even out lumpy demand or supply in the thin forex market; large lumpiness in demand is mainly on account of oil imports, leads and lags and external debt servicing on Government account. The entire sales or purchases are not control by a predetermine target or exchange rate.

The essence of portfolio management of reserves by the RBI is to ensure safety, liquidity and optimization of returns. The RBI in consultation with Government continuously reviews the reserve management strategies. In deploying reserves, attention is paid to the currency composition, duration and instruments. All of the foreign currency assets are invested in assets of top quality while a good proportion should be convertible into cash at short notice. The counterparties with whom deals are conducted are also subject to a rigorous selection process.

In assessing the returns from deployment, the total return (both interest and capital gains) is taken into consideration. Circumstances such as lumpy demand and supply in reserve accretion are countered through appropriate immunization strategies in deployment. One crucial area in the process of investment of the foreign currency assets in the overseas markets, relates to the risk involved in the process viz. credit risk, market risk and operational risk. While there is no set formula to meet all situations, RBI utilizes the accepted portfolio management principles for risk management.

Forex reserves and Quasi-fiscal activities

Central Banks perform a number of Quasi Fiscal Activities (QFAs). QFAs can be defined as an operation or measure carried out by a central bank with an effect that can, in principle, be duplicated by budgetary measures in the form of an explicit tax, subsidy or direct expenditure and that has or may have an impact on the financial operations of the central bank. In a broader sense, QFAs also include certain activities, such as, those relating to exchange rates, open market operations and cash reserve ratio, which have fiscal implications but cannot be obviously duplicated in terms of explicit taxes and subsidies in the budget.

Central banks' QFAs broadly arise from their role as a regulator of the financial system, as a banker to the government, and as a regulator of the foreign exchange system. QFAs of the central bank as a regulator of the foreign exchange often pertain to exchange rate and sterilized operations to offset the effect of unusual cross border capital flows. Impact of QFAs is difficult to quantify. First, the impact of QFAs is merged with the impact of other operations and thereby is reflected in the consolidated picture in the balance sheet of the central bank. It has not been possible to separate in the balance sheets the impact emerging exclusively from the QFAs from other operations. Secondly, market-clearing rates cannot be accurately predicted in an administered interest rate regime and therefore, it would be difficult to estimate the element of subsidy/tax involved in such operations.

Thirdly, the QFAs are performed on an ongoing basis covering innumerable transactions and, therefore, their measurement is virtually impossible. Fourthly, the impact of certain QFAs like credit ceiling and exchange related measures are not certain. On a very general plane it can be argued that sterilised intervention by the central bank to contain the liquidity impact of capital flows often involve a trade-off between low return assets and high return assets as far as the Central Bank is concerned. Earning from the deployment of foreign exchange is understandably lower than the interest loss on account of open market sale of government securities essentially due to interest rate differentials.

Communications Policies

Various issues regarding transparency and exposure include an important aspect of reserve management, within the broader framework of monetary, fiscal and financial polices. Thus, the policy as well as all relevant information are articulated through a variety of means from time to time, the most significant being the Monetary and Credit Policy Statements by Governor, RBI. The speeches of Governor and Deputy Governors are important sources of policy analysis, actions and intentions. The Annual Reports of RBI provide authentic version of RBI's perspective as approved by its Board. The Report on Currency and Finance provides research output from the professionals in RBI.

The periodical publications, Press Releases and Discussion Papers are also important sources of information. The RBI has been providing, on a regular basis, appropriate data directly relating to foreign exchange market operations. The RBI publishes daily data on exchange rates, forward premium, foreign exchange turnover etc. in the Weekly Statistical Supplement (WSS) of the RBI Bulletin with a time lag of one week, the movements in foreign exchange reserves of the RBI on a weekly basis are also published. The RBI publishes data on nominal effective exchange rate (NEER) and real effective exchange rate (REER), RBI's purchases and sales in the foreign exchange market along without standing forward liabilities on reserves, etc., in the RBI Bulletin with a time lag of one month. A5-country and a 36-country trade based NEER and REER is published in the RBI Bulletin.

The RBI has all along, been ahead of many developing and industrial country central banks, been publishing the size of its gross intervention (purchase and sale) per month and its net forward liability position. The daily reference rate of US dollar and Euro as well as the middle rates for four major currencies, viz., US dollar, GBP, Euro and Japanese yen are also available in the RBI website. As a part of the Special Data Dissemination Standards, IMF prescribed a data template for disclosure of the International reserves and foreign currency liquidity in respect of countries, which have subscribed to SDDS. India's approach to reserve management closely follows international standards and codes, especially with regard to transparency, disclosure, accountability and data dissemination of foreign s. India is among the 49 countries, which have adopted the SDDS template for publication of detailed data on forex reserves. The data template provides some information on a number of parameters including currency composition, deployment of forex reserves and forward positions. These data are made available on monthly basis in the RBI website as well as the country section of the IMF SDDS site, from the month of October, 2001.

Issues

It is proposed to consider five sets of issues covering policy matters; adequacy; costs and benefits; management aspects; and dissemination of information.

Policy matters

First, a critical issue is whether all the external assets are readily available for use. The management of foreign currency assets in India ensures such availability though in respect of a large part of gold which is a small part of official reserves, the quality is not in a form that is readily accepted in international financial markets. There is no likelihood of use of gold in reserves in the foreseeable future. Nevertheless, India has devised mechanisms by which a part of the gold holdings of RBI could be converted into usable foreign currency.

An incidental issue relates to the policy on enhancement or otherwise of gold component in the foreign exchange reserves and the way it is managed. The proportion of gold in our reserves is coming down in view of accretion to foreign currency reserves and the policy in regard to both holdings and management has been passive. Secondly, an issue common to many central banks is the advantage in clearly spelling out policy objectives in regard to forex reserves. The mandate as well as the practice in India clearly indicates that maintaining stability is an overriding objective but the detailing of objectives has to reckon the changing circumstances. As explained in the presentation on evolution of policy in India, a very dynamic view, based on multiple indicator approach has been adopted.

In this background, the practice of detailing of the context and objectives as is being done in the recent Monetary and Credit Policy Statements of Governor Jalan appears to be very appropriate; since such statements indicate the objectives ex ante, supplementing the earlier practice of reporting the policy and management, expost in the Annual Report. The major objective as articulated in recent Policy Statements appears to be to infuse and sustain confidence in the financial markets on our liquidity position and operate therein as appropriate, with a view to containing volatility in forex markets and contributing to financial stability.

Adequacy or appropriate level

First, the dominant concern of policy is maintaining confidence in our ability to provide liquidity and, there is no precise way of defining at what level the confidence factor would be undermined. In practice, policy makers should make judgements on (a) the difficulties in reviving confidence once it starts getting eroded; (b) the focus of market participants on incremental changes more than total size; and (c) demonstration of willingness to use the reserves when warranted without committing to do so and getting locked into a straight jacket situation. The issue of managing the level of reserves thus becomes, in many ways, as important as the level itself. Secondly, there are judgements involved in assessing whether the level of forex reserves provides comfort in the face of some weakness in domestic fundamentals.

Such a comfort will perhaps not be forthcoming if the current account deficit is not sustainable or exchange rate is highly overvalued. For example, it has been argued that high level of reserves could, under some circumstances, give comfort against weaknesses in the financial sector or high public debt or encourage laxity in financial and fiscal policies. Thirdly, many indicators of adequacy of reserves do, to a significant extent, capture the potential for drawdown by non-residents while the factors governing drawdown by residents through capital flight are not easily assessed.

Therefore, the domestic perceptions of level of reserves add to the comfort in withstanding drawdown through capital flight, and experience indicates that crisis of confidence in currency often originates among residents. Fourthly, the leads and lags in trade and even invisibles can significantly influence supply and demand in markets, particularly when markets are not fully developed. How should reserve adequacy be assessed with reference to prevalence of such leads and lags? If the leads and lags can be demonstrably impacted by discretionary administrative measures, the amount of reserves needed to moderate such leads and lags may be reduced. Fifthly, where there is lumpiness in demand and supply as is the case in India, the forex reserves have to be used for meeting the temporary mismatches in forex markets.

In such a condition, the incremental changes in the level of forex reserves may also be correspondingly large. There is a tendency among the analysts and media to react negatively to erosion in a more intensive way and positively to addition to reserves in a less intensive way. A higher level of reserves may possibly give greater scope for changes by making them appear marginal. Sixthly, it was widely felt that contingent credit lines from private sector could be negotiated and thus actual level of forex reserves to be maintained may be correspondingly brought down. The Contingency Credit Line (CCL) from the International Monetary Fund could also have similar effect. India had not accessed this facility, and in any case, experience of other countries has not been very satisfactory on this. Seventhly, bilateral or multilateral relations at government level do provide some indications, though on a judgmental basis, of the forex resources that may be readily accessed in case of difficulties. In other words, geopolitical factors do give different levels of comfort of ready availability of forex resources from official sector through bilateral or multilateral channels.

India has to constantly make and review its assessment of such access, noting that adequacy of forex reserves needs to be assessed with reference to changing perceptions of the economy in the market place as well as among governments or the official sector. In brief, a practical issue is, how much of judgemental, non-economic, and non-market considerations are relevant in assessing adequacy of forex reserves?

Cost and benefits

First, a major question on the level of reserves relates to the scope for measuring overall economic costs and benefits of holding reserves. While concepts of marginal social costs, or opportunity costs are useful for analytical purposes, computation is difficult though assessments are not impossible.

Second, if it is assumed that the direct financial cost of holding reserves is the difference between interest paid on external debt and returns on external assets in reserves, such costs have to be treated as insurance premium to assure and maintain confidence in the availability of liquidity. The benefits of such a premium are not merely in terms of warding off risks but also in terms of better credit rating and finer spreads that many private participants may get while contracting debt. The costs of comfort level in reserves are often met by some benefits, but both are difficult to measure, in financial or economic, and in quantitative terms.

Third, if the level of reserves is considered to be significantly in the high comfort zone, it may be possible to add greater weight to return on forex assets than on liquidity thus reducing net costs if any, of holding reserves.

Fourth, such calculations of costs of holding reserves by comparing return on forex reserve with costs of external debt may imply that addition to reserves has been made by contracting additional external debt. In India, almost the whole of addition to reserves in the last few years has been made while keeping the overall level of external debt almost constant.

Fifth, the costs and benefits of adding or not adding to reserves should be assessed with a medium-term view. For example, in case there is uncertainty about capacity to acquire needed reserves at a later date, a country may prefer to acquire them sooner than later. Indeed, an inter-temporal view of the adequacy as well as costs and benefits of forex reserves may be in order.

Finally, it is necessary to assess the costs of not adding to reserves through open market operations at a time when the capital flows are strong. In other words, the costs and benefits of forex reserves may have something to do with the open market operations, both in money and forex markets than merely the level itself. In brief, the costs and benefits arise as much out of open market operations of the central bank as out of management of levels of reserves.

Management aspects

First, sound legislative framework and institutional arrangements are fully in place, with RBI being the owner and custodian of reserves, but operating in consultations with government as necessary. There is no particular need for any changes in this regard.

Second, RBI does not have the legal authority to borrow or draw against external credit lines from the non-official sector. Should there be enabling changes in the law? Similarly, there are severe legal limitations on active management of gold reserves to optimise returns and should they be relaxed? Deep seated conservatism is reflected in hesitancy to alter the legislative framework.

Thirdly, there is close co-ordination between the RBI and Government with regard to magnitudes, composition and maturities of external debt, both in official and private sector. Such co-ordination as it exists today is clearly enhancing the effectiveness of reserve management.

Fourthly, co-ordination between monetary, exchange rate and reserve management is extremely important and it is ensured operationally and articulated publicly through the Monetary and Credit Policy Statements, in a comprehensive manner.

Random thoughts

First, there are important factors that contributed to the comfortable accretion to reserves in the last five years but often go unnoticed in any review of external sector policies in India.

(a) The liberalization of imports of gold has brought a large segment of unofficial imports and forex market into the official sector and reduced large transaction costs incurred in foreign exchange. In fact, this measure and consequently effectiveness of intervention in forex markets enhanced enabled meaningful development of forex markets.

(b) Furthermore, abolition of automatic monetization, and marketisation of Government borrowings provided opportunities to sterilize the capital inflows.

In other words, large capital flows could be absorbed into the forex reserves without seriously imparting volatility in forex or money markets because of simultaneous actions taken to develop these markets. In fact, there are occasions in recent years when RBI converted non-marketable government securities (ad-hoc treasury bills) in its portfolio into marketable ones by appropriate arrangements with government, to enhance its capacity to conduct open market operations. The criticality of the state of financial markets in the management of capital flows and forex reserves needs to be appreciated.

Second, it is justifiable to ask about the prospects for reserve levels increasing in future. It must be recognised that two factors are responsible for significant addition to reserves in the recent past viz., afar lower level of current account deficit (CAD) than the expected sustainable level of about 2 per cent of Gross Domestic Product (GDP) each year, and continued inflow of capital especially of non-debt creating flows as more or less planned. In this background, financing of an average CAD of about2.8 per cent of GDP as projected in the approach paper to the Tenth Five Year Plan, would require a minimum of two-fold increase in the size of annual capital flows from the present level.

As per the indication of the RBI Annual Report 2000-01, this would imply that the net capital flows would have to increase from about US $ 10 billion in the initial year of the Tenth Plan to about US $ 40 billion in the terminal year or an average of US $ 20 billion per annum during the Tenth Plan period. From a policy perspective, there are two facets of this coordination. To mobilise capital flows of this order, international investor confidence is critical. In order to maintain international confidence in the ability of the country's payment position, accumulation of reserves at a higher level is an important prerequisite. Moreover, in the event of capital flows of this order, the concern would be on absorption of such flows and its associated monetary impact. Policy coordination has to be put in place to synchronise the sustainable current account deficit with sustainable economic growth and maintain adequate forex reserves.

Third, in this regard, an interesting issue is whether there are circumstances when external borrowings need to be resorted to, merely to add to forex reserves. Review of literature certainly provides justification for such actions, especially when the issue of restoring or maintaining confidence in credit rating in external debt is involved. Similarly, such actions may be needed if sentiment in market needs to be influenced by the process. Finally, given the overall impact of increases in both forex reserves and external debt, it is possible to visualize circumstances when such operations are optimal. Fourth, are there alternatives to managing liquidity through maintaining reserves? In this regard, further explorations on the concept of "national liquidity" articulated in BIS Policy Papers No. 8, September 2000 appear to be useful.

Recent crises have shown that countries can be faced with liquidity problems not only because of the foreign assets and liabilities of the government and central bank, but also because of the foreign currency liabilities of the banks and even the corporate sector. A crucial difference between domestic and foreign currency debt is that the authorities can provide virtually unlimited domestic currency liquidity, but are tightly constrained in their provision of foreign currency liquidity. This has led to consideration of a broad concept of "national liquidity", though the relevance of a national balance sheet for policy purposes is controversial.

One polar view is that the external deficits and debt that are the result of decisions of the private sector – and not due to government borrowing – are of little concern to policymakers. Such a view may be taken by industrial countries since their access to international liquidity at zero risk spreads is normally assured. However, for emerging economies there are some arguments in favour of national balance sheet and national liquidity. Large net borrowings by some entities in the economy tend to increase country risk premia and thus raise the interest rate charged to all borrowers. One solution that has been suggested to counter any such externalities would be to internalise them through some form of tax on foreign borrowing or to impose some controls.

Furthermore, the exchange rate would overshoot if a country's access to capital markets dried up and it were suddenly forced to repay its foreign currency obligations, and this would cause a deep recession. Private sector external debt decisions have, in fact, impinged on fiscal management and balance sheets of official sector in several ways in the context of recent crises. Thus, an important policy aspect is the question of whether and how the official sector should take account of the maturity and currency mismatches of the private sector in structuring its own foreign assets and liabilities. The concept of a national balance sheet, of course, raises several tricky questions relating to private sector foreign assets offsetting liabilities, and the extent to which their foreign exchange exposures fully capture vulnerability. In spite of all these complexities that are involved in the national balance sheet approach, there is merit in exploring such an approach to provide guidance to policy relating to reserves, both in terms of adequacy and management. Finally, an idea which received some attention recently (March 2002) during the gathering on 'Finance for Development' in Monterrey, Mexico, is that, instead of holding their reserves in dollars, a new form of global money viz., 'global greenbacks' could be issued, which countries could hold in reserves.

The amount of money held by countries in 'global greenbacks' could be given to developing countries to finance their development programmes as well as global public goods like environmental projects, health initiatives, humanitarian assistance and so on. For countries that receive less than the amount that they need to put into reserves, the new 'global money' would go into reserves freeing dollars that these countries would otherwise set aside. Countries that receive more than they must put into reserves could exchange the new money for conventional currencies. Eventually, all the new money will find its way into reserves, which in effect represent a commitment by countries to help each other in times of trouble.

It has been argued that the greenbacks proposal envisages flow of funds to poor countries according to their need while contributing to global economic growth, stability and equity. Perhaps, as part of ongoing exercises relating to international financial architecture, this idea deserves to be deliberated. Treasury and Forex Management Treasury Management Treasury Management is increasingly being viewed as a specialised function in many corporate companies, and has already been assigned a separate status from the general financial functions. Treasury management asks for expertise on capital markets, money markets, instruments & investment avenues, treasury & risk management and related areas.

Forex management

In order to make the best use of opportunities to raise money outside India, one needs in-depth knowledge of international trade and the factors that influence the evaluation of overseas capital investment projects. The network of payments and international investments has elevated the study of finance to a multinational scale. Events in distant lands, whether they involve changes in the prices of oil and gold, election results, the outbreak of war, or the establishment of peace, have effects that instantly reverberate allover the globe. In this increasingly integrated and interdependent financial environment, the links between money and capital markets have become extremely close. To better understand this inter-linking and manage business in a better way, firms are hiring persons who can handle forex management and forecast rates accurately. Why the need? India is changing from an economy with strong socialistic leanings to a free-market one where the barriers to trade, both domestic and international, are fast vanishing. The transformation process that began in the early1990s has been put into overdrive.

While foreign firms are busy trying to get a foothold on Indian soil, Indian companies do not lag behind in attempting to penetrate foreign markets. There has been an unexpected rise in exports as well as imports, which has resulted in volatile exchange rates and more financial constraints. Given the inconsistency of exchange rates, the corporate and banking worlds are paying greater attention to treasury and foreign exchange management. Careers in treasury and forex management have suddenly been pitch-forked into the limelight. Banks have been scouting campuses of Indian B-schools with a view to recruiting for their treasury and forex functions. Shamita Ghosh, HR Manager, ICICI Bank says, "Of course we take fresh graduates for treasury and forex functions from the top B-schools in India."

The number of recruits getting placed in forex management operations has risen significantly. Shamita Ghosh adds, "Of the total recruitment By ICICI Bank at campuses from Indian B-schools, almost 8 per cent have been placed in treasury and forex operations at entry level positions." She however, declined to reveal the emoluments that have been offered to those recruited from campuses. Even students passing out of B-schools seem to be responding positively to the treasury sector. Rajiv Batra, MBA (Finance), Jamnalal Bajaj Institute of Management Studies, placed at Treasury department of IDBI Banksays, "I feel that the prospects for treasury and forex careers are very good. I had always wanted to pursue a career in treasury since the time I joined JBIMS. If you have excellent number crunching skills coupled with the ability to respond quickly to changing environments, then you are the right person to embark on this career." When asked for his advice to students who wish to take up a career in the treasury departments, Batra adds, "They should definitely opt for treasury and forex.

This sector sees a lull after every 2-3 years and therefore the chances of rising to the top are greater." Opportunities chiefly exist in the areas of: Corporate Finance Many Indian corporate are doing business internationally. They are also raising funds abroad, exposing them to greater risk due to deregulation of interest and exchange rates. To minimise these risks, it is necessary to handle forex and treasury related functions carefully. If neglected, it may lead to profit erosion. Corporate are on the look out for people with professional qualifications to handle all aspects pertaining to treasury and forex management.

Banks and Other Financial Institutions

Volatile exchange rate regimes and fickle interest rates are posing stiff challenges to financial institutions and banking organisations. They are also being offered myriad opportunities with the inter-linking of financial markets. Inconsistencies in lending rates require continuous monitoring and management of the asset-liability gap of these institutions. Clients are transacting more and more business with banks in foreign currencies. Thus, banks and financial institutions are also seeking professionally qualified persons to look after the treasury and forex management functions.

Forex Dealers Volatile foreign exchange rates have put forex dealers in a fix. Their forecasts have to be more accurate and the pace of transactions has to be quickened. Even as pressure is increasing in business, opportunities are becoming more lucrative. Firms that deal in foreign exchange are also seeking professionals with a good grip on areas of forex management for reducing risk levels of the business.

Treasury and forex consultancy

Corporate and banks are roping in experienced professionals as consultants for risk management. Opportunities as consultants are not only well paid but also satisfying. However, these positions demand sound experience. It is very natural to be curious about the kind of openings or careers that Treasury and Forex Management offers. Some of them are:

(a) *Treasury Analyst* : As a Treasury Analyst, you will support the Cash Management and Capital Markets department of the company. The candidate is expected to have a degree in business/finance and should demonstrate advanced analytical and system skills. He should be able to use these skills to develop sophisticated models and apply them to the treasury and accounting systems. Exposure to treasury workstation, ledger system, reporting and billing systems is an additional advantage.

(b) *Functional Support Analyst* : Functional Support Analysts are responsible for directly supporting treasury workstation functions. This includes modifying existing processes, clinching new business deals, reviewing old processes, upgrading systems, maintaining database, research of accounting data, end user training, and security control. They are also responsible for the documentation of all support processes. Financial Support Analysts will also respond to client support requests by resolving and diagnosing problems, and escalate (refer) complex ones to appropriate levels of expertise. They also maintain knowledge about Treasury banking systems and will serve as back-up support.

(c) *Cash Analyst* : Cash Analysts are responsible for everyday cash management for the company and its subsidiaries. They are also responsible for bank charge analysis, troubleshooting of credit card and direct debit problems as well as maintaining a database of quarterly and ad-hoc payments made. They will also serve as support to Treasury Operations, and assist in credit card charge backs and drafting of monthly reports. Cash Analysts will also follow up on sales and refinance distributions from partnerships.

(d) *Treasury Analyst-Business Solutions* : Here, treasury analysts may act as visionaries for world class business process reengineering. It will focus their efforts on establishing a world-class treasury organisation through documentation of business process flows and analysis of Treasury functions. They will analyse the benefits of using existing and future platforms to ensure that the Treasury Organisation is an enterprise solution and is compatible with existing Treasury processes and requirements. They also use their knowledge of treasury/business functions in association with IT experience to transform business requirements into software solutions.

(e) *Trade Specialist* : The specialists of the trade give support to Investment Managers and Clients through timely and accurate processing of trade instructions and related transactions. The varieties of trade instructions that require daily processing include global and domestic securities, derivatives, foreign exchange transactions and transfer of currency between accounts. They will maintain and strengthen the account's relationship while minimizing risk and maximising profitability. It will assist in the investment of cash and the research of currency balances, idle and overdrawn balance and the resolution of trade problems to ensure accurate client statements.

Forecasting Exchange Rates

Among the targets of studying the role of exchange rates is to be able to show exchange rates. The theories sometimes fail to provide a good approximation to the behavior of exchange rates. Forecasting exchange rates, therefore, seems to be a difficult task. This chapter analyses and evaluates the different methods used to forecast exchange rates. With the discussion of exchange rate volatility this chapter closes.

To show a future impact on the International transactions of Exchange Rates are usually settled in the near future. Exchange rate forecasts are necessary to evaluate the foreign denominated cash flows involved in international transactions. Thus, exchange rate forecasting is very important to evaluate the benefits and risks attached to the international business environment. For the forecasting of foreign exchange rates, two pure approaches are may be considered:

(1) The fundamental approach.

(2) The technical approach.

The fundamental approach is based on a wide range of data regarded as fundamental economic variables that determine exchange rates. These fundamental economic variables are taken from economic models. Usually included variables are GNP, consumption, trade balance, inflation rates, interest rates, unemployment, productivity indexes, etc. In general, the fundamental forecast is based on structural (equilibrium) models. These structural models are then modified to take into account statistical characteristics of the data and the experience of the forecasters. It is a mixture of art and science.

In the forecasting Work Practitioners generally use the fundamental approach to generate equilibrium exchange rates. The equilibrium exchange rates can be used for projections or to generate trading signals. A trading signal can be generated every time there is a significant difference between the forecasted exchange rate and the exchange rate observed in the market. If there is a significant difference between the forecast rate and the actual rate, the practitioner should decide if the difference is due to a mispricing or a heightened risk premium. If the practitioner decides the difference is due to mispricing, then a buy or sell signal is generated. There are two kinds of forecasts: in-sample and out-of-sample.

The first type of forecasts works within the sample at hand, while the latter works outside the sample. In-sample forecasting does not attempt to forecast the future path of one or several economic variables. In-sample forecasting uses today's information to forecast what today's spot rates should be. That is, we generate a forecast within the sample (in-sample). The fitted values estimated in a regression are in-sample forecasts. The fundamental approach generates an equilibrium exchange rate.

The foreign exchange rate in-sample fundamental forecasts are interpreted as equilibrium exchange rates. Equilibrium exchange rates can be used to generate trading signals. On the other hand, out-of sample forecasting attempts to use today's information to forecast the future behavior of exchange rates. That is, we forecast the path of exchange rates outside of our sample. In general, at time t, it is very unlikely that we know the inflation rate for time t+1. That is, in order to generate out-of-sample forecasts, it will be necessary to make some assumptions about the future behavior of the fundamental variables.

Forex Risk Management

Objectives behind forex management

- Cost reduction
- Contain losses
- Optimising exchange gain
- Protect operating profit
- Achieve budgets and targets
- Insure against adverse exchange rate movements

How to achieve these objectives?

- Determine the nature of exposure
- Evaluate the risks and rewards
- Decide targets & strategies to safeguard against currency risk

- Formulate policies for day-to-day operations
- Strong MIS Reporting system
- Periodical review of performance & strategy
- Single treasury concept for forex & money market

Key factors for an effective strategy

- Management's attitude towards risk
- Type of exposure – Tenure & Cost
- Firm's willingness to devote the amount and quality of resource to exposure management function
- Access to various markets & instruments such as forwards, options, futures etc and there implications
- Choice of currency - Dollar / Non- Dollar
- Gross or Net Exposure to be managed

Nature of risk

- *Currency risk*
  - † Dollar vs. INR - a) Spot b) Forward
  - † Cross Currency - DUAL Exposure
- **Interest rate risk**

  Domestic & International
- **Other economic risk**
  - † Competitor's pricing strategy
  - † Fluctuations in price of raw material
  - † Policy changes

Factors affecting risk

- Economic - Domestic & International
- Political / Country Risk
- Regulatory
- Spillover
- Other untoward events

Identifying risks

- Strong information system for Currency exposure
- Continuous flow of information, review of factors affecting

risk

- Continuous process involving reading, interaction, experience etc
- Prediction extremely difficult

Exchange rate and operating exposure

- Changes in revenues, costs, cash-flows and profits
- Effects competitiveness of the firm, attractiveness of various markets, relative cost of sourcing inputs
  - Information required on output market structure, competitor's cost structure, their likely response to exchange rate changes, own cost structure
- Participation of personnel across various functions like marketing, purchase, production and finance

Tools for hedging currency exposure

- FINANCIAL ENGINEERING PRODUCTS – Forwards, Options, Swaps, Futures, FRA's Exotic structured products etc
- INTERNAL HEDGING STRATEGIES:
  - † NETTING – receivables/payables can be netted out by matching amount. It reduces the amount of exposure to be covered hence reducing the banking costs
  - † LEADING & LAGGING – shift the timing of exposures by leading or lagging payables or receivables
  - † INVOICING – choice of currency for invoicing
  - † ASSET & LIABILITY MANAGEMENT – for e.g. increase exposed cash inflows in stronger currencies and vice-versa
- PRICE VARIATION

Financial engineering products

- ***Forwards, futures, options, swaps***

Some Myths:

- Complex pricing
- Greater loss due to complexities
- Difficult to manage
- Upfront Premia – Mental Block

- Zero Cost Options – Is there any free lunch anywhere?

Choosing the right product:

- Usage depends on market perception and individual requirement.

Options

A contract between two parties, which gives them, the right but not the obligation to buy/sell at an agreed price at a future date

- Call Option: Right to buy
- Put Option: Right to sell
- Exercise price: Set price between two parties
- Option premium: The price buyer pays to the seller
- Loss potential: Limited to premium
- Downside risks protected, upside gains unlimited
- Profit potential: Limited or unlimited depending on the strategy.

Options are best bet if markets are volatile and risks are asymmetric.

Swaps

- Swap is an agreement between two parties to exchange their liability (Interest, Principal)
- Interest rate swap exchange of periodic interest payments (No exchange of principal). Eg. from fixed rate of interest to floating rate and vice versa
- Currency Swap exchange of interest and principal in two different currencies.

Usage

- Asset/Liability management
- Issuing or reducing the burden of debt

Risk/reward

Gain

Loss

Fixed rate payer

Loss

Gain

Floating rate payer

Interest Rate Increases

Interest Rate Decreases

Risk/Reward profile of parties in Interest rate swap

3f's of the fx market

- FORWARDS – contract to sell/buy specific amount of currency at a future date against expected receivables/ payables at a pre-determined rate
- FORWARD RATE AGREEMENT (FRA) This is interest rate agreement for future dates between two parties on LIBOR/ LIBID
- FUTURES - simultaneous right and obligation to buy/sell a standard quantity of a specific financial instrument at a specified future date and at a price agreed between parties at the time of contract.

Operational strategy

- Setting optimum target rate
- Protecting benchmark rate
- Strong management information system
- Minimizing exchange risk
- While hedging protect operational profit
- Reducing interest burden
- Implementing sales policy on cost basis
- Minimizing foreign currency loan liability
- Trading positions
- Safeguard Operating Profit & Target
- Stop Loss / Take Profit Limit
- Lead & Lag Policy
- Continuous In & Out
- Options
- Review bench rate as per market trend

Advantages of integrated treasury management

- Reduces cost of domestic funds and forex
- Competitive cost advantage
- Optimum opportunity gains

- Asset/Liability management
- Easy availability of funds
- An edge over others

Regulatory implications

- Regulatory implications are controlled mainly by four agencies:
- MoF: Formulates the policies and directives.
- RBI
- ECD: Based on govt. policies, issues instructions and notifications.
- IECD: Manages export import credit regulations.
- FEDAI: Association of bankers which implements & decides operational procedures on the basis of RBI directions.
- Banks & Institutions: Based on overall directives as above under liberalized scenario decides their own policies and guidelines.

References

1. Office for National Statistics, International Passenger Survey; The UK National Tourist Boards, UK Tourism Survey.
2. Henley Centre for Forecasting, Hospitality into the 21st Century - a vision for the future.
3. Government Actuary's Department, Population projections.
4. Ferris, Ina Mobile. Words: Romantic Travel Writing and Print Anxiety. *Modern Language Quarterly*, 60:4 (1999): 451-68.
5. Fulford, Tim. *Landscape, Liberty, and Authority: Poetry, Criticism, and Politics from Thomson to Wordsworth*. Cambridge: Cambridge UP, 1996.
6. "Diversifying the Rural Economy: Tourism Development." Woods, Mike. 2000. *The Rural South: Preparing for the Challenges of the 21st Century*, No. 10: pp. 1-10. Jackson, Mississippi. Southern Rural Development Center, Mississippi State University.
7. Fesenmaier, Daniel R., Joseph T. O'Leary, and Muzaffer Uysal, eds. 1996. *Recent Advances in Tourism Marketing Research*. New York: Hawthorne Press.

8. "Developing a Rural Tourism Marketing Strategy Based on Visitor Profiles," Henning, Steven A. 1996. *Louisiana Agriculture,* Vol. 39, No. 1: pp. 8-9.

9. *The Influence of Rural Experience on Urbanites' Definition of Rurality*. Jacob, Steve, and A. E. Luloff. 1993. Radnor, Pennsylvania: Northeastern Forest Experiment Station. General Technical Report.

10. Kotler, Philip, John Bowen, and James Makens. 1998. Marketing for Hospitality and Tourism. 2nd ed. Upper Saddle River, New Jersey: Prentice-Hall.

11. "Rural Tourism: Special Marketing for a Special Place," Jones, Michael. 1990. Rural Development News, Vol. 14, No. 4: pp. 4-5.

3

Forex Risk Management Strategies

Unlike other markets, the Forex market shows a unique characteristic. The speed, volatility, and enormous size of the Forex market are unlike anything else in the financial world. Beware: the Forex market is uncontrollable - no single event, individual, or factor rules it. Enjoy trading in the perfect market. Like other speculative business the chances for a higher profit/loss is indicated by the increased risk. Generally currency markets are speculative highly and volatile. Any currency can become very expensive or very cheap in relation to any or all other currencies in a matter of days, hours, or sometimes, in minutes. This unpredictable nature of the currencies is what attracts an investor to trade and invest in the currency market. However, it may be asked, "How much am I ready to lose?" When you terminated, closed or exited your position, had you had understood the risks and taken steps to avoid them? Let's look at some foreign exchange risk management issues that may come up in your day-to-day foreign exchange transactions.

- Unexpected corrections in currency exchange rates
- Wild variations in foreign exchange rates
- Volatile markets offering profit opportunities
- Lost payments
- Delayed confirmation of payments and receivables
- Divergence between bank drafts received and the contract price

Exit the Forex market at profit targets

Limit orders, also known as profit take orders, allow Forex traders to exit the Forex market at pre-determined profit targets. If you are short (sold) a currency pair, the system will only allow you to place a limit order below the current market price because this is the profit zone. Similarly, if you are long (bought) the currency pair, the system will only allow you to place a limit order above the current market price. Limit orders help create a disciplined trading methodology and make it possible for traders to walk away from the computer without continuously monitoring the market.

Control risk by capping losses

Stop/loss orders allow traders to set an exit point for a losing trade. If you are short a currency pair, the stop/loss order should be placed above the current market price. If you are long the currency pair, the stop/loss order should be placed below the current market price. Stop/loss orders help traders control risk by capping losses. Stop/loss orders are counter-intuitive because you do not want them to be hit; however, you will be happy that you placed them. When logic dictates, you can control greed.

Place to stop and limit orders

Being an usual schedule of the thumb, traders should set stop/loss orders closer to the opening price than limit orders. If this rule is followed, a trader needs to be right less than 50% of the time to be profitable. For example, a trader that uses a 30 pip stop/loss and 100-pip limit orders, needs only to be right 1/3 of the time to make a profit. Where the trader places the stop and limit will depend on how risk-adverse he is. Stop/loss orders should not be so tight that normal market volatility triggers the order.

Likewise, limit orders should reflect a realistic expectation of gains based on the market's trading activity and the length of time one wants to hold the position. In the establishing the trade, the trader, should look to change the stop loss and set it at a rate in the 'middle ground' where they are not overexposed to the trade, and at the same time, not too close to the market. Among the experienced and trained investors, the trading foreign currencies are a demanding and potentially profitable opportunity. However, before deciding to participate in the Forex market, you should soberly reflect on the desired result of your investment and your level of experience. Hence, there is always significant risk in any deals of the foreign exchange. Any transaction involving currencies involves risks including, but not limited to, the potential for changing political and/or economic conditions, that may substantially affect the price or liquidity of a currency. In addition to this, the leveraged nature of FX trading implies that at any changes of the market there will always have an equally proportional effect on your deposited funds. This may work against you as well as for you. The possibility exists that you could sustain a total loss of your initial margin funds and be required to deposit additional funds to maintain your position.

If you fail to meet any margin call within the time prescribed, your position will be liquidated and you will be responsible for any resulting losses. 'Stop-loss' or 'limit' order strategies may lower an investor's exposure to risk. In order to achieve a lowest foreign currency rates and to take every opportunity to make or settle a transaction, Easy-Forex foreign exchange technology links around-the-clock to the world's foreign currency exchange trading floors. Knowledge about the fundamentals behind an investment needs awareness of the technical methodology of analysis. When your fundamental and technical signals point to the same direction, you have a good chance to have a successful trade, especially with good money management skills. Use simple support and resistance technical analysis, Fibonacci Retracement and reversal days. Be disciplined. Create a position and understand your reasons for having that position, and establish stop loss and profit taking levels. Discipline includes hitting your stops and not following the temptation to stay with a losing position that has gone through your stop/loss level.

When you buy, buy high. When you sell, sell higher. Likewise, when you sell, sell low. When you buy, buy lower. Rule of thumb: In a bull market, be either long or neutral - in a bear market, be short or neutral. If you forget this rule and trade against the trend, you will usually cause yourself to suffer psychological worries, and frequently, losses. And never add to a losing position. On Easy-Forex the trader can change their trade orders as many times as they wish free of charge, either as a stop loss or as a take profit. The trader can also close the trade manually without a stop loss or profit take order being hit. Majority of the traders set their stop loss price beyond the rate at which they made the trade so that the worst that can happen is that they get stopped out and make a profit.

Forex money management

It is a critical point that signifies differences between winners and losers. It was proved that if 100 traders start trading using a system with 60% winning odds, only 5 traders will be in profit at the end of the year. In spite of the 60% winning odds 95% of traders will lose because of their poor money management. Money management is the most significant part of any trading system. Majority of traders does not know the significance of it.

To understand the concept of money management and know the difference between it and trading decisions is very necessary. Money management represents the amount of money you are going to put on one trade and the risk your going to accept for this trade. There are different money management strategies. They all aim at preserving your balance from high risk exposure. Firstly, you should understand the term Core equity.

Core equity = Starting balance - Amount in open positions.

If you have a balance of 10,000$ and you enter a trade with 1,000$ then your core equity is 9,000$. If you enter another 1,000$ trade, your core equity will be 8,000$ It's important to understand what's meant by core equity since your money management will depend on this equity. We will explain here one model of money management that has proved high annual return and limited risk. The standard account that we will be discussing is 100,000$ accounts with 20:1 leverage. Anyway, you can adapt this strategy to fit smaller or bigger trading accounts.

India's Surging Forex Reserves

Is the foreign exchange reserves growth of India, a factor to worry about? In February 2004, India's Foreign exchange reserves touched $106 billion. Millions more are pouring in every day. The continuous surge in foreign exchange reserves is very encouraging keeping in mind the state of affairs in the early 1990s when the country was on the verge of defaulting on its foreign debt. As have stated, it is important to understand that in the present scenario effective utilization of the reserves is crucial. There was a sea change in the approach to foreign reserves management with the acceptance of the recommendations made by the Rangarajan Committee on Balance of Payments. The Committee emphasized on the maintenance of the target level of reserves and also emphasized that attention should be given to the payment obligations apart from the level of imports.

The Committee opinioned that the targets of foreign exchange should be fixed, in a manner by which it should be able to meet the import requirements for three months. The Committee proposed different factors, which are necessary to be addressed at determining the desirable level of reserves. The committee was of the opinion that a positive images regarding the country's capacity to honor its obligations needs to be built up in the international financial community. The Committee also recommended that a foreign currency reserve should be maintained to address any speculative tendencies by the players in the foreign exchange market. At the same time, the cost of carrying the liquidity should be minimal.

The importance of managing forex reserves

In the last few years the target on management of foreign exchange reserves has increased. Various reasons are behind it. Emergence of Euro as an alternate currency to dollar; change in the exchange rate regimes; change in perception on adequacy of reserves and its role in managing crisis; and operational use of "reserve targets" while calculating financing gaps by IMF. Apart from these there are various other reasons like increase in transparency and accountability at various levels. In addition to this, the IMF guidelines have increased focus on foreign exchange reserves management.

The Foreign exchange reserves are necessary to fulfill a unique set of objectives of a country. Central bank of a country acts as the reserve management entity. As the chief monetary authority of the country, it is central bank's responsibility to ensure a general macroeconomic financial stability. Because of happening the central bank to be the custodian of the foreign exchange reserves, it requires to control adequate liquidity, safety and yield on deployment of reserves. A survey done by IMF during 2000 signifies unique characteristics in the foreign exchange reserves management of various countries. It says that many countries maintain reserves to support monetary policy. The fundamental objectives of the countries, while maintaining the reserving are to cope up with the short-term fluctuations in exchange markets. Most of the countries use foreign exchange reserves for stability and integrity of the monetary and financial system as well.

The Indian context

From the Indian perspective, the RBI Act and the Foreign Exchange Management Act, 1999 set the legal provisions for governing the foreign exchange reserves. RBI acts as the chief monetary authority and the custodian of foreign exchange assets. RBI accumulates foreign currency reserves by purchasing from authorized dealers in the open market operations. Another source of Foreign exchange for RBI is deployment of foreign exchange reserves in appropriate instruments of select currencies. The type of instruments in which RBI can invest is stipulated in the RBI Act. All the financial matters received by the government also become a part of the reserves. The outflow of funds is resulted with the sale of foreign currency to the authorized dealers through open market operations. The consequences of the sale and purchase of foreign currency determines the level of foreign exchange reserves in a country.

The Surge in the forex reserves

The Asian crisis deals us about the suffering of the countries due to ill management of the foreign exchange reserves. Many countries foresaw the vulnerability to the external shocks and accumulated heavy foreign exchange reserves. Countries want to keep their exports competitive. Hence, they prefer to depreciate their currencies against dollars. In recent days, there has been a continuous appreciation of rupee vis-a-vis dollar. To avoid the appreciation of rupee, RBI has been continuously interfering in the money market. RBI is buying dollars from the market.

The dollars that are to be bought are added to the foreign exchange kitty. Unlike before, the NRI community is more dispersed now, not just confining to the Gulf. Due to software boom, Indians are heading towards new destinations. NRIs are doing well there and ploughing back their savings to India. In addition to this, foreign institutional investors are also making huge investments into Indian stocks. With the emergence of India as an offshore outsourcing hub have made new opportunities. There are huge dollar earnings for India. Further, India is also proving to be a worthy manufacturing hub for many companies. All these components played an optimistic role in the establishment of a huge foreign exchange reserve.

Costs and Benefits

It is always assessed the costs and outcomes of maintaining huge reserves. Holding sufficient reserves prevent a country from external shocks. Though excess foreign exchange reserves prevent a country from external shocks, it involves an opportunity cost as well. All the resources that have been used to maintain reserves could have been used to increase the domestic productivity. Similarly, the marginal productivity of domestic capital is the opportunity cost of holding reserves. Reserves management intends to minimize the opportunity costs against the benefits that results by holding the reserves. Putting a stop to accumulation of reserves can result in sharp appreciation of the rupee. A section of the exporters are worried about the appreciation of the rupee. They fear that India may lose its export competitiveness. But, according to the then RBI Governor, Bimal Jalan, export competitiveness of an exchange rate should be seen in parlance with trade-weighted exchange rate. It should not be just compared to US dollar alone. The appreciation of rupee is less compared to dollar. Therefore, exporters must try to communicate those markets, where the Indian exports are still competitive.

In order to acquire new technologies the foreign exchange reserves may be used. This would scale up the productivity of the industry. The government can even consider Indian companies to takeover can use raising the ceiling on the amount that or acquire a company across the world. It will help in the establishment and exploration of Indian multinational companies.

According to many analysts, though the growth of foreign exchange reserves is good, but the composition of the reserves is a matter of concern. In the first half of 2002, the inflows have grown by $11.5 and in the second half the total reserves increased by $12.3 billion. RBI was candid in admitting that these reserves were a result of current account transactions. These transactions were a result of the software exports and remittances from abroad. These transactions were considered to be better than portfolio investment and NRI deposits because in the case of any eventuality, the outflow of funds in the case of portfolio investment and NRI deposit would be faster.

The 2003 growth pattern of foreign exchange reserves has revealed a unique composition. The first six months of 2003 witnessed heavy inflows from NRIs. Around 42 percent of the total inflows during this period were from NRIs. The growth pattern continued in the period between April and June 2003. Of the $6.6 billion received during that period, $3.63 billion was because of NRI deposits.

The appropriate level

It is not an easy task to assess the appropriate level of quantity of reserves of foreign exchange for a country. Economists have come out with some models or methods by which the reserve adequacy can be assessed. There are certain parameters, which help in assessing the adequacy of foreign exchange reserves. The usual parameters are adequacy of foreign exchange reserves to take care of the future imports and whether reserves are enough to meet sudden withdrawals.

Many economists and analysts thought that the foreign exchange reserves of India are in surplus. Though RBI keeps justifying the accumulation of reserves saying that this can be used as a shield to protect the economy from capital flight and currency crises, but some economists do not buy this theory.

Previously, it has been revealed that countries enjoying on high foreign exchange reserves faced worst economic crisis. Thus one can say that no levels of foreign exchange reserves are enough to protect an economy from speculative capital attack.

The high reserves can be used to undergo smoothly the destabilizing movements. This can also be used as a shield to counter the currency fluctuations. Though, it is difficult for RBI to control the foreign exchange reserves accumulations, it can use these reserves for some productive purposes. Corporate can aggressively restructure their expensive foreign debt. Government on the other hand can also use them for repaying the high cost debts from various institutional sectors.

Familiarization Travel Related

Foreign Exchange Regulations

Foreign exchange regulations

Current Account Convertibility:

According to the present norms all receipts of foreign exchange under the current account both export earnings and inward receipts are fully convertible. As per the present policy of the Government all receipts of foreign exchange, under current transactions, both merchandise exports and invisible receipts, received by exporters and other recipients are required to be surrendered to an authorised dealer of foreign exchange. The authorised dealer converts 100% of the foreign exchange received into rupee at the free market.

From the point of export contracts entered into by exporters on CIF or C & F basis, the authorised dealers are required to obtain documentary proof of freight and insurance charges actually paid by the exporter, whether in foreign currency or rupees (to be notionally converted into foreign exchange at market rate for this purpose) and deduct this amount from the CIF value of exports to arrive at the FOB value of exports. The conversion of foreign currency into Indian Rupees is done on the basis of FOB value of Exports.

While from the free convertible portion, the exporters of goods and services have the option to retain upto 25% of the foreign exchange in Dollar Accounts, also called EEFC Accounts, with some commercial bank in India which is an authorised dealer of foreign exchange, to meet their current or contingent liability, and get only 75% of the foreign exchange converted into rupees at free market rates. However, as has been exempted before, all the 100% Export Oriented Units and Units set up in the Export Processing Zones / Free Trade Zones are allowed to get their entire proceeds from exports converted at market rates quoted by authorised dealers.

In importing raw materials, components, capital goods, etc. and for remittance of dividends, royalties, technical know-how fee, and repayment of overseas foreign exchange loans and/or interest therein, the foreign exchange has to be purchased by the remitter at market determined rates from the authorised dealers of foreign exchange in India. According to the necessity of the foreign exchange for any of these purposes, an application to the regional Exchange Control Department of RBI, under whose jurisdiction the unit is located, has to be made and permits have to be obtained.

In respect of the exports/imports in a convertible foreign currency to steamships/airline companies operating in India or to their Indian Agents, Indian exporters/importers can make payments towards freight charges. Such payments can be made either from their foreign currency accounts or by purchases of foreign exchange from authorised dealers at market rates quoted by them. It is open for Indian/Foreign Shipping lines/Airlines to open and maintain foreign agency accounts (EEFC accounts) and to credit up to 25% of the collections of the freight in foreign currencies to such accounts.

Because of all payments for deemed exports are settled in rupees, they are outside the purview of Liberalised Exchange Rate Mechanism (LERMS). Each foreign currency loans raised by Indian firms/Companies are converted into rupees at market rates. All remittances towards repayment/payment of principal/interest under commercial borrowings, supplier's credit, buyer's credit, lines of credit, etc and other incidental expenses connected therewith are also made at market rates.

There is permission from the RBI to the Indian parties who have raised foreign currency loans abroad to open ESCROW accounts with banks abroad and to assign the credit balance outstanding therein favour or the lenders. Such accounts can be funded through export earnings of the borrower to the extent permitted by the Reserve Bank of India. Any surplus inflows from these accounts into India are converted at market rates by their authorised dealers. Any foreign exchange received by Indian companies towards foreign equity contribution is converted at market rates.

If the foreign equity contribution is retained abroad, with the permission of the RBI, to finance import of capital goods, the unspent balance repatriated to India and surrendered to an authorised dealer is converted into rupees at market rates. The proceeds of Imports into India and exports from India have to be credited to or paid from the US Dollar Excrow account maintained with the bank in India.

References

1. Acciaioli, G. 1985. Culture as Art: From Practice to Spectacle in Indonesia. Canberra Anthropology 8:148-172.
2. Adams, J. 1972. Why the American Tourist Abroad is Cheated: A Price Theoretical Analysis. Journal of Political Economics 80:203-207.
3. Adams, Kathleen M. 1997a Ethnic Tourism and the Renegotiation of Tradition in Tana Toraja (Sulawesi, Indonesia). Ethnology 36:309-320.
4. "Strategic Initiatives in Tourism and Travel Established for Cooperative Extension," Sadowske, Sue, and Phil Alexander. 1992. *Rural Development News*, Vol. 16, No. 5: p. 7.
5. "Regional Tourism Marketing: An Analogical Approach to Organizational Framework Development," Shields, Peggy O., and Timothy J. Schibik. 1995. *Journal of Travel and Tourism Marketing*, Vol. 4, No. 1: pp. 105-113.
6. *Rural Tourism Handbook: Selected Case Studies and Development Guide*. U.S. Department of Commerce, United States Travel and Tourism Administration. 1993.
7. *Enhancing Kansas Communities*. Albright, K. B. 1991. Manhattan, Kansas: Cooperative Extension Service, Kansas State University. Report No. 839.
8. Harris, Thomas R., Jeffrey E. Englin, Shawn W. Stoddard, Tom R. MacDiarmid, and Gary M. Veserat. 1996. "An Analysis of Visitation Potential and Corresponding Economic Impacts of the Great Basin National Park," *Journal of the Community Development Society*, Vol. 27, No. 2: pp. 248-260.

4

Foreign Exchange Regulation Act, 1973

An Act to consolidate and amend the law regulating certain payments, dealings in foreign exchange and securities, transactions indirectly affecting foreign exchange and the import and export of currency, for the conservation of the foreign exchange resources of the country and the proper utilisation thereof in the interests of the economic development of the country. BE it enacted by Parliament in the Twenty-fourth Year of the Republic of India as follows:

Short Title, Extent, Application and Commencement

(1) This Act may be called the Foreign Exchange Regulation Act, 1973.

(2) It extends to the whole of India.

(3) It applies also to all citizens of India outside India and to branches and agencies outside India of companies or bodies corporate, registered or incorporated in India.

(4) It shall come into force on such date as the Central Government may, by notification in the Official Gazette, appoint in this behalf:

"Provided that different dates may be appointed for different provisions of this Act and any reference in any such provision to the commencement of this Act shall be construed as a reference to the coming into force of that provision."

Definitions

In this Act, unless the context otherwise requires, -

(a) "Appellate Board" means the Foreign Exchange Regulation Appellate Board constituted by the Central Government under sub-section(1) of section 52;

(b) "authorised dealer" means a person for the time being

authorised under section 6 to deal in foreign exchange;

(c) "bearer certificate" means a certificate of title to securities by the delivery of which (with or without endorsement) the title to the securities is transferable;

(d) "certificate of title to a security" means any document used in the ordinary course of business as proof of the possession or control of the security, or authorising or purporting to authorise, either by an endorsement or by delivery, the possessor of the document to transfer or receive the security thereby represented;

(e) "coupon" means a coupon representing dividends or interest on a security;

The provisions of F.E.R. (Amendment) Act, 1993 (hereafter referred to as Act 29 of 1993) came into force on the 8th day of January 1993.

(f) "currency" includes all coins, currency notes, banks notes, postal notes, postal orders, money orders, cheques, drafts, traveller's cheques, letters of credit, bills of exchange and promissory notes;

(g) "foreign currency" means any currency other than Indian currency;

(h) "foreign exchange" means foreign currency and includes -

(i) all deposits, credits and balances payable in any foreign currency, and any drafts, traveller's cheques, letters of credit and bills of exchange, expressed or drawn in Indian currency but payable in any foreign currency;

(ii) any instrument payable, at the option of the drawee or holder thereof or any other party thereto, either in Indian currency or in foreign currency or partly in one and partly in the other;

(i) "foreign security" means any security created or issued elsewhere than in India, and any security the principal of or interest on which is payable in any foreign currency or elsewhere than in India;

(j) "Indian currency" means currency which is expressed or drawn in Indian rupees but does not include special bank notes and special one-rupee notes issued under section 28A of the Reserve Bank of India Act, 1934;

(k) "Indian custom waters" means the waters extending into the sea to a distance of twelve nautical miles measured from the appropriate base line on the coast of India and includes any bay, gulf, harbour, creek or tidal river;.

(l) "money-changer" means a person for the time being authorised under section 7 to deal in foreign currency;

(m) "overseas market", in relation to any goods, means the market in the country outside India and in which such goods are intended to be sold;

(n) "owner", in relation to any security, includes any person who has power to sell or transfer the security, or who has the custody thereof or who receives, whether on his own behalf or on behalf of any other person, dividends or interest thereon, and who has any interest therein, and in a case where any security is held on any trust or dividends or interest thereon are paid into a trust fund, also includes any trustee or any person entitled to enforce the performance of the trust or to revoke or vary, with or without the consent of any other person, the trust or any terms thereof, or to control the investment of the trust moneys;

(o) "person resident in India" means -

(i) a citizen of India, who has, at any time after the 25th day of March, 1947, been staying in India but does not include a citizen of India who has gone out of, or stays outside, India, in either case— (a) for or on taking up employment outside India, or (b) for carrying on outside India a business or vocation outside India, or (c) for any other purpose, in such circumstances as would indicate his intention to stay outside India for an uncertain period;

(ii) a citizen of India, who having ceased by virtue of paragraph (a) or paragraph (b) or paragraph (c) of sub-clause (I) to be resident in India, returns to, or stays in, India, in either case -(a) for or on taking up employment in India, or (b) for carrying on in India a business or vocation in India, or.(c) for any other purpose, in such circumstances as would indicate his intention to stay in India for an uncertain period;

(iii) a person, not being a citizen of India, who has come to, or stays in, India, in either case -(a) for or on taking up employment in India, or (b) for carrying on in India a business or vocation in India, or (c) for staying with his or her spouse, such spouse being a person resident in India, or (d) for any other purposes, in such circumstances as would indicate his intention to stay in India for an uncertain period;

(iv) a citizen of India, who, not having stayed in India at any time after the 25th day of March, 1947, comes to India for any of the purposes referred to in paragraphs (a), (b) and (c) of sub-clause (iii) or for the purpose and in the circumstances referred to in paragraph (d) of that sub-clause or having come to India stays in India for any such purpose and in such circumstances.

Explanation - A person, who has, by reason only of paragraph (a) or paragraph (b) or paragraph (d) of sub-clause (iii) been resident in India, shall, during any period in which he is outside India, be deemed to be not resident in India;

(p) "person resident outside India" means a person who is not resident in India;

(q) "precious stone" includes pearl and semi-precious stone and such other stone or gem as the Central Government may for the purposes of this Act, notify in this behalf in the Official Gazette;

(r) "prescribed" means prescribed by rules made under this Act;

(s) "Reserve Bank" means the Reserve Bank of India;.

(t) "security" means shares, stocks, bonds, debentures, debenture stock, Government securities as defined in the Public Debt Act, 1944, savings certificates to which the Government Savings Certificates Act, 1959 applies, deposit receipts in respect of deposits of securities, and units or sub-units of unit trusts and includes certificates of title to securities, but does not include bills of exchange or promissory notes other than Government promissory notes;

(u) Deleted by Act 29 of 1993

(v) "transfer", in relation to any security, includes transfer by way of loan or security.

Classes of officers of enforcement

There shall be the following classes of officers of Enforcement, namely:-

(a) Directors of Enforcement;

(b) Additional Directors of Enforcement;

(c) Deputy Directors of Enforcement;

(d) Assistant Directors of Enforcement; and

(e) Such other class of officers of Enforcement as may be appointed for the purposes of this Act.

Appointment and powers of officers of enforcement

(1) The Central Government may appoint such persons as it thinks fit to be officers of Enforcement.

(2) Without prejudice to the provisions of sub-section (1), the Central Government may authorise a Director of Enforcement or an Additional Director of Enforcement or a Deputy Director of Enforcement or an Assistant Director of Enforcement to appoint officers of Enforcement below the rank of an Assistant Director of Enforcement.

(3) Subject to such conditions and limitations as the Central Government may impose, an officer of Enforcement may exercise the powers and discharge the duties conferred or imposed on him under this Act.

Entrustment of Functions of Director

The Central Government may, by order and subject to such conditions and limitations as it thinks fit to impose, authorise any officer of customs or any Central Excise Officer or any police officer or any other officer of the Central Government or a State Government to exercise such of the powers and discharge such of the duties of the Director of Enforcement or any other officer of Enforcement under this Act as may be specified in the order.

Authorised dealers in foreign exchange

(1) The Reserve Bank may, on an application made to it in this behalf, authorise any person to deal in foreign exchange.

(2) An authorisation under this section shall be in writing and

(i) may authorise transactions of all descriptions in foreign currencies or may be restricted to authorising dealings in specified foreign currencies only;

(ii) may authorise dealings in all foreign currencies or may be restricted to authorising specified transactions only;

(iii) may be granted to be effective for a specified period, or within specified amounts;

(iv) may be granted subject to such conditions as may be specified therein.

(3) Any authorisation granted under sub-section (1) may be revoked by the Reserve Bank at any time if the Reserve Bank is satisfied that, -

(i) it is in the public interest to do so;or

(ii) the authorised dealer has not complied with the conditions subject to which the authorisation was granted or has contravened any of the provisions of this Act or of any rule, notification, direction or order made thereunder:

Provided that no such authorisation shall be revoked on the ground specified in clause (b) unless the authorised dealer has been given a reasonable opportunity for making a representation in the matter.

(4) Any authorised dealer shall, in all his dealings in foreign exchange and in the exercise and discharge of the powers and of the functions delegated to him under section 74, comply with such general or special directions or instructions as the Reserve Bank may, from time to time, think fit to give, and, except with the previous permission of the Reserve Bank, an authorised dealer shall not engage in any transaction involving any foreign exchange which is not in conformity with the terms of his authorisation under this section.

(5) An authorised dealer shall, before undertaking any transaction in foreign exchange on behalf of any person, require that person to make such declarations and to give such information as will reasonably satisfy him that the transaction will not involve, and is not designed for the purpose of, any contravention or evasion of the provisions of this Act or of any rule, notification, direction or order made thereunder, and where the said person refuses to comply with any such requirement or makes only unsatisfactory compliance therewith, the authorised dealer shall refuse to undertake the transaction and shall, if he has reason to believe that any such contravention or evasion as aforesaid is contemplated by the person, report the matter to the Reserve Bank.

Money-changers

(1) The Reserve Bank may, on an application made to it in this behalf, authorise any person to deal in foreign currency.

(2) An authorisation under this section shall be in writing and (i) may authorise dealings in all foreign currencies or may be restricted to authorising dealings in specified foreign currencies only;

(ii) may authorise transactions of all descriptions in foreign currencies or may be restricted to authorising specified transactions only;

(iii) may be granted with respect to a particular place where alone the money changer shall carry on his business;

(iv) may be granted to be effective for a specified period, or within specified amounts;

(v) may be granted subject to such conditions as may be specified therein.

(3) Any authorisation granted under sub-section (1) may be revoked by the Reserve Bank at any time if the Reserve Bank is satisfied that -

(i) it is in the public interest to do so; or

(ii) the money-changer has not complied with the conditions subject to which the authorisation was granted or has contravened any of the provisions of this Act or of any rule, notification, direction or order made thereunder:

Provided that no such authorisation shall be revoked on the ground specified in clause (ii) unless the money-changer has been given a reasonable opportunity for making a representation in the matter.

(4) The provisions of sub-sections (4) and (5) of section 6 shall, in so far as they are applicable, apply in relation to a money-changer as they apply in relation to an authorised dealer.

Explanation - In this section, "foreign currency" means foreign currency in the form of notes, coins or traveller's cheques and "dealing" means purchasing foreign currency in the form of notes, coins or traveller's cheques or selling foreign currency in the form of notes or coins.

Restrictions on dealing in foreign exchange

(1) Except with the previous general or special permission of the Reserve Bank, no person other than an authorised dealer shall in India, and no person resident in India other than an authorised dealer shall outside India, purchase or otherwise acquire or borrow from, or sell, or otherwise transfer or lend to or exchange with, any person not being an authorised dealer, any foreign exchange:

Provided that nothing in this sub-section shall apply to any purchase or sale of foreign currency effected in India between any person and a money-changer.

Explanation - For the purposes of this sub-section, a person, who deposits foreign exchange with another person or opens an account in foreign exchange with another person, shall be deemed to lend foreign exchange to such other person.

(2) Except with the previous general or special permission of the Reserve Bank, no person, whether an authorised dealer or a money-changer or otherwise, shall enter into any transaction which provides for the conversion of Indian currency into foreign currency or foreign currency into Indian currency at rates of exchange other than the rates for the time being authorised by the Reserve Bank.

(3) Where any foreign exchange is acquired by any person, other than an authorised dealer or a money-changer, for any particular purpose, or where any person has been permitted conditionally to acquire foreign exchange, the said person shall not use the foreign exchange so acquired otherwise than for that purpose or, as the case may be, fail to comply with any condition to which the permission granted to him is subject, and where any foreign exchange so acquired cannot be so used or the conditions cannot be complied with, the said person shall, within a period of thirty days from the date on which he comes to know that such foreign exchange cannot be so used or the conditions cannot be complied with, sell the foreign exchange to an authorised dealer or to a money-changer.

(4) For the avoidance of doubt, it is hereby declared that where a person acquires foreign exchange for sending or bringing into India any goods but sends or brings no such goods or

does not send or bring goods of a value representing the foreign exchange acquired, within a reasonable time or sends or brings any goods of a kind, quality or quantity different from that specified by him at the time of acquisition of the foreign exchange, such person shall, unless the contrary is proved, be presumed not to have been able to use the foreign exchange for the purpose for which he acquired it or, as the case may be, to have used the foreign exchange so acquired otherwise than for the purposes for which it was acquired.

(5) Nothing in this section shall be deemed to prevent a person from buying from any post office, in accordance with any law or rules made thereunder for the time being in force, any foreign exchange in the form of postal orders or money orders.

Restrictions on payments

(1) Save as may be provided in and in accordance with any general or special exemption from the provisions of this sub-section which may be granted conditionally or unconditionally \by the Reserve Bank, no person in, or resident in, India shall -

(a) make any payment to or for the credit of any person resident outside India;

(b) receive, otherwise than through an authorised dealer, any payment by order or on behalf of any person resident outside in India.

Explanation - For the purposes of this clause, where any person in, or resident in, India receives any payment by order or on behalf of any person resident outside India through any other person (including an authorised dealer) without a corresponding inward remittance from any place outside India, then, such person shall be deemed to have received such payment otherwise than through an authorised dealer;

(c) draw, issue or negotiate any bill of exchange or promissory note or acknowledge any debt, so that a right (whether actual or contingent) to receive a payment is created or transferred in favour of any person resident outside India;

(d) make any payment to, or for the credit of, any person by order or on behalf of any person resident outside India;

(e) place any sum to the credit of any person resident outside India;

(f) make any payment to, or for the credit of, any person or receive any payment for, or by order or on behalf of, any person as consideration for or in association with -(i) the receipt by any person of a payment or the acquisition by any person of property outside India, (ii) the creation or transfer in favour of any person of a right (whether actual or contingent) to receive payment or acquire property outside India;

(g) draw, issue or negotiate any bill of exchange or promissory note, transfer any security or acknowledge any debt, so that a right (whether actual or contingent) to receive a payment is created or transferred in favour of any person as consideration for or in association with any matter referred to in clause (f).

(2) Nothing in sub-section (1) shall render unlawful -(a) the making of any payment already authorised either with foreign exchange obtained from an authorised dealer or a money-changer under section 8 or with foreign exchange retained by a person in pursuance of an authorisation granted by the Reserve Bank; (b) the making of any payment with foreign exchange received by way of salary or payment for services not arising from any business in, or anything done while in, India.

(3) Save as may be provided in, and in accordance with, any general or special exemption from the provisions of this sub-section, which may be granted conditionally or unconditionally by the reserve Bank, no person shall remit or cause to be remitted any amount from any foreign country into India except in such a way that the remittance is received in India only through an authorised dealer.

(4) Nothing in this section shall restrict the doing by any person of anything within the scope of any authorisation or exemption granted under this Act.

(5) For the purposes of this section and section 19, "security" includes coupons or warrants representing dividends or interest and life or endownment insurance policies.

Blocked accounts

(1) Where an exemption from the provisions of section 9 is granted by the Reserve Bank in respect of payment of any sum to any person resident outside India and the exemption is made subject to the condition that the payment is made to a blocked account -(a) the payment shall be made to a blocked account in the name of that person in such manner as the Reserve Bank may, by general or special order, direct; (b) the crediting of that sum to that account shall, to the extent of the sum credited, be a good discharge to the person making the payment.

(2) No sum standing at the credit of a blocked account shall be drawn on except in accordance with any general or special permission which may be granted conditionally or otherwise by the Reserve Bank.

(3) In this section, "blocked account" means an account opened, whether before or after the commencement of this Act, as a blocked account at any office or branch in India of a bank authorised in this behalf by the Reserve Bank, or an account blocked, whether before or after such commencement, by order of the Reserve Bank.

Restrictions on import and export of certain currency

(1) The Central Government may, by notification in the Official Gazette, order that, subject to such exemption, if any, as may be specified in the notification, no person shall, except with the general or special permission of the Reserve Bank and on payment of the fee, if any, prescribed, bring or send into India any foreign exchange or any Indian currency. Explanation - For the purposes of this sub-section, the bringing or sending into any port or place in India of any such article as aforesaid intended to be taken out of India without being removed from the ship or conveyance in which it is being carried shall nonetheless be deemed to be a bringing, or, as the case may be, sending, into India of that article.

(2) No person shall, except with the general or special permission of the Reserve Bank or the written permission of a person authorised in this behalf by the Reserve Bank, take or send out of India any Indian currency or foreign exchange other than foreign exchange obtained by him from an authorised dealer or from a money-changer.

Acquisition by Central Government of Foreign Exchange

The Central Government may, by notification in the Official Gazette, order every person in, or resident in, India -(a) who owns or holds such foreign exchange as may be specified in the notification, to offer it, or cause it to be offered, for sale to the Reserve Bank on behalf of the Central Government or to such person, as the Reserve Bank may authorise for the purpose, at such price as the Central Government may fix, being a price which is not less than the price calculated at the rate of exchange for the time being authorised by the Reserve Bank; (b) who is entitled to assign any right to receive such foreign exchange as may be specified in the notification, to transfer that right to the Reserve Bank on behalf of the Central Government on payment of such consideration therefore as the Central Government may fix having regard to the rate for the time being authorised by the Reserve Bank in pursuance of sub-section (2) of section 8 for conversion into Indian currency of the foreign currency in which such foreign exchange is expressed:

Provided that the Central Government may, by the said notification or by a separate order, except any person or class of persons from the operation of the order made in the said notification:

Provided further that nothing in this section shall apply to any foreign exchange acquired by a person from an authorised dealer or from a money-changer and retained by him with the permission of the Reserve Bank for any purpose.

Duty of persons entitled to receive foreign exchange

(1) No person who has a right to receive any foreign exchange or to receive from a person resident outside India a payment in rupees shall, except with the general or special permission of the Reserve Bank, do or refrain from doing anything, or take or refrain from taking any action, which has the effect of securing - (a) that the receipt by him of the whole or part of that foreign exchange or payment is delayed, or (b) that the foreign exchange or payment ceases in whole or in part to be receivable by him.

(2) Where a person has failed to comply with the requirements of sub-section (1) in relation to any foreign exchange or payment in rupees, the Reserve Bank may give to him such directions as appear to be expedient for the purposes of

securing the receipt of the foreign exchange or payment, as the case may be.

Payment for exported goods

(1) (a) The Central Government may, by notification in the Official Gazette, prohibit the taking or sending out by land, sea or air (hereafter in this section referred to as export) of all goods or of any goods or class of goods specified in the notification from India directly or indirectly to any place so specified unless the exporter furnishes to the prescribed authority a declaration in the prescribed form supported by such evidence as may be prescribed or so specified and true in all material particulars which, among others, shall include the amount representing:

(i) the full export value of the goods; or

(ii) if the full export value of the goods is not ascertainable at the time of export, the value which the exporter, having regard to the prevailing market conditions, expects to receive on the sale of the goods in the overseas market, and affirms in the said declaration that the full export value of the goods (whether ascertainable at the time of export or not) has been, or will within the prescribed period be, paid in the prescribed manner.

(b) If the Central Government is of opinion that it is necessary or expedient in the public interest so to do, it may, by notification in the Official Gazette, specify any goods, from among those goods to which a notification under clause (a) applies, and direct that in respect of the goods so specified, where an exporter makes a declaration under sub-clause (ii) of clause (a) of the value which he, having regard to the prevailing market conditions expects to receive on the sale of such goods in the overseas market, he shall not, except with the permission of the Reserve Bank on an application made to the Reserve Bank by the exporter in this behalf, authorise or permit or allow or in any manner be a party to, the sale of such goods for a value less than that declared:

Provided that no permission shall be refused by the Reserve Bank under this clause unless the exporter has been given a reasonable opportunity for making a representation in the matter:

Provided further that where the exporter makes an application to the Reserve Bank for permission under this clause and the Reserve Bank does not, within a period of twenty days from the date of receipt of the application, communicate to the exporter that permission applied for has been refused, it shall be presumed that Reserve Bank has granted such permission.

Explanation - In computing the period of twenty days for the purposes of the second proviso, the period, if any, taken by the Reserve Bank for giving an opportunity to the exporter for making a representation under the first proviso shall be excluded.

(2) Where any export of goods, to which a notification under clause (a) of sub-section (1) applies, has been made, no person shall, except with the permission of the Reserve Bank, do or refrain from doing anything, or take or refrain from taking any action, which has the effect of securing:

(A) in a case falling under sub-clause (i) or sub-clause (ii) of clause (a) of sub-section(1), -(a) that payment for the goods -(i) is made otherwise than in the prescribed manner, or (ii) is delayed beyond the period prescribed under clause (a) of sub-section (1), or (b) that the proceeds of sale of the goods exported do not represent the full export value of the goods subject to such deductions, if any, as may be allowed by the Reserve Bank; and

(B) in a case falling under sub-clause (ii) of clause (a) of sub-section (1), also that the sale of the goods is delayed to an extent which is unreasonable having regard to the ordinary course of trade:

Provided that no proceedings in respect of any contravention of the provisions of this sub-section shall be instituted unless the prescribed period has expired and payment for the goods representing the full export value has not been made in the prescribed manner within the prescribed period.

(3) Where in relation to any goods to which a notification under clause (a) of sub-section (1) applies the prescribed period

has expired and payment therefore has not been made as aforesaid, it shall be presumed, unless the contrary is proved by the person who has sold or is entitled to sell the goods or to procure the sale thereof, that such person has not taken all reasonable steps to receive or recover the payment for the goods as aforesaid and he shall accordingly be presumed to have contravened the provisions of sub-section(2).

(4) Where in relation to any goods to which a notification under clause (a) of sub-section (1) applies the prescribed period has expired and payment therefore has not been made as aforesaid, the Reserve Bank may give to any person who has sold the goods or who is entitled to sell the goods or procure the sale thereof, such directions as appear to it to be expedient for the purpose of securing –

(i) if the goods have been sold, the payment therefore, or

(ii) if the goods have not been sold, either the sale of the goods and payment therefore as aforesaid, or the re-import of the goods into India as the circumstances permit, within such period as the Reserve Bank may specify in this behalf and without prejudice to the generality of the foregoing provision, may direct that the goods, the right to receive the payment therefore or any other right to enforce such payment shall be transferred or assigned to the Central Government or to a person specified in the directions.

(5) Where any goods or a right to receive payment or any other right to enforce such payment, are or is transferred or assigned in accordance with sub-section (4), the Central Government shall pay to the person transferring or assigning the same, the amount recovered by or on behalf of the Central Government in respect of the goods, after deducting all costs, charges and expenses incurred by the Central Government in selling the goods or in recovering or realising the amount in respect of such goods.

(6) Without prejudice to the provisions of sub-section(1), where the value of the goods specified in the declaration furnished under that sub-section is less than the amount which in the opinion of the Reserve Bank, in a case falling under sub-clause (i) of clause (a) of that sub-section, represents the full export value of those goods, or in a case falling under sub-

clause (ii) of that clause, the value which the exporter can, having regard to the prevailing market conditions, expect to receive on the sale of the goods in the overseas market, the Reserve Bank may issue an order requiring the person holding the shipping documents to retain possession thereof until such time as the exporter of the goods has made arrangements for the Reserve Bank or a person authorised by the Reserve Bank to receive on behalf of the exporter payment in the prescribed manner of an amount which in the opinion of the Reserve Bank represents the full export value of such goods or the value which the exporter, having regard to the prevailing market conditions, can be expected to receive on the sale of the goods in the overseas market.

(7) For the purpose of ensuring compliance with provisions of this section and any order or direction made there under, the Reserve Bank or the prescribed authority referred to in sub-section (1) may require any person making any export of goods to which a notification under clause (a) of that sub-section applies to exhibit contracts with his foreign buyer or other evidence to show that the full export value of the goods, or, as the case may be, the value which the exporter, having regard to the prevailing market conditions, expects to receive on the sale of the goods in the overseas market, has been, or will within the prescribed period be, paid in the prescribed manner.

(8) Without prejudice to the provisions of sub-section (1), where the Reserve Bank has permitted any authorised dealer to accept for negotiation or collection of shipping documents covering exports from his constituent [not being a person who has signed the declaration in terms of sub-section (1)], such authorised dealer shall, before accepting such documents for negotiation or collection, require the constituent concerned also to sign such declaration and thereupon such constituent shall be bound to comply with such requisition and the original declaration and such constituent signing the declaration shall each be considered to be the exporter for the purposes of this section, and shall be governed by the provisions thereof accordingly.

(9) Without prejudice to the provisions of sub-section (1), in relation to export of goods to which a notification under clause (a) of that sub-section applies, the Reserve Bank may, for the purpose of ensuring that the full export value of the

goods or, as the case may be, the value which the exporter, having regard to the prevailing market conditions, expects to receive on the sale of the goods in the overseas market, is received in proper time or without delay, by general or special order, direct from time to time, that in respect of export of goods to any destination or any class of export transactions or any class of goods or class of exporters, the exporter shall, prior to the export of the goods, comply with any or all of the following conditions as may be specified in the order, namely:-

(a) that any contract or other arrangement for the sale of the goods shall be registered in such manner and with such authority or organisation as may be specified in the order;

(b) that the payment for the goods is covered by an irrevocable letter of credit or by such other arrangement or document as may be specified in the order;

(c) that a copy of the declaration to be furnished to the prescribed authority under sub-section(1) shall be submitted to such authority or organisation as may be specified in the order for certifying that the value of the goods specified in such declaration represents the proper value thereof;

(d) that any declaration to be furnished to the prescribed authority under sub-section (1) shall be submitted to the Reserve Bank for its prior approval, which may, having regard to the circumstances, be given or withheld or may be given subject to such conditions as the Reserve Bank may deem fit to impose. Provided that no approval shall be withheld by the Reserve Bank under this clause unless the exporter has been given a reasonable opportunity for making a representation in the matter.

(10) Where the Central Government is of opinion that, in respect of any goods or class of goods or class of exporters, or in respect of export to any destination, the practice of exporting goods in accordance with any term to the effect that the goods will be sold on account of the exporter and the account of such sales rendered to the exporter has resulted or is likely to result in the full export value of the goods not being

brought into India in the prescribed manner or within the prescribed period, it may, by general or special order, prohibit the export, in accordance with such term, of such goods or class of goods or by such exporters or to such destination.

Payment for lease, hire or other arrangement

No individual shall, except with the general or special permission of the Reserve Bank, take or send out by land, sea or air any goods from India to any place on lease or hire or under any arrangement other than sale or disposal in any other manner of such goods.

Regulation of export and transfer of securities

(1) Notwithstanding anything contained in section 81 of the Companies Act, 1956, no person shall, except with the general or special permission of the Reserve Bank, -

(a) take or send any security to any place outside India;

(b) transfer any security, or create or transfer any interest in a security, to or in favour of a person resident outside India;

(c) issue, whether in India or elsewhere, any security which is registered or to be registered in India, to a person resident outside India;

(d) acquire, hold or dispose of any foreign security.

(2) Where the holder of a security is a nominee, neither he nor any person through whose agency the exercise of all or any of the holder's rights in respect of the security is controlled shall, except with the general or special permission of the Reserve Bank, do any act, whereby he recognises or gives effect to the substitution of another person as the person from whom he directly receives instructions, unless both the person previously instructing and the person substituted for that person were, immediately before the substitution, resident in India.

(3) The Reserve Bank may, for the purpose of securing that the provisions of this section are not evaded, require that the person transferring any security and the person to whom such security is transferred shall subscribe to a declaration that the transferee is not resident outside India.

(4) Notwithstanding anything contained in any other law, no person shall, except with the permission of the Reserve such

Bank:

(a) enter any transfer of securities in any register or book in which securities are registered or inscribed if he has any ground for suspecting that the transfer involves any contravention of the provisions of this section, or

(b) enter in any such register or book, in respect of any security whether in connection with the issue or transfer of the security or otherwise, an address outside India except by way of substitution for any such address in the same country or for the purpose of any transaction for which permission has been granted under this section with knowledge that it involves entry of the said address.

(5) Notwithstanding anything contained in any other law, no transfer of any share, bond or debenture of a company registered in India made by a person resident outside India or by a national of a foreign State to another person resident in India shall be valid unless such transfer is confirmed by the Reserve Bank on an application made to it in this behalf by the transferor or the transferee.

(6) If the Reserve Bank is of opinion that it is necessary or expedient in the public interest so to do, it may, by general or special permission exempt any transfer referred to in sub-section (5) or any class of such transfers from the operation of the provisions of that sub-section, subject to such conditions, if any, as may be specified in such permission.

(7) For the purposes of this section:

(a) "holder", in relation to a bearer security, means the person having physical custody of the security; provided that, where a bearer security is deposited with any person in a locked or sealed receptacle from which the person with whom it is deposited is not entitled to remove it without the authority of some other person, that other person shall be deemed to be the holder of the security;.

(b) "nominee" means a holder of any security (including a bearer security) or any coupon representing dividends or interest who, as respects the exercise of any rights in respect of the security or coupon, is not entitled to exercise those rights except in accordance with the instructions given by some other person, and a person holding a security or coupon as a nominee shall be deemed to act as nominee for the person who is entitled to give instructions either directly or through the agency of one or more persons, as to the exercise by the holder of the security or coupon of any rights in respect thereof and is not, in so doing, himself under a duty to comply with instructions given by some other person.

Restrictions on issue of bearer securities

Except with the general or special permission of the Reserve Bank, no person shall, in India, and no person resident in India shall, outside India, create or issue any bearer certificate or coupon or so alter any document that it becomes a bearer certificate or coupon.

Restriction on settlement etc.

No individual resident in India shall, except with the general or special permission of the Reserve Bank, settle, or make a gift of, any property so that a person who at the time of the settlement or the making of the gift is resident outside India, elsewhere than in the territories notified in this behalf by the Reserve Bank, will have an interest in the property, or exercise any power for payment in favour of a person who at the time of the exercise of the power is resident outside India elsewhere than in such notified territories:

Provided that any settlement or gift made or any power exercised as aforesaid without the permission of the Reserve Bank shall not be invalid merely on the ground that such permission has not been obtained.

Restriction on holding of immovable property outside India

(1) No Individual resident in India shall, except with the general or special permission of the Reserve Bank, acquire or hold or transfer or dispose of by sale, mortgage, lease, gift, settlement or otherwise, any immovable property situate outside India:

Provided that nothing in this sub-section shall apply to the acquisition or transfer of any such immovable property by way of lease for a period not exceeding five years.

(2) Any personnel who is residing in India and holding any immovable property outside India at the commencement of this Act shall, before the expiry of a period of three months from such commencement or such further period as the Reserve Bank may allow in this behalf, declare such holding

to the Reserve Bank in such form and containing such particulars as may be specified by the Reserve Bank.

(3) Nothing in this section shall apply to a national of a foreign State.

Continuance of proceeding in the event of death or insolvency

(1) Where -(i) a penalty has been imposed under section 50 read with section 51 by the adjudicating officer on any person and no appeal against the order imposing such penalty has been preferred to the Appellate Board; or

(ii) any such appeal has been preferred to the Appellate Board, and:

(a) in a case referred to in clause (i), such person dies or is adjudicated an insolvent before preferring an appeal to the Appellate Board; or

(b) in a case referred to in clause (ii), such person dies or is adjudicated an insolvent during the pendency of the appeal, then, it shall be lawful for the legal representatives of such person, or the official assignee or the official receiver, as the case may be, to prefer an appeal to the Appellate Board, or as the case may be, to continue the appeal before the Appellate Board, in place of such person and the provisions of section 52 shall, so far as may be, apply or continue to apply to such appeal.

(2) Where -(i) after the passing of a decision or order by the Appellate Board, no appeal has been preferred to the High Court under section 54; or

(ii) any such appeal has been preferred to the High Court, and -(a) in a case referred to in clause (i), the person entitled to file the appeal dies or is adjudicated an insolvent before preferring an appeal to the High Court; or (b) in a case referred to in clause (ii), the person who had filed the appeal dies or is adjudicated an insolvent during the pendency of the appeal before the High Court, then, it shall be lawful for the legal representatives of such person, or the official assignee or the official receiver, as the case may be, to prefer an appeal to the High Court or to continue the appeal before the High Court in place of such person and the provisions of section 54 shall, so far as may be, apply or continue to apply to such appeal.

(3) The powers of the official assignee or the official receiver under sub-section (1) or sub-section (2) shall be exercised by him subject to the provisions of the Presidency-towns Insolvency Act, 1909, or the Provincial Insolvency Act, 1920, as the case may be.

Offences and prosecutions

(1) Without prejudice to any award of penalty by the adjudicating officer under this Act, if any person contravenes any of the provisions of this Act [other than section 13, clause (a) of sub-section (1) of section 18, section 18A clause (a) of sub-section (1) of section 19, sub-section (2) of section 44 and sections 57 and 58], or of any rule, direction or order made thereunder, he shall, upon conviction by a court, be punishable, -(i) in the case of an offence the amount or value involved in which exceeds one lakh of rupees, with imprisonment for a term which shall not be less than six months, but which may extend to seven years and with fine:

Provided that the court may, for any adequate and special reasons to be mentioned in the judgement, impose a sentence of imprisonment for a term of less than six months; (ii) in any other case, with imprisonment for a term which may extend to three years or with fine or with both.

(2) If any person convicted of an offence under this Act [not being an offence under section 13 or clause (a) of sub-section (1) of section 18 or section 18A or clause (a) of sub-section (1) of section 19 or sub/section (2) of section 44 or section 57 or section 58] is again convicted of an offence under this Act [not being an offence under section 13 or clause (a) of sub-section (1) of section 18 or section 18A or clause (a) of sub-section (1) of section 19 or sub-section (2) of section 44 or section 57 or section 58], he shall be punishable for the second and for every subsequent offence with imprisonment for a term which shall not be less than six months but which may extend to seven years and with fine:

Provided that the court may, for any adequate and special reasons to be mentioned in the judgement, impose a sentence of imprisonment for a term of less than six months.

(3) Where a person having been convicted of an offence under this Act [not being an offence under section 13 or clause (a) of sub-section (1) of section 18 or section 18A or clause:

(a) of sub-section (1) of section 19 or sub-section (2) of section 44 or section 57 or section 58] is again convicted of an offence under this Act [not being an offence under section 13 or clause (a) of sub-section (1) of section 18 or section 18A or clause (a) of sub-section (1) of section 19 or sub-section (2) of section 44 or section 57 or section 58], the court by which such person is convicted may, in addition to any sentence which may be imposed on him under this section, by order, direct that that person shall not carry on such business as the court may specify, being a business which is likely to facilitate the commission of such offence, for such period not exceeding three years, as may be specified by the court in the order.

(4) For the purposes of sub-sections (1) and (2), the following shall not be considered as adequate and special reasons for awarding a sentence of imprisonment for a term of less than six months, namely:

(i) the fact that the accused has been convicted for the first time of an offence under this Act;

(ii) the fact that in any proceeding under this Act, other than a prosecution, the accused has been ordered to pay a penalty or the goods in relation to such proceedings have been ordered to be confiscated or any other penal action has been taken against him for the same offence;

(iii)the fact that the accused was not the principal offender and was acting merely as a carrier of goods or otherwise was a secondary party in the commission of the offence;

(iv)the age of the accused.

(5) For the purposes of sub-sections (1) and (2), the fact that an offence under this Act has caused no substantial harm to

the general public or to any individual shall be an adequate and special reason for awarding a sentence of imprisonment for a term of less than six months.

(6) Nothing in the proviso to section 188 of the Code of Criminal Procedure, 1973, shall apply to any offence punishable under this section.

Power of Central Government to give directions

For the purposes of this Act, the Central Government may, from time to time, give to the Reserve Bank such general or special directions as it thinks fit, and the Reserve Bank shall, in the discharge of its functions under this Act, comply with any such directions. Factors to be taken into account by the Central Government and the Reserve Bank while giving or granting permissions or licences under the Act. Save as otherwise expressly provided in this Act, the Central Government or the Reserve Bank, as the case may be, shall, while giving or granting any permission or licence under this Act, have regard to all or any of the following factors, namely:

(i) conservation of the foreign exchange resources of the country;

(ii) all foreign exchange accruing to the country is properly accounted for;

(iii) the foreign exchange resources of the country are utilised as best to subserve the common good; and

(iv) such other relevant factors as the circumstances of the case may require.

Certain officers to assist officers of enforcement

The following officers are hereby empowered and required to assist the officers of Enforcement in the enforcement of this Act, namely:

(a) officers of the Customs Department;

(b) officers of the Central Excise Department;

(c) officers of Police;

(d) officers of the Central or State Government employed at any port or airport;

(e) such other officers of the Central or State Government or a local authority as are specified by the Central Government in this behalf by notification in the Official Gazette.

Bar of legal proceedings

No suit, prosecution or other legal proceeding shall lie against the Central Government or the Reserve Bank or any officer of Government or of the Reserve Bank or any other person exercising any powers or discharging any functions or performing any duties under this Act, for anything in good faith done or intended to be done under this Act or any rule, direction or order made thereunder.

Power to make rules

(1) The Central Government may, by notification in the Official Gazette, make rules for carrying out the provisions of this Act.

(2) With the partiality to the generalisation of the foregoing power, such rules may -(a) prescribe the forms and the circumstances of their use for the purposes of this Act; (b) prescribe the procedure to be followed by the authorised dealers and money-changers and by persons applying for permission to do anything for the doing of which permission is necessary under this Act; (c) prescribe the manner in which inquiries may be held, and orders may be served, under this Act and the procedure to be followed in respect of the proceedings before the adjudicating officer or the Appellate Board; (d) provide, subject to such conditions as may be specified therein, for the publication of names and other particulars of persons who have been found guilty of any contravention of the provisions of this Act, or of any rule, direction or order made thereunder; (f) prescribe the fee payable by a person preferring appeal to the Appellate Board under sub-section (2) of section 52; (e) provide for any other matter which is to be or may be prescribed under this Act.

(3) Each rule made under this Act shall be laid, as soon as may be after it is made, before each House of Parliament, while it is in session, for a total period of thirty days which may be comprised in one session or in two or more successive sessions, and if before the expiry of the session immediately following the session or the successive sessions aforesaid both Houses agree in making any modification in the rule, or both Houses agree that the rule should not be made, the rule shall, thereafter have effect only in such modified form or be of no effect, as the case may be; so, however, that any such modification or annulment shall be without prejudice

to the validity of anything previously done under that rule. If any difficulty arises in giving effect to the provisions of this Act, the Central Government may, by order, do anything not inconsistent with such provisions for the purpose of removing the difficulty:

Provided that no such order shall be made after the expiration of two years from the commencement of this Act.

Repeal and saving

(1) The Foreign Exchange Regulation Act, 1947 is hereby repealed

(2) Notwithstanding such repeal -

(a) anything done or any action taken or purported to have been done or taken (including any rule, notification, inspection, order or notice made or issued, or any appointment, confirmation or declaration made or any licence, permission, authorisation or exemption granted or any document or instrument executed or any direction given or any proceedings taken or any confiscation adjudged or any penalty or fine imposed) under the Act hereby repealed shall, in so far as it is not inconsistent with the provisions of this Act, be deemed to have been done or taken under the corresponding provisions of this Act;

(b) the provisions of section 60 of this Act shall apply in relation to the contravention of any of the provisions of the Act hereby repealed or of any rule, direction or order made thereunder;

(c) any appeal preferred to the Foreign Exchange Regulation Appellate Board under sub-section (2) of section 23E of the Act hereby repealed but not disposed of before the commencement of this Act and any appeal that may be preferred to the said Board against any order made or to be made under section 23 of the Act hereby repealed may be disposed of by any member of the Appellate Board constituted under this Act in accordance with the provisions of sub-section (6) of section 52 of this Act:

(d) every appeal from any decision or order of the Foreign Exchange Regulation Appellate Board under sub-section (3) or sub-section (4) of Section 23E of the Act hereby repealed shall, if not filed before the commencement of this Act, be filed before the High Court within a period of sixty days of such commencement;

Provided that the High Court may entertain any such appeal after the expiry of the said period of sixty days if it is satisfied that the appellant was prevented by sufficient cause from filing the appeal within the said period. (3) The mention of particular matters in sub-section (2) shall not be held to prejudice or affect the general application of section 6 of the General Clauses Act, 1897 with regard to the effect of repeal.

Currency Conversions

The Indian Rupee is the currency in India (IN, IND). The symbol for INR can be written Rs, IRs, and Rp. The Indian Rupee is divided into 100 paise. The exchange rate for the Indian Rupee was last updated on April 2, 2008 from The International Monetary Fund. The INR conversion factor has 6 significant digits. Large amounts of Rupees are expressed in lakh rupees or crore rupees.

A Lakh Rupee is one hundred thousand rupees and a crore rupee is ten million rupees. Dollar is the currency in American Samoa in The United States (AS, ASM), British Virgin Islands (VG, VGB, BVI), El Salvador (SV, SLV), Guam (GU, GUM), Marshall Islands (MH, MHL), Micronesia (Federated States of Micronesia, FM, FSM), Northern Mariana Islands (MP, MNP), Palau (PW, PLW), Puerto Rico (PR, PRI), United States (United States of America, US, USA), Turks and Caicos Islands (TC, TCA), Virgin Islands (VI, VIR), Timor-Leste, Ecuador (EC, ECU), Johnston Island, Midway Islands, and Wake Island.

The United States Dollar is also known as the American Dollar, and the US Dollar. The symbol for USD can be written $. The United States Dollar is divided into 100 cents. The exchange rate for the United States Dollar was last updated on April 2, 2008 from The International Monetary Fund. The USD conversion factor has 6 significant digits. For conversion, a calculator is used.

Significant figures

Usually conversion factors have six significant figures, but some may have as few as three. The number of significant figures in the result will depend on the number of significant figures in the input and in the conversion factors. (Entering 2.00 INR will give more accurate results than entering 2 INR.) If significant figures are not used for rounding the results may have more significant digits than the input or conversion factor.

Rounding to smallest currency unit

The results are rounded to the nearest amount that can be expressed in coins and notes. For example, US Dollars are rounded to the penny and New Zealand Dollars are rounded to the nearest ten cents.

Foreign currency exchange in India

With the Foreign Exchange Management Act, 1999 (FEMA) which came into operation as of 1st June 2000, foreign exchange transactions in India have become more liberalized. Foreign exchange dealers in India today have been given powers of making all types of remittances in foreign exchange subject to present rules. The previous requirements of seeking Reserve Bank of India permission has been eliminated for most transactions.

Application for remittances in foreign currency

A person, firm or bank may apply to an Authorized Dealer for remittances in any foreign currency to a beneficiary abroad. Application should be made in FORM -A1, if the purpose of remittance is import of goods into India.

The Authorized Dealer may sell the foreign Exchange applied for provided the purpose of the request is an approved one.

Mode of payment of rupees against sale of foreign exchange

It is necessary to note that transactions amounting to Rupees 20,000 or more should be made by cheque payments. Payment can also be accepted in the form of a Banker's cheque / Pay Order / Demand Draft. Receipt of Payment in cash in case of such sale of foreign Exchange or remittance in foreign Exchange is strictly prohibited.

Travellers cheque negotiable only in India

Outside India there is no provision to cashed for the Rupee Travelers cheque, if they are issued solely for use within India. In such a case they cannot be taken or sent out of India.

Reconversion of Indian Currency

Foreign currency may be sold against Indian Rupees held by persons who are not resident of India but are passing through or leaving India after a visit, at the time of their departure from India.

With this purpose, a Bank or Encashment certificate issued by an Authorized Dealer, Exchange bureau or Authorized Money changer in form BCI, ECF OR ECR, is required to show that the rupee had been acquired by sale of foreign Exchange to an Authorized Dealer or money changer in India. A certificate of such kind is valid for reconversion i.e. a period of three months is not over from the date of sale of the foreign currency by the traveler.

Rates of exchange

Each Authorized dealers and their Exchange bureau may purchase from and sell to public foreign currency notes and coins at rates of exchange determined by market conditions.

Dealings in foreign currency notes and coins between authorized dealers and between authorized dealers and moneychangers would also be at rates determined by market conditions.

References

1. Galperin, William. The Return of the Visible in British Romanticism. Baltimore & London: John Hopkins UP, 1993.
2. Garrard, Greg. Radical Pastoral? Studies in Romanticism, 35.3 (1996 Fall), 449-65.
3. Hipple, Walter John. *The Beautiful, the Sublime, and the Picturesque in Eighteenth-Century British Aesthetic Theory*. Carbondale, IL: Southern Illinois University Press, 1957.
4. Janowitz, Anne. *England's Ruins: Poetic Purpose and the National Landscape*. Oxford: Basil Blackwell, 1990.
5. *The Literature of Images: Narrative Landscape from Julie to Jane Eyre*- Kadish, Doris. New Brunswick: Rutgers UP, 1986.
6. Labbe, Jacqueline M. *Romantic Visualities: Landscape, Gender, and Romanticism*. New York: St. Martin's P, 1997.
7. Litz, A. Walton. The Picturesque in *Pride and Prejudice*. *Persuasions: Journal of the Jane Austen Society of North America*, 13-15 (1979 Dec. 1): 20-24.
8. Moir, Esther. *The Discovery of Britain: The English Tourists 1540-1840*. London: Routledge & Kegan Paul, 1964.
9. "Employment in Tourism: A Review," Johnson, Peter, and Barry Thomas. 1990a. *Industrial Relations Journal*, Vol. 21, No. 1: pp. 36-48.

10. "Measuring the Local Employment Impact of a Tourist Attraction: An Empirical Study," Johnson, Peter, and Barry Thomas. 1990b. *Regional Studies* Vol. 24, No. 5: pp. 395-403.

11. "Tourism Means More than Money to the Host Community," Jurowski, Claudia. 1996. *Parks and Recreation*, Vol. 31, No. 9: pp. 110-118.

5

Tariff Terminology

Terminology

Some of the principles are very helpful in the interpretation and terminology of the Tariff. First, it is essential to remember that because the main body and structure of the Tariff is based on the international Nomenclature, a lot of the wording used will not match the type of terminology commonly used in Canada, but will often sound a bit more British. Second, the updating of the Tariff tends to lag behind technological innovation. The descriptions of some products, especially those of a technologically sophisticated nature, might seem a little old-fashioned or out of date. For example, "computers" are referred to as "electronic data processing machines". Moreover, certain phrases and punctuation patterns have very specific uses and meanings. These are given in detailed in the following sections.

Terminology in Tariff Item Descriptions

Punctuation: Punctuation is important in interpreting the wording of the Tariff. Semi-colons, colons and commas are used for very specific purposes. A semi-colon in a Tariff Item indicates a full stop and that the portions of the Tariff Item divided by means of a semi-colon are separate and distinct from each other. Take, for example, a description such as that given for heading 84.21:

Centrifuges, including centrifugal dryers; filtering or purifying machinery and apparatus, for liquids or gases. This description refers to two separate product groups centrifuges and filtering or purifying machinery and apparatus. The qualifying phrase, including centrifugal dryers refers only to the first product group, whereas the qualifying phrase for liquids or gases refers only to the second.

Colons are used to indicate that additional information follows, which pertain to the goods, specified. Most commonly, it means that the product being described at one level is further divided at the next level down by some characteristic such as the material it is made of or whether it includes a certain part or performs a certain function. For example, the text for Subheading 8501.30 is worded Other DC motors, DC generators. It is further divided into a second level of Subheadings that describes various types of motors and generators i.e. 8501.31, Of an output not exceeding 750 W, 8501.32,Of an output exceeding 750 W but not exceeding 75 kW, etc. Commas are used to separate a list or series of goods within the product groups delineated by the semi-colons. At the end of a product group, a comma is used to separate the descriptor phrase from the list of goods to which it applies.

And/Or: And is used in the same way as a comma, to connect items in a series which are all to be included together. And may also be used when there is more than one condition which pertains to an item as in footwear with outer soles of leather and uppers of canvas. This means that the footwear must satisfy both conditions in order to be classified here. The word Or is generally used to show that alternatives exist. For example, in heading 73.20, Springs and leaves for springs, of iron or steel, the product in question can be made of either metal in order to be classified in that Heading. Other: The word "Other" is very necessary in the Tariff and can be a little tricky. It may occur on any level. At each level of the Tariff, the product in question is divided into groups. Typically, the first few groups on a given level are described specifically, with products that don't fit into any of these groups put into an Other category. For example, the Heading 73.20 refers to springs and leaves for springs, of iron or steel. It is divided at the six digit level into 7320.10.00, Leaf springs and leaves therefore, 7320.20, Helical springs and 7320.90, other. The other refers to springs that do not fit into the other two groups.

The Tariff

Tariff Classification is a highly specific area that includes multi-levels of item classification. Making use of the correct tariff classifications requires accurate and detailed knowledge, not only of the item being classified but also of the classification system itself. The following information outlines the importance of tariff classification and a description of the purpose of the Harmonized System of Tariff Classification. There are also very specific rules of interpretation for classifying your goods under the Harmonized System. The fundamental division of goods in the Tariff is into Sections and Chapters. There are altogether 21 Sections, consisting of 98 Chapters. The Harmonized System is a global classification system where products are grouped according to what they are, what they are made of, and how they are manufactured or processed. These sections and chapters are accompanied by both Legal Notes and Explanatory Notes.

Legal Notes define the precise scope and limits of each Chapter, Section, Heading or Subheading. Explanatory Notes are included to aid in the understanding of the classification. Within Chapter, goods are enlisted on the basis of their hierarchical classification system, broken down into finer and finer categories. The lowest breakdown level is called the Classification Number. This is the number that must be used on the Customs documents. There is a Classification Number for every product that anyone could ever wish to import. The proper classification of items can be complicated and specific item descriptions apply. The preceding Tariff Resources may help you to know and make sense of the multi-level Harmonized System of Tariff Classification.

The Significance of Tariff Classification

Every goods imported should be classified as to have duties and taxes assessed. Tariff classification enables governments to identify goods imported into the country for purposes of duty and tax collection, as well as gathering statistical information for economic planning, trade negotiation, and the enforcement of national and international laws. A global "Harmonized System" for the description and classification of goods was created in 1988, and soon after adopted by nations around the world. The broad, core specifics and structure of Harmonized System classifications is universal, with each participating country eligible to add and define specific detail items, and to create and assign rates of duty in any required categories for all classifications.

To an importer, it is a legal responsibility to classify correctly of goods, and also often saves money on both duties and taxes. In some countries, it also speeds customs release. When examining a company's past imports, customs consultants nearly always find that overall, too much duty has been paid, indicating that the importer (or their broker) did not take full advantage of provisions in the Tariff. Making use of these provisions requires a precise and thorough knowledge of the product to be classified, as well as knowledge of the Tariff and the principles of classification. The way of classification of goods is based on the minute technical details of their composition and manufacture.

Whether they are eligible for any of the special provisions of the Tariff that allow for lower duty rates usually depends on the use or purpose for which they are being imported, or on the availability of certificates of origin. The importer is in the best position to know these facts, and increasingly importers are becoming aware of this and choosing to classify their own goods, or verify the work of third parties (in particular, their customs broker).

Importers who use custom brokers should not leave classification of their goods entirely up to the broker. By understanding how the tariff classification process works, they will be able to work together with their broker to ensure that their goods are classified correctly. Brokers, on the other hand, should insist on getting complete, accurate product descriptions, including intended use, from the importer.

The Harmonized System of Tariff Classification

It should be properly classified for all the imported goods by using the Harmonized System of Tariff Classification. Tariff classification enables governments to identify goods imported into the country for purposes of duty and tax collection, as well as gathering statistical information for economic planning, trade negotiation, and the enforcement of national and international laws. The Harmonized System of Tariff Classification is used worldwide. The core specifics and structure of tariff classifications are universal, with each participating country eligible to define specific detail items and assign applicable rates of duty to any required category.

The Descriptions of Harmonized Commodity and Coding System were designed to fulfill the following goals:

- The systematic classification of all goods found in international trade.
- Classification of all goods on a uniform basis in the tariffs of all countries adopting this Nomenclature.
- The adoption of a common internationally accepted Customs language.
- Simplicity and certainty of meaning in the negotiation,

application and interpretation of trade agreements.

- An internationally uniform basis for the collection of trade statistics.

General Rules of Interpretation

There are six General Rules of Interpretation. Rules one to four are related and must be applied in sequence. Rules five and six stand on their own to be applied whenever necessary. A discussion of the individual rules follows:

RULE 1: The Sections titles, Chapters and sub-Chapters are provided for ease of reference only; for legal purposes, classification shall be determined according to the terms of the headings and any relative Section or Chapter Notes and, provided such headings or Notes do not otherwise require, according to the following provisions [that is, GIRs 2 to 6]:

Explanation: For the classification of product it plays an important role. For practical purposes, this means that the Section and Chapter titles can be used as guidelines to point the way to the area of the Tariff in which the product to be classified is likely to be found. However, articles may be included in or excluded from a Section or Chapter even though the titles might lead one to believe otherwise. Thus in order to classify a product, one must carefully check the Notes associated with any Sections and Chapters under consideration to see if the product is mentioned specifically as being included or excluded. Then it is necessary to go down to the Heading level and find a Heading that is worded in such a way as to include the product in question. Many goods should be correctly classifiable by reference to Rule 1 alone. If the results of this process are ambiguous, then Rule 2 should be applied.

Example: Suppose if you were importing Christmas tree candles, it appears to be logical to classify them with Classification Number 9505.10.00.90: Other, articles for Christmas festivities. In fact, we must classify them with the Classification Number 3406.00.00.00: Candles, tapers and the like.

RULE 2: (a) Each cited references in a heading to an article shall be taken to include a reference to that article incomplete or unfinished, provided that, as presented, the incomplete or unfinished article has the essential character of the complete or finished article. It shall also be taken to include a reference to that article complete or finished (or falling to be classified as complete or finished by virtue of this Rule), presented unassembled or disassembled.

(b) Those references in a heading to a material or substance shall be taken to include a reference to mixtures or combinations of that material or substance with other materials or substances. Any reference to goods of a given material or substance shall be taken to include a reference to goods consisting wholly or partly of such material or substance. The classification of goods consisting of more than one material or substance shall be according to the principles of Rule 3.

Explanation: Rule 2 (a). It deals with the classification of incomplete, unfinished, unassembled or disassembled goods. Unfinished and incomplete goods can be classified under the same Heading as the same goods in a finished state provided that they have the essential character of the complete or finished article. As well, unassembled or disassembled goods may also be classified the same as the complete finished product. This rule does not apply if the text of the Heading or the relevant Legal Notes excludes the unfinished or unassembled product in question.

Example: An automobile missing only its wheels would be classified the same as if it were complete.

Explanation: Rule 2 (b) emphasises to the groundwork for dealing with products, not classifiable through the use of Rule 1 or Rule 2 (a), which are composed of a mixture of materials or substances. It basically states that a Heading referring to a given material or substance includes mixtures of that substance with others. Likewise, a reference to a product composed of a given material or substance includes products composed either wholly or partly of the material or substance. This means that a mixed product may seem to be eligible for classification under two or more Headings.

Example: If you were importing dicalcium citrate, the Tariff does not specifically state this compound. However, it is a compound containing more than one material and its essential character is that of a salt of citric acid.

RULE 3: When by application of Rule 2 (b) or for any other reason, goods are, prima facie, classifiable under two or more headings, classification shall be effected as follows:

(a) The heading which provides the most specific description shall be preferred to headings providing a more general description. However, when two or more headings each refer to part only of the materials or substances contained in mixed or composite goods or to part only of the items in a set put up for retail sale, those headings are to be regarded as equally specific in relation to those goods, even if one of them gives a more complete or precise description of the goods.

(b) Mixtures, composite goods consisting of different materials or made up of different components, and goods put up in sets for retail sale, which cannot be classified by reference to 3(a), shall be classified as if they consisted of the material or component which gives them their essential character, insofar as this criterion is applicable.

(c) When goods cannot be classified by reference to 3(a) or 3(b), they shall be classified under the heading which occurs last in numerical order among those which equally merit consideration.

Explanation: Rule 3 (a) states that where 2 or more Headings seem to apply, the one which provides the most specific description of the product in question should be used. This means that a Heading which names the actual product should be used in preference to one which only names a category to which the product could belong. Similarly, a Heading that describes the whole product should be used in preference to one which describes part of it. However, where two Headings both only describe part of the product, this rule cannot be used to tell which one to use even if one seems more specific or detailed than the other.

Example: It is not stated specifically the mint tea, as a product, in the Tariff. Although the product descriptions available are mint and tea, the importer must classify mint tea under the appropriate tea heading because it provides the most specific product description and mint is only the flavour of the tea.

Explanation: Rule 3 (b) Usually applies to mixtures, composite goods and sets that cannot be classified by use of the previous Rules. These should be classified as if they consisted of the material or component which gives them their essential character.

Example: An importer bringing in "liquor gift sets" (that include the bottle of liquor and glasses) must classify the goods under the appropriate liquor Heading. The essential character of the item is the liquor itself and not the glasses contained within the set.

Explanation: Rule 3 (c) is for use in cases in which a good seems to fit in more than one Heading and the essential character cannot be determined. In this case, the product should be classified under the Heading which occurs last in numerical order.

Example: A gift set which includes socks and ties cannot be classified by the previous rule since neither item gives the gift set its essential character. The gift set must be classified under the Heading number for ties which is the Heading that occurs last in numerical order.

RULE 4: Those goods items which cannot be classified with reference to the above Rules shall be classified under the heading appropriate to the goods to which they are most akin.

Explanation: This is a "last resort" rule, most often used with new products.

RULE 5: In addition to the above provisions, the following Rules shall apply in respect of the goods referred to therein:

(a) Those specially shaped or fitted to contain a specific article or set of articles, suitable for long-term use and presented with the articles for which they are intended, such as Camera cases, musical instrument cases, gun cases, drawing instrument cases, necklace cases and similar containers etc shall be classified with such articles when of a kind normally sold therewith. This Rule does not, however, apply to containers which give the whole its essential character.

(b) Subject to the above Rule 5 (a) above, packing materials and packing containers presented with the goods therein shall be classified with the goods if they are of a kind normally used for packing such goods. However, this provision does not apply when such packing materials or packing containers are clearly suitable for repetitive use.

Explanation: Rule 5 highlights about the classification of containers which:

- are shaped or fitted for the article they will contain,
- are suitable for long-term use,
- protect the article when not in use,
- are of a kind normally sold with such articles,
- are presented with the articles they are designed to contain.

The containers which have the above characteristics can be classified with the products which they contain. However, in cases where the container gives the product its essential character, it would be the container which would have to be classified.

Example: Rule 5 (a) would apply to flute cases because flutes are normally sold with their cases (due to their specific shape) and are intended for long term use.

Explanation: Rule 5 (b) deals with other types of containers and packing materials. These should be classified with the goods they contain if they are of a kind normally used for packing such goods and are not suitable for repetitive use. Example: An importer bringing in goods and using Styrofoam chips for padding fits well into Rule 5 (b). Styrofoam chips are normally used for the padding and insulation of many goods, however they are rarely reused and are therefore classified with the goods when they enter Canada.

RULE 6: For legal purposes, the classification of goods in the subheadings of a heading shall be determined according to the terms of those subheadings and any related Subheading Notes and mutatis mutandis, to the above Rules, on the understanding that only subheadings at the same level are comparable. For the purpose of this Rule the relative Section and Chapter Notes also apply, unless the context otherwise requires. Explanation: Once goods have been classified to the Heading level by the use of international Rules 1 to 5, then classification to the Subheading level can now take place by repeating international Rules 1 to 5 and taking into account any related Legal Notes.

Legal Notes

In the Harmonized Tariff, Notes precede some of the Sections and Chapters. These are known as Legal Notes because they have legal force as an integral part of the Harmonized System. Section Notes, Chapter Notes and Subheading Notes are included in the international core of the Harmonized System Nomenclature. The international Legal Notes define the precise scope and limits of each Chapter, Section, Heading or Subheading. Specifically, they perform the following functions:

(1) Define the limits of a Heading.

(2) Provide lists of goods included in a particular Section, Chapter, Heading or group of Headings.

(3) Provide lists of goods excluded from a particular Section, Chapter or Heading.

(4) Direct the user to the appropriate Section, Chapter or Heading for a particular product.

(5) Subheading Notes specifically define what is to be included in or excluded from given Subheadings after classification to the Heading level has taken place.

Legal Notes Terminology

Throughout the Nomenclature: This is used in case in which words or expressions are defined in the notes for a specific Chapter or Heading, but the definition will apply throughout the whole Tariff. On the other hand, if these words are not used in a definition given in the notes for a particular Section or Chapter, the definition should be taken as applying only to that Section or Chapter.

Inter Alia: This implies "among other things". Basically it is used with a list of similar objects to illustrate that the list is not exhaustive, and the classification is not restricted to just what is listed.

Mutatis Mutandis: The literal meaning is "making due alteration for detail". If this wording is found in the Tariff, it permits a person to make alterations for small specific details in order to complete classifying the item being imported.

Context: The phrases Except where the context otherwise requires and Unless the context mean that in those cases in which the Chapter or Section Notes are incompatible with the Heading/Subheading Notes or the text of Headings and Subheadings, the lower level notes and text will prevail.

Sections and Chapters

It has already mentioned that the primary division of goods in the Tariff is consisted of 21 Sections and 98 chapters.

Agricultural products

- Section I: Live animals; animal products
- Section II: Vegetable products
- Section III: Animal or vegetable fats and oils and their cleavage products; prepared edible fats; animal or vegetable waxes
- Section IV: Prepared foodstuffs; beverages, spirits and vinegar; tobacco and manufactured tobacco substitutes

Mineral products

- Section V: Mineral products

Chemical and related products

- Section VI: Products of the chemical or allied industries
- Section VII: Plastics and articles thereof; rubber and articles thereof

Non-consumable animal and plant products

- Section VIII: Raw hides and skins, leather, furskins and articles thereof; saddlery and harness; travel goods, handbags and similar containers; articles of animal gut (other than silk-worm gut)
- Section IX: Wood and articles of wood; wood charcoal; cork and articles of cork; manufactures of straw, of esparto or of other plaiting materials; basket ware and wickerwork
- Section X: Pulp of wood or of other fibrous cellulosic material; waste and scrap of paper or paperboard; paper and paperboard and articles thereof

Textiles and apparel

- Section XI: Textiles and textile articles
- Section XII: Footwear, headgear, umbrellas, sun umbrellas, walking-sticks, seat-sticks, whips, riding crops and parts thereof; prepared feathers and articles made therewith; artificial flowers; articles of human hair

Non-metallic mineral products

- Section XIII: Articles of stone, plaster, cement, asbestos, mica or similar materials; ceramic products; glass and glassware

Metals and manufactured articles made mostly of metal

- Section XIV: Natural or cultured pearls, precious or semi-precious stones, precious metals, metals clad with precious metal and articles thereof; imitation jewelry; coin
- Section XV: Base metal and articles of base metal
- Section XVI: Machinery and mechanical appliances; electrical equipment; parts thereof; sound recorders and reproducers, television image and sound recorders and reproducers, and parts and accessories of such articles
- Section XVII: Vehicles, aircraft, vessels and associated transport equipment

- Section XVIII: Optical, photographic, cinematographic, measuring, checking, precision, medical or surgical instruments and apparatus; clocks and watches; musical instruments; parts and accessories thereof
- Section XIX: Arms and ammunition; parts and accessories thereof

Other highly manufactured and special-purpose goods

- Section XX: Miscellaneous manufactured articles
- Section XXI: Works of art, collectors' pieces and antiques

Explanatory Notes

In order to understand clearly, the international version of the Harmonized System has Explanatory Notes associated with it. The Notes are arranged in the same order as the Tariff itself. They can be used to assist in classification but have no legal force. They typically contain more detailed descriptions of the products or groups of products to be included in a given area of the Tariff often including detailed accounts of the manufacturing processes to be used.

The classification number

It has already been discussed that goods are listed according to a hierarchical classification system, broken down into finer and finer categories. The lowest breakdown level is called the Classification Number. This is the number that must be used on the Customs documents. There is a Classification Number for every product that anyone could ever wish to import. The Classification Number is put together in a very logical manner. Consisting of 10 digits, each digit provides specific data used to systematically produce an increasingly accurate description of the item. Because the Harmonized System was designed to be used on a global basis, the first 6 digits fulfill the international requirements while the last 4 have been designated for Country-specific Tariff and statistical purposes.

Example: 0406.20.90.20 Cheese, as an animal product, is found in Section I: Live Animals; Animal Products. Classification down to the 10 digit level can be reached as follows:

04 is the Chapter designation indicating that the item: dairy produce; birds' eggs; natural honey; edible products of animal origin not elsewhere specified or included. 0406.20 is the Subheading indicating the type of cheese or curd: grated or powdered cheese of

all kinds. Note that the decimal in between the first two digits and last two digits of the Heading level moves to after the first four digits in the Subheading level and below. 0406.20.90 is the Tariff Item, describing the variety of grated or powdered cheese: other than cheddar and cheddar types. The Canadian duty rate is assessed at this level. The official unit of measurement is assigned, where applicable, at this level when the Statistical Suffix is 00.

0406.20.90.20 is the Classification Number, specifying the exact type of grated or powdered cheese other than cheddar: Romano. The classification number is built by adding a two digit code, the Statistical Suffix (in this case 20) to the Tariff Item. Note that all Classification Numbers belonging to a given Tariff Item will have the same duty rate. As well, the official unit of measurement is assigned, where applicable, at this level when the Statistical Suffix is other than 00. It may appears to be more complicated in the classification of an item. Often, the digits at a given level are filled in with zeros indicating that no further breakdown is required at that level. For example, look at 8502.20.00.00 the Classification Number for "Generating sets with spark-ignition internal combustion piston engines."

It may be noted that the digits for the Tariff Item and Classification Number levels are zeros. This indicates that no further breakdown beyond the Subheading is required and that the same number encompasses all the Subheading, Tariff Item and Classification Number levels. It is quite common for the last 2 digits of the Classification Number to be filled in with zeros to indicate that the duty rates and statistical classification are to be determined at the same level of detail. On the contrary, when a more complex breakdown than that shown in the powdered cheese example, above, is required, both digits of one or more levels are filled in with non-zero digits. It may be noted that the first Tariff Item on the page, 8413.30.10, is broken down into 5 Classification Numbers by adding the pairs of digits, 10, 20, 30, 40, 90, respectively. These are known as first level Classification Numbers.

The second Tariff Item shown, 8413.30.90 breaks down differently. Below the Tariff Item is the Classification Number 8413.30.90.10 with the description, Fuel pumps. This is a first level Classification Number. Below this are the numbers 8413.30.90.11 to 8413.30.90.19, each with a description. These are second level Classification Numbers. Where there are second levels Classification Numbers, the first level Classification Number at the top of a group of second level Classification Numbers is simply a Heading for the group of second level Classification Numbers.

Another important feature of the Tariff is the dash or series of dashes preceeding the Subheading and Subheading description lines. At the time of classification, one must always classify within like description categories that have the same number of dashes. The minimum number of dashes is one; the maximum is 6.

Description of Goods — is an explanatory statement verifying the characteristics of the item. Often the descriptions for a few levels above the Classification Number must be examined in order to verify that the description associated with the Classification Number really refers to the product in question.

Unit of Measure Code — indicated by abbreviated units measuring the item by volume/capacity, weight, area, number, etc. The unit of measure is used to determine the value for duty on goods which have a specific or compound rate of duty.

For example. KGM—imported quantities of Quinacridone Violet are measured by weight in kilograms.

Trade Agreements and Associated Duty Rates — the rates of duty imposed upon the item according to tariff agreements in effect with the country of origin are shown here. Duty is calculated in the following ways: on an ad valorem rate (which is a percentage of the value of the goods), on a specific rate per measure, or on a compound rate (which is a combination of both).

For example. If this commodity was being imported from a country where the Most Favoured Nation Tariff applies and provided all the conditions are met, duty is assessed on an ad valorem rate of 5%. Both the General Preferential Tariff rate and the United States Tariff rate are free.

Accelerated tariff elimination: When the duties of the import duties are decreased, faster than was originally agreed upon or projected. For instance, under NAFTA, tariffs on goods traded between the US and Canada were phased out earlier than was initially planned.

Ad valorem tariff: The tariff levied on imports, defined in terms of a fixed percentage of the goods' value. For instance, if India imposes an ad valorem tariff of 40% on butter, it means that the tariff will be 40% of the value of the butter being imported.

Applied tariffs: The present tariff rates are to be charged on the product imports.. Applied tariffs may be below or equal to bound tariffs, but may not exceed them. For instance, the applied tariff in Pakistan for coffee was 20%, while the bound tariff rate was 100%.

Average tariff : The simple average of all applied ad valorem tariffs (tariffs based on the value of the import) applicable to the bilateral imports of countries. This rate is calculated by adding up all the tariff rates and dividing this by the number of import categories.

Bound tariffs : In the WTO, when there is an agreement to open their markets to goods and services, they "bind" their commitments. For goods, these bindings amount to ceilings on customs tariff rates. Sometimes countries tax imports at rates that are lower than the bound rates. This rate is legally binding under the WTO and applies on a Most Favoured Nation (MFN) basis. If a WTO member raises a tariff above the bound rate, affected countries have the right to retaliate against an equivalent value of the offending country's exports, or receive compensation, usually in the form of reduced tariffs on other products they export to the "offending" country. India has bound 72% of its tariff lines, with all agricultural products bound and some 68% of tariff lines bound with respect to industrial goods. India bound products particularly such as textiles and clothing, which were previously unbound.

Compound tariff : A combination of ad valorem and specific tariffs (such as 10% plus $ 5 per kilogram).

GATT (General Agreement on Tariffs and Trade) : In 1947 this agreement was first drafted in order to establish "free trade" between nations by limiting or eliminating tariffs and quotas on international trade. The Uruguay Round of the GATT, completed in December 1993, substantially expanded the scope of the agreement and created the World Trade Organisation (WTO).

GSP (Generalised System of Preferences) : A system where developed countries grant preferential treatment to eligible products imported from developing countries, so that the exports of developing countries are able to compete in the markets of developed countries.

The purpose of the GSP is to enable developing countries' exports to be competitive in developed country markets. It involves reduced MFN tariffs or duty-free entry of eligible products exported by beneficiary countries to the markets of donor countries. European Union (EU) member countries have allowed equal preferential treatment in duties in the range of 2.5% on imports of clothing from both Pakistan and India under the new Generalised System of Preferences (GSP) scheme, effective from January 1, 2006.

Harmonised system (HS) : It is specialised to serve as a universally accepted classification system for goods so that countries can run customs programmes and collect trade data on exports and imports. It was designed to replace the varied tracking methods used by countries and create a common classification system by which to track trade and apply tariffs.

Usually the system uses a six-digit number in order to identify basic commodities. Each country is allowed to add additional digits for statistical purposes. In Canada , two additional digits are used for exports and four additional digits for imports. The US uses a 10-digit system for both exports and imports. The system was developed by the World Customs Organisation (WCO).

HS is a classification of commodity system where articles are grouped largely based on the nature of the materials they are made of. The system contains approximately 5,000 heads and sub-heads covering all articles of trade. These provisions are organised into 96 chapters, arranged in 21 sections that, along with the interpretive rules and legal notes to the chapters and sections, form the legal text of the harmonised system. The code is made up of three parts — the first two digits identify the chapter and the next two, groupings within the chapter; the last two are the most specific.

Industrial tariffs : The import taxes which are applied to manufactured products such as textiles and clothing, leather, wood pulp and transport equipment. They have the effect of raising the price for consumers and hence discouraging them from buying imported goods.

Mixed tariff : A choice between ad valorem and/or specific tariffs depending on the condition attached (for example, 10% or $ 5 per kilogram, whichever is greater).

Most Favoured Nation (MFN) rate : The quantity of duty for a product originating from an MFN supplier. A product originating from non-MFN suppliers may be subject to a different rate of duty from the MFN rate, depending on whether the suppliers are from a territory outside of the WTO (the rate may be higher), covered by a GSP or GSTP (Generalised System of Trade Preferences) scheme (the rate is often lower) or a customs union or free trade area (a final rate of zero for covered products).

Prohibitive tariff : Tariff at a level that discourages the import of a product in any quantity. For instance, in 1995, average tariffs in OECD countries stood at 214% for wheat and 154% for barley. Similarly, Senegal levies prohibitive tariffs on imported cycles to protect a small domestic manufacturer that sells only 2,000 bikes annually.

Simple average applied tariff rate: It is the average of a country's applied tariff rates. The applied average tariff is calculated by dividing the total of applied tariffs with the number of tariff lines. For instance, if a country's tariff rate under the non-agricultural import category for three products is 10%, 25% and 33% respectively, then the average applied tariff rate for that country, under the non-agricultural import category, would be 22.67%.

Simple average bound tariff rate: The average of a country's bound tariff rates divided by the number of tariff lines. For instance, if there are three tariff lines with a bound tariff rate of 100.7%, 63.8% and 90% in a country, the simple average bound tariff rate will be 84.33% for that country.

Specific tariff : Tariff that is levied at a specific rate per physical unit of a particular item. For instance, a tariff of $ 10 on every kilogram of butter imported.

Tariff: It is the tax imposed on the import or export of goods. In general parlance, however, it refers to "import duties" charged at the time goods are imported. Tariffs have three primary functions: to serve as a source of revenue, to protect domestic industry, and to remedy trade distortions. Tariffs can be ad valorem or specific or mixed.

Tariff bands : It is the tiers of tariff under certain slabs. Illustrations of two bands: tariffs between 0% and 10% and tariffs between 11% and 25%. Tariffs are put into bands to decide the percentage of tariff reduction. For instance, there can be an agreement for no tariff cuts in the 0-10% band, a 25% cut for tariffs in the 11-50% band, and a 50% cut for tariffs in bands above this. India pursued a policy of tariff reduction and rationalisation of the tariff structure notably by reducing the number of tariff bands. By 2004-5, there were two bands —10% for raw materials and intermediate goods, and 20% for final products.

Tariff binding : It is necessary in the setting of a maximum tariff rate on an imported product. While the applied tariff rate charged by an importing country could vary, an importing country cannot exceed the bound rate without re-negotiating its WTO commitments. Tariff binding comprises two sets of issues. First is the issue of tariff binding coverage, implying the number of tariff lines to be bound. The second relates to the rate at which unbound tariff lines should be bound. Developed countries have been keen that developing countries and Least Developed Countries (LDCs) increase their tariff binding coverage to 100% or near 100%. Increasing tariff binding coverage implies binding more tariff lines, thereby giving up the flexibility of being able to increase tariff rates on a particular product beyond a certain point.

Tariff classifications : National based tariffs are organised in a tabular form which consists of "tariff classification numbers" assigned to goods, and a corresponding tariff rate. The way in which an item is classified for tariff purposes will have an important and palpable effect on the duties charged. When classifications are applied in an arbitrary fashion, they can in effect nullify rate reductions. The GATT contains no rules regarding tariff classifications. In the past, countries had their own individual systems. However, as trade expanded, countries began to recognise the need for more uniform classifications, which resulted in the drafting, in 1988, of the Harmonised Commodity Description and Coding System, or the HS system. Nowadays, majority of the countries uses a harmonised system of six-digit tariff numbers.

Tariff cuts : It is the percentage reduction in tariffs. Various formulae are proposed different tariff cuts. For instance under a fixed percentage formula, the tariffs for all products are cut by a single rate, whether the starting tariff is high or low. Under this formula all tariffs can be cut by 25% in equal steps over five years. On the other hand, the Swiss formula proposes steeper cuts for higher tariffs. This means that a tariff of, say, 150% will face a higher cut than a tariff of 80%.

Tariff escalation : In case of a country wants to protect its processing or manufacturing industry, it can set low tariffs on imported materials used by the industry (cutting industry costs) and set higher tariffs on finished products to protect goods produced by the industry. When importing countries escalate their tariffs in this way, they make it more difficult for countries producing raw materials to process and manufacture value-added products for export.

Tariff enhances in the existing of both developed and developing countries. A country may choose to impose no tariff on the import of raw materials, but increase tariffs on semi-processed and final goods. For instance, the tariff average in developed countries for rubber increases from 0.0% for raw rubber to 3.3% for semi-processed products to 5.1% for finished products.

Tariff line : It is the single item in a country's tariff schedule.

Tariff peaks : Most import tariffs are now quite low while for a few products that governments may consider to be sensitive, tariffs remain high. These are "tariff peaks". Some affect exports from developing countries. There are two kinds of tariff peaks:

- *International tariff peaks* : The percentage of tariff lines in a country that has a bound tariff rate of more than 15%. For instance, in Pakistan, 33.2% of the total tariff lines have bound tariff rates that exceed 15%.
- *National tariff peak* : The percentage of tariff lines in a country that have bound tariff rates at least three times higher than the country's average tariff. In the case of dairy products as well as fruits and vegetables, developed countries impose peak tariffs that are, on average, more than three times the peak tariff applied in India.

Tariff rate quotas : A combination of an import tariff and an import quota whereby imports below a specified quantity enter at a low (or zero) tariff, and imports above that quantity enters at a higher tariff. For India, the EU and US have committed a tariff rate quota of 20,000 tonnes and 9,000 tonnes respectively, which means that imports above this quantity will be charged higher import duty.

Tariff revenue : The revenue generated for the government from tariffs.

Tariff schedule : A database maintained by the WTO Secretariat that contains, among other things, members' commitments to reducing bound rates.

Tariff valuation : When countries assign arbitrary values for tariff purposes, they render tariff rates meaningless. GATT Article VII and the Agreement on Implementation of Article VII (Custom Valuation Agreement) define international rules for valuation.

Tariff war : When one nation increases tariffs on goods imported from or exported to another country and that country then retaliates by also raising tariffs.

Tariffication : Conversion of NTBs (Non-Tariff Barriers) to tariffs at the level of their tariff equivalent. In the Uruguay Round, agricultural NTBs were tariffied and bound, to replace unwieldy NTBs with tariffs that could then become the subject of negotiation.

Weighted average tariffs : An assessment that weighs each tariff by the share of total imports in that import category. Thus, if a country has most of its imports in a category with very low tariffs, but has many import categories with high tariffs but virtually no imports, then the trade-weighted average tariff would indicate a low level of protection. The standard way of calculating this tariff rate is to divide total tariff revenue by the total value of imports. Since many countries regularly report this data, this is a common way to report average tariffs.

Tariff Reduction Formulae and Approaches

Linear tariff cut formula : Decreasing tariffs by an equal percentage across the entire class of products. Linear tariff cuts can be contrasted with tariff harmonisation, which brings different countries' measures in line with each other by requiring relatively large cuts in higher tariffs and smaller cuts in lower tariffs. Developing countries argue that their reduction commitments must be based on a linear formula, as tariff protection is their only means of safeguarding their developmental needs and protecting themselves against international price shocks. The linear tariff cut formula isT1 = T0-(C*T0), where T1 = final rate, T0 = initial rate and C = reduction coefficient.

Swiss formula : Decreasing tariffs by using a harmonising coefficient that cuts higher tariffs more steeply, in proportion to lower tariffs, and establishes a maximum final rate no matter how high the original tariff was. Under a simple Swiss formula, the higher the tariff, the greater the cut. Developing countries are generally opposed to the Swiss formula, as they tend to have higher tariffs on industrial goods than their richer counterparts.

The Swiss formula is T1 = (C*T0)/(C+T0) where T1 = new tariff rate, T0 = initial tariff rate and C = reduction coefficient.

Modified Swiss formula : A modification in the Swiss formula, as proposed by the Cairns Group of agriculture commodity exporting countries. The reduction coefficient proposed for developed countries under this formula is 25 (that is, C = 25). For developing countries the formula proposes that using the Swiss formula with a coefficient of 50 should reduce tariffs between 0% and 50%. For tariffs between 50% and 250%, it proposes a linear cut of 50%, and for tariffs above 250% it proposes an across-the-board reduction to a maximum of 125%.

Blended formula : Tariff reduction formula proposed by the EC and the US. It encompasses, on a self-declaratory basis, a proportion of tariff lines subject to the Uruguay Round tariff reduction formula; a proportion of tariff lines subject to the Swiss formula, and a proportion of tariff lines to be made duty-free. This formula is not supported by developing countries like India and other members of the G20. By this formula, tariff reductions are much higher for developing countries.

Girard formula : Tariff reduction formula that takes into account the interests of developing countries by incorporating each country's average tariff. The equation for the formula is T1 = B*T2*T0/B*T2+T0, where T1 is the final bound rate, T2 is the average of the base rates, T0 is the base rate and B is the coefficient. The higher the value of B, the less the rate of tariff reduction. For example, in the case of India, the bound tariff rate for fish and fish products is 100.7%. If the tariff reduction for this category takes place with a lower value of B, say 0.5, then the tariff rate after reduction will be 14.6%. If the value of B is changed to 1, the tariff rate after reduction would be 25.5%.

Tiered formula (banded formula) : Tariff reduction formula that classifies tariffs into various bands for subsequent reduction from bound rates, the higher tariffs being cut more than the lower ones. The actual modalities number of bands, threshold for defining bands, and type of tariff reductions within each band remain subject to negotiation. The role of a tariff cap with distinct treatment for sensitive products also remains subject to negotiation.

Uruguay Round formula : Tariff reduction formula designed to allow varied levels of tariff protection across products but nonetheless subjecting all tariff lines to a minimum degree of cuts in a linear fashion. Developed countries had to impose an average cut of 36%, with a minimum 15% cut. The corresponding figures for developing countries were 24% and 10% respectively. Developing countries contended that the Uruguay Round approach allowed developed countries to focus the largest reductions on the lowest tariffs, while allowing them to maintain high tariffs on lines that were of interest to developing country exports.

Sectoral approach : Tariff reduction approach, also called the sector-by-sector approach, whereby tariff rates on all products of export interest to developing countries and LDCs are eliminated and bound. The sectoral approach essentially means cutting or eliminating tariffs on certain sectors independent of the tariff cutting formula that is followed for other sectors. India has not made any submission on the issue of sectoral liberalisation. India's argument is that the sectoral approach should be voluntary in nature and should be taken up only after the issue of a tariff reduction formula is settled.

Zero-for-zero approach : Tariff reduction approach which implies that in identified sectors all countries should bring down their tariff rates to zero. This implies losing policy flexibility. For instance, in the fish and fish products category, India and Pakistan have 87%

and 90% of tariff lines unbound. When such a high proportion of tariff lines is unbound in a sensitive sector it would not be prudent for these countries to support the zero-for-zero approach.

EC tariff reduction approach : Modified Swiss formula proposed at NAMA negotiations, in March 2005, by the European Commission (EC). The EC formula is T1 = (X*T0)/(T0+X) where T1 is the final tariff, X is the given coefficient and T0 is the initial tariff. The EC approach implies flexibility: while there would be an overall tariff reduction, each country would be free to determine the level of tariffs on individual products, subject to the overall reduction.

US tariff reduction approach : Modified Swiss formula proposed by the US with dual coefficients: one coefficient for developed countries and another for developing countries. The US proposal also states that the two coefficients must be "within sight of each other," which means that the coefficient for developed countries should not be significantly greater than the coefficient for developing countries.

Norway tariff reduction approach: Proposed by Norway, this is a non-linear tariff cutting formula with two coefficients that include a simple and transparent system of credits. The formula is T1 = (A*T0)/A+C), where T1 is the new bound tariff after the formula cut, T0 is the old bound tariff, A is the coefficient indicating the level of ambition. 'A' will have different values for developed and developing countries. 'C' is the credit that the country gets for binding 100% tariff lines and participating in the sectoral approach to tariff reduction.

Argentina, Brazil and India (ABI) approach : Girard formula of tariff reduction proposed by Argentina, Brazil and India.

Pakistan tariff reduction proposal : Simple Swiss formula for tariff reduction proposed by Pakistan, with two coefficients. Based on existing bound average tariff rates, the coefficient for developed countries would be six and that for developing countries 30. This would have the effect of harmonising tariffs in both bands while retaining the difference in average tariff levels between the groups. According to Pakistan, its proposal would reduce developing countries' average bound rates of 35% and applied rates of 25% to around 15%, while developed countries' average bound and applied rates would be cut roughly by 4%.

Tariff Reduction

In the preceding years, countries had their own individual systems. However, as trade expanded countries recognized the need for more uniform classifications, which resulted in the drafting in 1988 of the "Harmonized Commodity Description and Coding System" or "HS" system. Today, most countries use a Harmonized system of six-digit tariff numbers.

Valuation : It is the final component in tariffs to valuation of goods for tariff purposes. When countries assign arbitrary values for tariff purposes, they render tariff rates meaningless. GATT Article VII and the "Agreement on Implementation of Article VII" (Custom Valuation Agreement) define international rules for valuation 4.

Legal framework

The WTO bans, in principle, all quantitative restrictions, but allows for the imposition of tariffs. It then attempts to reduce the barrier posed by tariffs in "tariff negotiations" among member countries, whereby they agree to "bind" themselves to maximum rates ("bound rates") for individual items (in principle following the tariff classification nomenclature) and negotiate for their progressive reduction.

(a) GATT Disciplines: GATT Article II obligates Member countries to apply tariff rates that are no higher than their bound rates. GATT Article XXVIII specifies that when Members wish to raise their bound rates or withdraw tariff concessions, they must negotiate and reach agreements with other Members with whom they had initially negotiated and enter into consultation with major supplying countries that have a substantial interest in any change in the bound rate.

(b) Disciplines on Tariff Classifications: Article 3.1 of the International Convention on the Harmonized Commodity Description and Coding System (HS Convention) stipulates that the signatories "shall not modify the scope of the sections, chapters, headings, or subheadings of the Harmonized System." This is done in order to maintain uniform administration of the HS. The HS classifications are reviewed on a 4 Customs Valuation Agreement states that "the primary basis for customs value under this Agreement is "transaction value" as defined in Article 1...together with Article 8...adjustments."

This is an explicit affirmation that the price actually paid is to be used as the basis for customs valuation. Article 2 of the Agreement provides for the transaction prices of similar goods to be used in exceptional cases regular basis so as to keep pace with technological development. If, as a result of these reviews, the classification of a good changes in such a way as to raise its bound rate, countries must enter into negotiations under the terms of GATT Article XXVIII.

(c) The Importance of "Binding": It would be obvious from the discussion so far that there are not much problems in regards to WTO rules in the in setting of high bound rates or in not agreeing to be bound at all. The WTO rules therefore allow countries to raise effective tariff rates within the scope of their bound rates, and to raise tariff rates at will for non-bound items. Regardless of whether it is permitted by the rules, however, a sudden hike in tariff rates will obviously have a detrimental impact on trade.

Similarly, not binding tariff rates also runs against the grain of the WTO, which, as we have observed, is based on the idea of using "binding" to reduce tariffs? From this perspective, the significance of binding must be emphasized. As a result of the Uruguay Round, the percentage of industrial products subject to bound rates in Japan, the United States, the EU, and Canada (total value of imports subject to bound tariffs divided by total value of imports) is now about 100 percent. The percentage of other countries and regions is somewhat lower, or in some cases substantially lower: Korea (89 percent), Indonesia (92 percent), Thailand (70 percent), Malaysia (79 percent), Singapore (73 percent), and Hong Kong (23 percent).

Economic implications

Here in this section it analyses some of the basic economic issues associated with tariffs, specifically, why they are preferable to quantitative restrictions, and why it is desirable that they be reduced. This section then considers the importance of international tariff-reduction negotiations at the WTO.

(a) The Effect of tariffs :

The most fundamental effect that an import tariff has is to raise domestic prices in the country imposing the tariff. In "small countries" (defined for our purposes as countries that do not have an influence on international prices), the rise in domestic price is equivalent to the amount of the tariff. In "large countries" (those that have an impact on international prices), the price rises somewhat less than the amount of the tariff because part of the tariff is reflected in a reduction in international prices. A tariff-induced price rise creates a gap between prices in the importing and exporting countries. This in turn supplies (production) to rise in the importing country, while demand (consumption) falls, which are the essence of the "industrial protection" function of tariffs. Obviously, a tariff also generates revenues for the government of the importing country (revenue function). Tariffs therefore benefit the government and producers of the importing country in the form of tax revenues and producer surpluses at the expense of its consumers in the form of higher prices. Because tariffs bring different benefits and costs to different groups,5 the net cost to the importing country is the "cost to consumers minus profits to producers minus government revenues." It shows an equality to the sum of the "efficiency loss" caused by distortions to the pricing system and the "profits from improved terms of trade" brought by a reduction in international prices. Therefore, for "small countries" which see no improvement in their terms of trade because their tariffs have no influence on international prices, the benefits from a tariff will necessarily be negative. However, for "large countries" that can expect an improvement in terms of trade because part of the tariff will lead to a reduction in international prices, the pros and cons are not so easily weighted. Many economists sometimes refer to "optimal tariffs" that are low enough for the improvement in the terms of trade to exceed the costs, thereby maximizing economic welfare. The degree of protection afforded by a tariff (the effective protection rate) is not equal to the tariff rate. The first reason for this is because of the potential influence from an improvement in the terms of trade. The second reason is that the effective protection rate will differ depending on which stage of the production process the tariff is applied (tariffs on parts or tariffs on finished goods). We must therefore point out that even a relatively low tariff rate can function adequately as a means of protecting domestic industry.

(b) The Effect of quantitative restrictions :

The Quantitative restrictions taking into many forms, import quotas are the most common one. The effect of quotas is the same as that of import tariffs higher domestic prices for imported goods. Quotas differ from tariffs because the importing country's government gains no revenue from quotas while importers to whom the quotas are allocated obtain excessive profits ("rents") from them. The cost of quotas to importing country governments is therefore higher than the cost of tariffs. Moreover, when there is a monopoly in the domestic market, an import quota results in higher domestic prices than an import tariff that achieves the same import volume. From the fact point of view, it is difficult to gauge the net effect of tariffs in any strict sense because different people will assign different values to the same profits in absolute terms. We will therefore forgo further discussion here. We should note, however, that this point becomes important in real-world discussions, considers "weighted social welfare" later in this chapter. For an industry with an added-value rate of 25% (purchases parts for $75 and assembles them into a finished good worth $100), a tariff of 25% on finished goods (resulting in a domestic price of $125) will increase the costs that can be tolerated by the industry from $25 to $50, which gives an effective protection rate of 100%.

(c) Tariffs in the Quantitative restrictions :

It has been noted that the WTO Agreement bans in principle all quantitative restrictions while permitting tariffs to be used to protect domestic industries. One of the reasons for this is because it is easier to negotiate tariffs down than it is to negotiate a reduction in quantitative restrictions in all their many forms. Tariffs are also preferable from an economic standpoint because unlike quantitative restrictions, tariffs have a revenue generating function and less of a distorting effect on markets where monopolies or oligopolies exist. In addition, import quotas may not always be administered fairly. Finally, exporters can respond to tariffs by boosting their efficiency to levels that negate the effective protection rate of the tariff.

(d) Justifications for tariff reductions :

When the WTO Agreements allows tariffs as a protective industrial means (unlike quantitative restrictions, which it bans outright), it also seeks to gradually reduce those tariffs through negotiations among Member countries. Below is a summary of the economic rationale for tariff reductions.

Reducing tariffs mitigates the "loss of efficiency" costs generated by the distortions to the price system that the tariff causes. Reducing the degree of market protection also expands the market, allowing producers in exporting countries to enjoy economies of scale and bringing benefits to the economy as a whole. There are also arguments against reducing tariffs. Many large countries might give comments regarding the tariffs have certain benefits since they improve the terms of trade (the "optimal tariff" debate). Likewise, when the domestic market fails, tariffs might be seen as a means of increasing welfare. These rebuttals might themselves be rebutted by questioning whether the hypothesis of "large countries" is reasonable and significant, or by questioning whether market failures can be measured.

(e) Income redistribution and the importance of international negotiations :

From the angle of Economic point, it would appear to infer that the decrease of tariff are basically beneficial in that they increase economic efficiency, and therefore tariff reductions are undisputably desirable for all countries other than "large countries" (in practical terms, the vast majority of countries), and for the world economy as a whole. It is rare, however, for countries to completely eliminate their tariffs. In point of practice, countries often impose tariffs not for the purpose of increasing macroeconomic welfare from a purely economic standpoint, but for the purpose of redistributing income. As a result of lobbying by various interest groups, policy-makers assess marginal benefits differently depending on which group is benefiting (the "weighted social welfare" debate). When tariffs are brought down for domestic reasons such as these, domestic political interests often will outweigh "greater economic welfare" in the view of the government, making it more difficult to reduce tariffs. This domestic political reality is what makes international negotiations to reduce tariffs, the basic strategy of the WTO, so important. When international negotiations are conditional upon mutual benefits, governments are more likely to forego the marginal benefits that positively effect one sector to obtain the broader general welfare benefits that effect a group of sectors.

Problems of Trade Policies and Measures in Individual Countries

Here in this section we will consider the problems of the trade policies and assessment of the individual countries in the light of the discussion above. We look both at measures that clearly violate the WTO and at measures that are within the scope of WTO rules but nonetheless have a detrimental impact on trade. Chief among the measures considered is high tariff rates and low bound rates. We also touch upon examples of voluntary reductions in effective tariff rates by individual countries when the evidence is clear and discussion is warranted.

We have already noted that countries must go through the procedures outlined in GATT Article XXVIII and obtain approval for a hike in their bound rates before they are able to raise their tariffs to levels in excess of the current bound rate. Raising tariffs beyond the bound rate without going through these procedures constitutes a clear violation of GATT Article II. The WTO Councils and Disputes Settlement Mechanism addresses such violations. When changes in tariff classification result in what for all purposes is a tariff hike, the case must be referred to the Customs Co-operation Council (CCC; also known as the "World Customs Organization" or "WCO") for a judgement on the reclassification.

High tariffs, low percentage of bound items, and tariff hikes (within bound rates) are not, strictly speaking, "unfair trade policies and measures in violation of WTO rules," but they nevertheless have a detrimental impact on trade when they are resorted to too easily or too often. In light of the goals of the WTO, which are to promote free trade, these are actions that countries should remedy voluntarily.

(1) European Union

Even after implementation of the Uruguay Round commitments, the EU tariff rate on some trucks remains high at 22 percent.

(2) United States

After the implementation of the Uruguay Round there will be high US tariffs on some items such as watch parts (maximum 2.16 dollars each (121 percent)), woolen fabrics (maximum 25 percent), glassware (maximum.38 percent), some ceramics (maximum 25 percent), and trucks (maximum 25 percent).

(3) Korea

After the implementation of the Uruguay Round, the internationally-competitive "textiles and textile products" sector will have, on average, high tariffs (between 16.3 percent and 35 percent). Moreover, there will be high tariffs on some items such as automobiles (maximum 80 percent), glass fibers (maximum 25 percent), copper products (maximum 13 percent), and aluminum products (maximum 13 percent). The bound rate for electrical equipment is 62.4 percent, and the binding rate for industrial goods as a whole is 86 percent. The efforts of the Korea to pushing forward liberalization, including dropping its 80 percent high-end bound rate for automobiles to a flat rate of eight percent in February 1999, is appreciated. However, taking into account its status in the current world trade system and the fact that, by participating in the OECD, Korea should be in a position to promote free-trade as a developed country, further steps toward trade liberalization is expected.

(4) Australia

In Australia the tariffs on non-agricultural products remain high even after the implementation of the Uruguay Round. Items such as certain clothes (maximum 55 percent), automobiles (maximum 40 percent), electrical machinery (maximum 23 percent), and glass (maximum 23 percent) have high tariffs. Australia began a unilateral program of phased-in tariff reductions in 1998, and effective rates will be either zero or 5 percent by 1 July 1996 excluding passenger cars, textiles, clothing, and footwear. As a result, with the implementation of the Uruguay Round offer, the average applied tariff rate will be 2.9 percent in 2001 according to Australia's government.

(5) Indonesia

In Indonesia the Uruguay Round show improvement to the Indonesia's bound rate to 92 percent of its tariff items, a development that Japan welcomes. However, the bound tariff rates for the vast majority of items remain extraordinarily high, at levels of 30-40 percent. Effective tariff rates are also high, at an average of 27.8 percent for textiles and textile products, 30.6 percent for transportation equipment, and 26.1 percent for electric equipment. In its "Individual Action Plan" for APEC, Indonesia made an explicit commitment to begin in 1995 to reduce effective tariffs of less than 20 percent to less than 5 percent by 2000, and those in excess of 20 percent to 20 percent by 1998 and to less than 10 percent by 2003.

(6) Canada

High Tariff Goods: In the case of Canada it is estimated that the average tariff rate on non-agricultural products will be 4.9 percent after the implementation of Uruguay Round commitments, somewhat higher rates than those of Japan, the United States, and the EU. Tariffs on glass (maximum 15.7 percent) are an example of high tariffs. In addition to its concession in the Uruguay Round, Canada's APEC "Individual Action Plan" provides that Canada will phase in reductions in effective tariff rates on 714 items by 1999 and another 64 items by 2004. Modification of Schedules, Procedural Violation: As to adjust or change customs tariffs and tariff classifications, Canada amended its national legislation and made modifications to the schedules of concessions (implemented in January 1998). In case of modification of the schedules, as prescribed by GATT Article XXVIII, Canada has a legal obligation to negotiate, in advance, with Members. It is also concerned that it violates GATT Article II due to the fact that, by the time of the completion of the amendment procedure, there were already dozens of goods whose applied rates were set according to national laws, exceeded their pre-amendment bound rates. However, because these above-mentioned goods only affected the Members slightly, some Members merely expressed objections at the WTO General Council, and this procedure in Article XXVIII was then carried out. To simply overlook such a procedural violation would lead to similar violations by other Members. Therefore, in the light of WTO rules, we need to take strict measures against these violations.

(7) Thailand

The levels of tariffs in sectors such as transportation equipment (average 47.6 percent) and electronics (average

31.6 percent) are still high even after the implementation of the Uruguay Round commitment. Copper products (maximum 30 percent) and polyethylene (maximum30 percent) also have high tariffs. Thailand has agreed to bind a relatively low percentage of its tariff goods. For example, only 15.7 percent of transportation equipment is bound while only about 70 percent of industrial goods as a whole is bound.

(8) Malaysia

High Tariff Goods, Bound Rates: The Uruguay Round ensued in an average bound rate (trade-weighted average) of 9.1 percent for imports of industrial goods into Malaysia. This is a low level for a developing country, and one that Japan welcomes. There are, however, some areas that are subject to high tariffs, for example, textile products (average 21.5 percent) and transportation equipment (average 22.6 percent). Other high-tariff items include electrical equipment and glass, which have maximum tariffs of 30 percent. We would also note that Malaysia's bound rate covers only 79 percent of tariff items.

(9) Philippines

The Philippines still has several high-tariff items, including textile products (maximum of 50 percent), watches and clocks (maximum of 50 percent), and electrical equipment (maximum of 50 percent) even after implementation of its Uruguay Round commitments. The percentage of bound items is only 66 percent of tariff lines. We note, however, that the Philippines has been reforming its tariff structure since 1980 and has announced that it will enact a uniform effective tariff rate of 5 percent for all items except selected agricultural products by 2004.

(10) India

(a) High Tariff Goods, Bound Rates: with the implementation of its Uruguay Round commitments, India will have a stationary uniform tariff rates for virtually all bound items: high rates will be 40 percent; low rates, 25 percent. Almost all textiles are subject to 40 percent tariffs, which are high given India's competitiveness and international standing in this sector. Likewise, the percentage of bound items is only 68 percent of tariff line, which leaves substantial room for improvement.

(b) The Introduction of Special Additional Customs Duty: In August 1998, India established a new special additional customs duty. Because of this additional duty, applied rates of some goods have exceeded the bound rates, which may be regarded as a violation of GATT Article II. Thus Japan has participated as a third party in the consultations which were requested by the EU pursuant to based on GATT Article XXII. India argues that the introduction of the special additional duty is aimed at providing a level playing-field to the domestic industry, which is compatible with WTO rules. However, it is still necessary to evaluate the facts related to this issue to see whether these new special additional duties violate the WTO rules or not, and if they violate the WTO rules, we need to request India to take a remedial measure at an early stage.

References

1. Amor, F., C. Calabuig, J. Abell‡n, and V. M. Monfort. 1994. Barriers Found in Repositioning a Mediterranean "Sun and Beach" Product: The Valencian Case.
2. In Tourism: The State of the Art. A. V. Seaton, ed. Pp. 428-435. Chichester, England: Wiley.
3. Anderson, Nels. 1961. Work and Leisure. New York: Free Press of Glencoe.
4. Moore, Hugh. The Southern Landscape of William Bartram: A Terrible Beauty. *Essays in Arts and Sciences*, 10:1 (1981 May): 41-50.
5. *Mountain Gloom and Mountain Glory: The Development of the Aesthetics of the Infinite:* Nicolson, Marjorie. Ithaca: Cornell UP, 1959.
6. Leones, Julie, and Douglas Dunn. 1991. *Strategies for Monitoring Tourism in Your Community's Economy*. Arizona Cooperative Extension Bulletin.
7. "Economic Impacts of Tourism." Stynes, Daniel J. 2000.
8. "Economic Impact of Travel in the U.S., 2000." Travel Industry Association of America. 2001b.
9. "Tourism Development: A Potential for Economic

Growth," Weaver, Glenn. 1986 in *New Dimensions in Rural Policy: Building Upon our Heritage,* Subcommittee on Agriculture and Transportation of the Joint Economic Committee, U.S. Congress, pp. 440-444.

10. *Heritage Tourism: Partnership and Possibilities*. American Association for State and Local History, and National Trust for Historic Preservation. 1994. Nashville, Tennessee.

6

Foreign Exchange Management Act, 1999

Short Title, Extent, Application and Commencement

An Act to consolidate and amend the law relating to foreign exchange with the objective of facilitating external trade and payments and for promoting the orderly development and maintenance of foreign exchange market in India.

BE it enacted by Parliament in the Fiftieth Year of the Republic of India as follows:

(1) This Act may be called the Foreign Exchange Management Act, 1999.

(2) It extends to the whole of India.

(3) It shall also apply to all branches, offices and agencies outside India owned or controlled by a person resident in India and also to any contravention thereunder committed outside India by any person to whom this Act applies.

(4) It shall come into force on such date as the Central Government may, by notification in the Official Gazette, appoint:

'Provided that different dates may be appointed for different provisions of this Act and any reference in any such provision to the commencement of this Act shall be construed as a reference to the coming into force of that provision.'

In this Act, unless the context otherwise requires,—

(a) "Adjudicating Authority" means an officer authorised under sub-section (1) of section 16;

(b) "Appellate Tribunal" means the Appellate Tribunal for Foreign Exchange established under section 18;

(c) "authorised person" means an authorised dealer, money changer, off-shore banking unit or any other person for the time being authorised under sub-section (1) of section 10 to deal in foreign exchange or foreign securities;

(d) "Bench" means a Bench of the Appellate Tribunal;

(e) "capital account transaction" means a transaction which alters the assets or liabilities, including contingent liabilities, outside India of persons resident in India or assets or liabilities in India of persons resident outside India, and includes transactions referred to in sub-section (3) of section 6;

(f) "Chairperson" means the Chairperson of the Appellate Tribunal;

(g) "chartered accountant" shall have the meaning assigned to it in clause (b) of sub-section (1) of section 2 of the Chartered Accountants Act, 1949 (38 of 1949);

(h) "currency" includes all currency notes, postal notes, postal orders, money orders, cheques, drafts, travellers cheques, letters of credit, bills of exchange and promissory notes, credit cards or such other similar instruments, as may be notified by the Reserve Bank;

(i) "currency notes" means and includes cash in the form of coins and bank notes;

(j) "current account transaction" means a transaction other than a capital account transaction and without prejudice to the generality of the foregoing such transaction includes:-

(i) payments due in connection with foreign trade, other current business, services, and short-term banking and credit facilities in the ordinary course of business,

(ii) payments due as interest on loans and as net income from investments,

(iii) remittances for living expenses of parents, spouse and children residing abroad, and

(iv) expenses in connection with foreign travel, education and medical care of parents, spouse and children;

(k) "Director of Enforcement" means the Director of Enforcement appointed under sub-section (1) of section 36;

(l) "export", with its grammatical variations and cognate expressions, means—

(i) the taking out of India to a place outside India any goods,

(ii) provision of services from India to any person outside India;

(m) "foreign currency" means any currency other than Indian currency;

(n) "foreign exchange" means foreign currency and includes,—

(i) deposits, credits and balances payable in any foreign currency,

(ii) drafts, travellers cheques, letters of credit or bills of exchange, expressed or drawn in Indian currency but payable in any foreign currency,

(iii) drafts, travellers cheques, letters of credit or bills of exchange drawn by banks, institutions or persons outside India, but payable in Indian currency;

(o) "foreign security" means any security, in the form of shares, stocks, bonds, debentures or any other instrument denominated or expressed in foreign currency and includes securities expressed in foreign currency, but where redemption or any form of return such as interest or dividends is payable in Indian currency;

(p) "import", with its grammatical variations and cognate expressions, means bringing into India any goods or services;

(q) "Indian currency" means currency which is expressed or drawn in Indian rupees but does not include special bank notes and special one rupee notes issued under section 28A of the Reserve Bank of India Act, 1934 (2 of 1934);

(r) "legal practitioner" shall have the meaning assigned to it in clause (i) of sub-section (1) of section 2 of the Advocates Act, 1961 (25 of 1961);

(s) "Member" means a Member of the Appellate Tribunal and includes the Chairperson thereof;

(t) "notify" means to notify in the Official Gazette and the expression "notification" shall be construed accordingly;

(u) "person" includes—

(i) an individual,

(ii) a Hindu undivided family,

(iii) a company,

(iv) a firm,

(v) an association of persons or a body of individuals, whether incorporated or not,

(vi) every artificial juridical person, not falling within any of the preceding sub-clauses, and

(vii) any agency, office or branch owned or controlled by such person

Regulation and Management of Foreign Exchange

Dealing in Foreign Exchange, etc.

Save as otherwise provided in this Act, rules or regulations made thereunder, or with the general or special permission of the Reserve Bank, no person shall:

(a) deal in or transfer any foreign exchange or foreign security to any person not being an authorised person;

(b) make any payment to or for the credit of any person resident outside India in any manner;

(c) receive otherwise through an authorised person, any payment by order or on behalf of any person resident outside India in any manner;

Explanation.—With the purpose of this clause, where any individual in, or residing in, India enjoys any receives any payment by order or on behalf of any person resident outside India through any other person (including an authorised person) without a corresponding inward remittance from any place outside India, then, such person shall be deemed to have received such payment otherwise than through an authorised person;

(d) enter into any financial transaction in India as consideration for or in association with acquisition or creation or transfer of a right to acquire, any asset outside India by any person.

Explanation.— With the purpose of this clause, "financial transaction" implies making any payment to, or for the credit of any person, or receiving any payment for, by order or on behalf of any person, or drawing, issuing or negotiating any bill of exchange or promissory note, or transferring any security or acknowledging any debt.

Holding of foreign exchange, etc.

Save as otherwise provided in this Act, no person resident in India shall acquire, hold, own, possess or transfer any foreign exchange, foreign security or any immovable property situated outside India.

Current account transactions

Any individual may person may deal or draw foreign exchange to or from an authorised person if such sale or drawal is a current account transaction :

Furnishing that, the Central Government may, in public interest and in consultation with the Reserve Bank, impose such reasonable restrictions for current account transactions as may be prescribed.

Capital account transactions

(1) A matter of subject to the provisions of sub-section (2), any individual may deal or draw foreign exchange to or from an authorised person for a capital account transaction.

(2) The Reserve Bank may, in consultation with the Central Government, specify:

(a) any class or classes of capital account transactions which are permissible;

(b) the limit up to which foreign exchange shall be admissible for such transactions :

Provided that the Reserve Bank shall not impose any restriction on the drawal of foreign exchange for payments due on account of amortization of loans or for depreciation of direct investments in the ordinary course of business.

(3) Without prejudice to the generality of the provisions of sub-section (2), the Reserve Bank may, by regulations, prohibit, restrict or regulate the following:

(a) transfer or issue of any foreign security by a person resident in India;

(b) transfer or issue of any security by a person resident outside India;

(c) transfer or issue of any security or foreign security by any branch, office or agency in India of a person resident outside India;

(d) any borrowing or lending in foreign exchange in whatever form or by whatever name called;

(e) any borrowing or lending in rupees in whatever form or by whatever name called between a person resident in India and a person resident outside India;

(f) deposits between persons resident in India and persons resident outside India;

(g) export, import or holding of currency or currency notes;

(h) transfer of immovable property outside India, other than a lease not exceeding five years, by a person resident in India;

(i) acquisition or transfer of immovable property in India, other than a lease not exceeding five years, by a person resident outside India;

(j) giving of a guarantee or surety in respect of any debt, obligation or other liability incurred:

(i) by a person resident in India and owed to a person resident outside India; or

(ii) by a person resident outside India.

(4) A person resident in India may hold, own, transfer or invest in foreign currency, foreign security or any immovable property situated outside India if such currency, security or property was acquired, held or owned by such person when he was resident outside India or inherited from a person who was resident outside India.

(5) A person resident outside India may hold, own, transfer or invest in Indian currency, security or any immovable property situated in India if such currency, security or property was acquired, held or owned by such person when he was resident in India or inherited from a person who was resident in India.

(6) Without prejudice to the provisions of this section, the Reserve Bank may, by regulation, prohibit, restrict, or regulate establishment in India of a branch, office or other place of business by a person resident outside India, for carrying on any activity relating to such branch, office or other place of business.

Export of goods and services

(1) Every exporter of goods shall:

(a) Providing to the Reserve Bank or to such other

authority a declaration in such form and in such manner as may be specified, containing true and correct material particulars, including the amount representing the full export value or, if the full export value of the goods is not ascertainable at the time of export, the value which the exporter, having regard to the prevailing market conditions, expects to receive on the sale of the goods in a market outside India;

(b) Provide to the Reserve Bank of such kind information which may be required by the Reserve Bank for the purpose of ensuring the realisation of the export proceeds by such exporter.

(2) For the purpose of ensuring that the full export value of the goods or such reduced value of the goods as the Reserve Bank determines, having regard to the prevailing market conditions, is received without any delay, direct any exporter to comply with such requirements as it deems fit.

(3) All exporter of services shall provide to the Reserve Bank or to such other authorities a declaration in such form and in such manner as may be specified, containing the true and correct material particulars in relation to payment for such services.

Realisation and repatriation of foreign exchange

Save as otherwise provided in this Act, where any amount of foreign exchange is due or has accrued to any person resident in India, such person shall take all reasonable steps to realise and repatriate to India such foreign exchange within such period and in such manner as may be specified by the Reserve Bank.

Exemption from realisation and repatriation in certain cases

The provisions may not apply to the following:

(a) possession of foreign currency or foreign coins by any person up to such limit as the Reserve Bank may specify;

(b) foreign currency account held or operated by such person or class of persons and the limit up to which the Reserve Bank may specify;

(c) foreign exchange acquired or received before the 8th day of July, 1947 or any income arising or accruing thereon which is held outside India by any person in pursuance of a general or special permission granted by the Reserve Bank;

(d) foreign exchange held by a person resident in India up to such limit as the Reserve Bank may specify, if such foreign exchange was acquired by way of gift or inheritance from a person referred to in clause (c), including any income arising therefrom;

(e) foreign exchange acquired from employment, business, trade, vocation, services, honorarium, gifts, inheritance or any other legitimate means up to such limit as the Reserve Bank may specify; and

(f) such other receipts in foreign exchange as the Reserve Bank may specify.

Authorised Person

(1) The Reserve Bank may, on an application made to it in this behalf, authorise any person to be known as authorised person to deal in foreign exchange or in foreign securities, as an authorised dealer, money changer or off-shore banking unit or in any other manner as it deems fit.

(2) An authorisation under this section shall be in writing and shall be subject to the conditions laid down therein.

(3) An authorisation granted under sub-section (1) may be revoked by the Reserve Bank at any time if the Reserve Bank is satisfied that

  (a) it is in public interest so to do; or

  (b) the authorised person has failed to comply with the condition subject to which the authorisation was granted or has contravened any of the provisions of the Act or any rule, regulation, notification, direction or order made there under:

  Provided that no such authorisation shall be revoked on any ground referred to in clause (b) unless the authorised person has been given a reasonable opportunity of making a representation in the matter.

(4) A person who is given authorization shall, in all his dealings in foreign exchange or foreign security, comply with such general or special directions or orders as the Reserve Bank may, from time to time, think fit to give, and, except with the previous permission of the Reserve Bank, an authorised person shall not engage in any transaction involving any foreign

exchange or foreign security which is not in conformity with the terms of his authorisation under this section.

(5) A person who is given authorization shall, before undertaking any transaction in foreign exchange on behalf of any person, require that person to make such declaration and to give such information as will reasonably satisfy him that the transaction will not involve, and is not designed for the purpose of any contravention or evasion of the provisions of this Act or of any rule, regulation, notification, direction or order made thereunder, and where the said person refuses to comply with any such requirement or makes only unsatisfactory compliance therewith, the authorised person shall refuse in writing to undertake the transaction and shall, if he has reason to believe that any such contravention or evasion as aforesaid is contemplated by the person, report the matter to the Reserve Bank.

(6) Any person, other than an authorised person, who has acquired or purchased foreign exchange for any purpose mentioned in the declaration made by him to authorised person under sub-section (5) does not use it for such purpose or does not surrender it to authorised person within the specified period or uses the foreign exchange so acquired or purchased for any other purpose for which purchase or acquisition of foreign exchange is not permissible under the provisions of the Act or the rules or regulations or direction or order made thereunder shall be deemed to have committed contravention of the provisions of the Act for the purpose of this section.

Reserve Bank's powers to issue directions to authorised person

(1) The Reserve Bank may, for the purpose of securing compliance with the provisions of this Act and of any rules, regulations, notifications or directions made thereunder, give to the authorised persons any direction in regard to making of payment or the doing or desist from doing any act relating to foreign exchange or foreign security.

(2) The Reserve Bank may, for the purpose of ensuring the compliance with the provisions of this Act or of any rule, regulation, notification, direction or order made thereunder, direct any authorised person to furnish such information, in such manner, as it deems fit.

(3) Where any authorised person contravenes any direction given by the Reserve Bank under this Act or fails to file any return as directed by the Reserve Bank, the Reserve Bank may, after giving reasonable opportunity of being heard, impose on the authorised person a penalty which may extend to ten thousand rupees and in the case of continuing contravention with an additional penalty which may extend to two thousand rupees for every day during which such contravention continues.

Power of Reserve Bank to inspect authorised person

(1) The Reserve Bank may, at any time, cause an inspection to be made, by any officer of the Reserve Bank specially authorised in writing by the Reserve Bank in this behalf, of the business of any authorised person as may appear to it to be necessary or expedient for the purpose of:

(a) verifying the correctness of any statement, information or particulars furnished to the Reserve Bank;

(b) obtaining any information or particulars which such authorised person has failed to furnish on being called upon to do so;

(c) securing compliance with the provisions of this Act or of any rules, regulations, directions or orders made thereunder.

(2) It shall be the duty of every authorised person, and where such person is a company or a firm, every director, partner or other officer of such company or firm, as the case may be, to produce to any officer making an inspection under sub-section (1), such books, accounts and other documents in his custody or power and to furnish any statement or information relating to the affairs of such person, company or firm as the said officer may require within such time and in such manner as the said officer may direct.

Contravention and Penalties

Penalties

(1) If any person contravenes any provision of this Act, or contravenes any rule, regulation, notification, direction or order issued in exercise of the powers under this Act, or

contravenes any condition subject to which an authorisation is issued by the Reserve Bank, he shall, upon adjudication, be liable to a penalty up to thrice the sum involved in such contravention where such amount is quantifiable, or up to two lakh rupees where the amount is not quantifiable, and where such contravention is a continuing one, further penalty which may extend to five thousand rupees for every day after the first day during which the contravention continues.

(2) Any Adjudicating Authority adjudging any contravention under sub-section (1), may, if he thinks fit in addition to any penalty which he may impose for such contravention direct that any currency, security or any other money or property in respect of which the contravention has taken place shall be confiscated to the Central Government and further direct that the foreign exchange holdings, if any of the persons committing the contraventions or any part thereof, shall be brought back into India or shall be retained outside India in accordance with the directions made in this behalf.

Explanation.—For the purposes of this sub-section, "property" in respect of which contravention has taken place, shall include:

(a) deposits in a bank, where the said property is converted into such deposits;

(b) Indian currency, where the said property is converted into that currency; and

(c) any other property which has resulted out of the conversion of that property.

Cadjudication and Appeal

Appointment of Adjudicating Authority

(1) For the purpose of adjudication under section 13, the Central Government may, by an order published in the Official Gazette, appoint as many officers of the Central Government as it may think fit, as the Adjudicating Authorities for holding an inquiry in the manner prescribed after giving the person alleged to have committed contravention under section 13, against whom a complaint has been made under sub-section (2) (hereinafter in this section referred to as the said person) a reasonable

opportunity of being heard for the purpose of imposing any penalty:

Provided that where the Adjudicating Authority is of opinion that the said person is likely to abscond or is likely to evade in any manner, the payment of penalty, if levied, it may direct the said person to furnish a bond or guarantee for such amount and subject to such conditions as it may deem fit.

(2) The Central Government shall, while appointing the Adjudicating Authorities under sub-section (1), also specify in the order published in the Official Gazette, their respective jurisdictions.

(3) No Adjudicating Authority shall hold an enquiry under sub-section (1) except upon a complaint in writing made by any officer authorised by a general or special order by the Central Government.

(4) The said person may appear either in person or take the assistance of a legal practitioner or a chartered accountant of his choice for presenting his case before the Adjudicating Authority.

(5) Every Adjudicating Authority shall have the same powers of a civil court which are conferred on the Appellate Tribunal under sub-section (2) of section 28 and—

(a) all proceedings before it shall be deemed to be judicial proceedings within the meaning of sections 193 and 228 of the Indian Penal Code (45 of 1860);

(b) shall be deemed to be a civil court for the purposes of sections 345 and 346 of the Code of Criminal Procedure, 1973 (2 of 1974).

(6) Every Adjudicating Authority shall deal with the complaint under sub-section (2) as expeditiously as possible and endeavour shall be made to dispose of the complaint finally within one year from the date of receipt of the complaint:

Provided that where the complaint cannot be disposed off within the said period, the Adjudicating Authority shall record periodically the reasons in writing for not disposing off the complaint within the said period.

Appeal to special director (Appeals)

(1) The Central Government shall, by notification, appoint one or more Special Directors (Appeals) to hear appeals against

the orders of the Adjudicating Authorities under this section and shall also specify in the said notification the matter and places in relation to which the Special Director (Appeals) may exercise jurisdiction.

(2) Any person aggrieved by an order made by the Adjudicating Authority, being an Assistant Director of Enforcement or a Deputy Director of Enforcement, may prefer an appeal to the Special Director (Appeals).

(3) Every appeal under sub-section (1) shall be filed within forty-five days from the date on which the copy of the order made by the Adjudicating Authority is received by the aggrieved person and it shall be in such form, verified in such manner and be accompanied by such fee as may be prescribed:

Provided that the Special Director (Appeals) may entertain an appeal after the expiry of the said period of forty-five days, if he is satisfied that there was sufficient cause for not filing it within that period.

(4) On receipt of an appeal under sub-section (1), the Special Director (Appeals) may after giving the parties to the appeal an opportunity of being heard, pass such order thereon as he thinks fit confirming, modifying or setting aside the order appealed against.

(5) The Special Director (Appeals) shall send a copy of every order made by him to the parties to appeal and to the concerned Adjudicating Authority.

(6) The Special Director (Appeals) shall have the same powers of a civil court which are conferred on the Appellate Tribunal under sub-section (2) of section 28 and:

(a) all proceedings before him shall be deemed to be judicial proceedings within the meaning of sections 193 and 228 of the Indian Penal Code (45 of 1860);

(b) shall be deemed to be a civil court for the purposes of sections 345 and 346 of the Code of Criminal Procedure, 1973 (2 of 1974).

Establishment of Appellate Tribunal

The Central Government shall, by notification, establish an Appellate Tribunal to be known as the Appellate Tribunal for Foreign Exchange to hear appeals against the orders of the Adjudicating Authorities and the Special Director (Appeals) under this Act.

Appeal to Appellate Tribunal

(1) Save as provided in sub-section (2), the Central Government or any person aggrieved by an order made by an Adjudicating Authority, other than those referred to sub-section (1) of section 17, or the Special Director (Appeals), may prefer an appeal to the Appellate Tribunal:

Provided that any person appealing against the order of the Adjudicating Authority or the Special Director (Appeals) levying any penalty, shall while filing the appeal, deposit the amount of such penalty with such authority as may be notified by the Central Government:

Provided further that where in any particular case, the Appellate Tribunal is of the opinion that the deposit of such penalty would cause undue hardship to such person, the Appellate Tribunal may dispense with such deposit subject to such conditions as it may deem fit to impose so as to safeguard the realisation of penalty.

(2) Every appeal under sub-section (1) shall be filed within a period of forty-five days from the date on which a copy of the order made by the Adjudicating Authority or the Special Director (Appeals) is received by the aggrieved person or by the Central Government and it shall be in such form, verified in such manner and be accompanied by such fee as may be prescribed:

Provided that the Appellate Tribunal may entertain an appeal after the expiry of the said period of forty-five days if it is satisfied that there was sufficient cause for not filing it within that period.

(3) On receipt of an appeal under sub-section (1), the Appellate Tribunal may, after giving the parties to the appeal an opportunity of being heard, pass such orders thereon as it thinks fit, confirming, modifying or setting aside the order appealed against.

(4) The Appellate Tribunal shall send a copy of every order made by it to the parties to the appeal and to the concerned Adjudicating Authority or the Special Director (Appeals), as the case may be.

(5) The appeal filed before the Appellate Tribunal under sub-section (1) shall be dealt with by it as expeditiously as

possible and endeavour shall be made by it to dispose of the appeal finally within one hundred and eighty days from the date of receipt of the appeal:

Provided that where any appeal could not be disposed of within the said period of one hundred and eighty days, the Appellate Tribunal shall record its reasons in writing for not disposing of the appeal within the said period.

(6) The Appellate Tribunal may, for the purpose of examining the legality, propriety or correctness of any order made by the Adjudicating Authority under section 16 in relation to any proceeding, on its own motion or otherwise, call for the records of such proceedings and make such order in the case as it thinks fit.

Composition of Appellate Tribunal

(1) The Appellate Tribunal shall consist of a Chairperson and such number of Members as the Central Government may deem fit.

(2) Subject to the provisions of this Act :

(a) the jurisdiction of the Appellate Tribunal may be exercised by Benches thereof;

(b) a Bench may be constituted by the Chairperson with one or more Members as the Chairperson may deem fit;

(c) the Benches of the Appellate Tribunal shall ordinarily sit at New Delhi and at such other places as the Central Government may, in consultation with the Chairperson, notify;

(d) the Central Government shall notify the areas in relation to which each Bench of the Appellate Tribunal may exercise jurisdiction.

(3) Notwithstanding anything contained in sub-section (2), the Chairperson may transfer a Member from one Bench to another Bench.

(4) If at any stage of the hearing of any case or matter it appears to the Chairperson or a Member that the case or matter is of such a nature that it ought to be heard by a Bench consisting of two Members, the case or matter may be transferred by the Chairperson or, as

the case may be, referred to him for transfer, to such Bench as the Chairperson may deem fit.

Qualifications for appointment of Chairperson, member and Special Director (Appeals)

(1) A person shall not be qualified for appointment as the Chairperson or a Member unless he—

(a) in the case of Chairperson, is or has been, or is qualified to be, a Judge of a High Court; and

(b) in the case of a Member, is or has been, or is qualified to be, a District Judge.

(2) A person shall not be qualified for appointment as a Special Director (Appeals) unless he:

(a) has been a member of the Indian Legal Service and has held a post in Grade I of that Service; or

(b) has been a member of the Indian Revenue Service and has held a post equivalent to a Joint Secretary to the Government of India.

Term of office

The Chairperson and every other Member shall hold office as such for a term of five years from the date on which he enters upon his office:

Provided that no Chairperson or other Member shall hold office as such after he has attained:

(a) in the case of the Chairperson, the age of sixty-five years;

(b) in the case of any other Member, the age of sixty-two years.

Terms and conditions of service

The salary and allowances payable to and the other terms and conditions of service of the Chairperson, other Members and the Special Director (Appeals) shall be such as may be prescribed:

Provided that neither the salary and allowances nor the other terms and conditions of service of the Chairperson or a Member shall be varied to his disadvantage after appointment.

Vacancies

If, for reason other than temporary absence, any vacancy occurs in the office of the Chairperson or a Member, the Central Government shall appoint another person in accordance with the provisions of this Act to fill the vacancy and the proceedings may be continued before the Appellate Tribunal from the stage at which the vacancy is filled.

Resignation and removal

(1) The Chairperson or a Member may, by notice in writing under his hand addressed to the Central Government, resign his office:

Provided that the Chairperson or a Member shall, unless he is permitted by the Central Government to relinquish his office sooner, continue to hold office until the expiry of three months from the date of receipt of such notice or until a person duly appointed as his successor enters upon his office or until the expiry of term of office, whichever is the earliest.

(2) The Chairperson or a Member shall not be removed from his office except by an order by the Central Government on the ground of proved misbehaviour or incapacity after an inquiry made by such person as the President may appoint for this purpose in which the Chairperson or a Member concerned has been informed of the charges against him and given a reasonable opportunity of being heard in respect of such charges.

Procedure and powers of Appellate Tribunal and Special Director (Appeals)

(1) The Appellate Tribunal and the Special Director (Appeals) shall not be bound by the procedure laid down by the Code of Civil Procedure, 1908 (5 of 1908) but shall be guided by the principles of natural justice and, subject to the other provisions of this Act, the Appellate Tribunal and the Special Director (Appeals) shall have powers to regulate its own procedure.

(2) The Appellate Tribunal and the Special Director (Appeals) shall have, for the purposes of discharging its functions under this Act, the same powers as are vested in a civil court under the Code of Civil Procedure, 1908 (5 of 1908); while trying a suit, in respect of the following matters, namely :

(a) summoning and enforcing the attendance of any person and examining him on oath;

(b) requiring the discovery and production of documents;

(c) receiving evidence on affidavits;

(d) subject to the provisions of sections 123 and 124 of the Indian Evidence Act, 1872 (1 of 1872) requisitioning any public record or document or copy of such record or document from any office;

(e) issuing commissions for the examination of witnesses or documents;

(f) reviewing its decisions;

(g) dismissing a representation of default or deciding it ex parte;

(h) setting aside any order of dismissal of any representation for default or any order passed by it ex parte; and

(i) any other matter which may be prescribed by the Central Government.

(3) An order made by the Appellate Tribunal or the Special Director (Appeals) under this Act shall be executable by the Appellate Tribunal or the Special Director (Appeals) as a decree of civil court and, for this purpose, the Appellate Tribunal and the Special Director (Appeals) shall have all the powers of a civil court.

(4) Notwithstanding anything contained in sub-section (3), the Appellate Tribunal or the Special Director (Appeals) may transmit any order made by it to a civil court having local jurisdiction and such civil court shall execute the order as if it were a decree made by that court.

(5) All proceedings before the Appellate Tribunal and the Special Director (Appeals) shall be deemed to be judicial proceedings within the meaning of sections 193 and 228 of the Indian Penal Code (45 of 1860) and the Appellate Tribunal shall be deemed to be a civil court for the purposes of sections 345 and 346 of the Code of Criminal Procedure, 1973 (2 of 1974)

Distribution of business amongst Benches

Where Benches are constituted, the Chairperson may, from time to time, by notification, make provisions as to the distribution of the business of the Appellate Tribunal amongst the Benches and also provide for the matters which may be dealt with by each Bench.

Power of Chairperson to transfer cases

On the application of any of the parties and after notice to the parties, and after hearing such of them as he may desire to be heard, or on his own motion without such notice, the Chairperson may transfer any case pending before one Bench, for disposal, to any other Bench.

Decision to be by majority

If the Members of a Bench consisting of two Members differ in opinion on any point, they shall state the point or points on which they differ, and make a reference to the Chairperson who shall either hear the point or points himself or refer the case for hearing on such point or points by one or more of the other Members of the Appellate Tribunal and such point or points shall be decided according to the opinion of the majority of the Members of the Appellate Tribunal who have heard the case, including those who first heard it.

Directorate of Enforcement

Directorate of Enforcement

(1) The Central Government shall establish a Directorate of Enforcement with a Director and such other officers or class of officers as it thinks fit, who shall be called officers of Enforcement, for the purposes of this Act.

(2) Without prejudice to provisions of sub-section (1), the Central Government may authorise the Director of Enforcement or an Additional Director of Enforcement or a Special Director of Enforcement or a Deputy Director of Enforcement to appoint officers of Enforcement below the rank of an Assistant Director of Enforcement.

(3) Subject to such conditions and limitations as the Central Government may impose, an officer of Enforcement may exercise the powers and discharge the duties conferred or imposed on him under this Act.

Power of Search, Seizure, Etc.

(1) The Director of Enforcement and other officers of Enforcement, not below the rank of an Assistant Director, shall take up for investigation the contravention referred to in section 13.

(2) Without prejudice to the provisions of sub-section (1), the Central Government may also, by notification, authorise any officer or class of officers in the Central Government, State Government or the Reserve Bank, not below the rank of an Under Secretary to the Government of India to

investigate any contravention referred to in section 13.

(3) The officers referred to in sub-section (1) shall exercise the like powers which are conferred on income-tax authorities under the Income-tax Act, 1961 (43 of 1961) and shall exercise such powers, subject to such limitations laid down under that Act.

Empowering other officers

(1) The Central Government may, by order and subject to such conditions and limitations as it thinks fit to impose, authorise any officer of customs or any central excise officer or any police officer or any other officer of the Central Government or a State Government to exercise such of the powers and discharge such of the duties of the Director of Enforcement or any other officer of Enforcement under this Act as may be stated in the order.

(2) The officers referred to in sub-section (1) shall exercise the like powers which are conferred on the income-tax authorities under the Income-tax Act, 1961 (43 of 1961), subject to such conditions and limitations as the Central Government may impose

Rules and regulations to be laid before Parliament

Every rule and regulation made under this Act shall be laid, as soon as may be after it is made, before each House of Parliament, while it is in session for a total period of thirty days which may be comprised in one session or in two or more successive sessions, and if, before the expiry of the session immediately following the session or the successive sessions aforesaid, both Houses agree in making any modification in the rule or regulation, or both Houses agree that the rule or regulation should not be made, the rule or regulation shall thereafter have effect only in such modified form or be of no effect, as the case may be; so, however, that any such modification or annulment shall be without prejudice to the validity of anything previously done under that rule or regulation.

Repeal and saving

(1) The Foreign Exchange Regulation Act, 1973 (46 of 1973) is hereby repealed and the Appellate Board constituted under sub-section (1) of section 52 of the said Act (hereinafter referred to as the repealed Act) shall stand dissolved.

(2) On the dissolution of the said Appellate Board, the person appointed as Chairman of the Appellate Board and every other person appointed as Member and holding office as such immediately before such date shall vacate their respective offices and no such Chairman or other person shall be entitled to claim any compensation for the premature termination of the term of his office or of any contract of service.

(3) Notwithstanding anything contained in any other law for the time being in force, no court shall take cognizance of an offence under the repealed Act and no adjudicating officer shall take notice of any contravention under section 51 of the repealed Act after the expiry of a period of two years from the date of the commencement of this Act.

(4) Subject to the provisions of sub-section (3) all offences committed under the repealed Act shall continue to be governed by the provisions of the repealed Act as if that Act had not been repealed.

(5) Notwithstanding such repeal :

(a) anything done or any action taken or purported to have been done or taken including any rule, notification, inspection, order or notice made or issued or any appointment, confirmation or declaration made or any licence, permission, authorization or exemption granted or any document or instrument executed or any direction given under the Act hereby repealed shall, in so far as it is not inconsistent with the provisions of this Act, be deemed to have been done or taken under the corresponding provisions of this Act;

(b) any appeal preferred to the Appellate Board under sub-section (2) of section 52 of the repealed Act but not disposed of before the commencement of this Act shall stand transferred to and shall be disposed of by the Appellate Tribunal constituted under this Act;

(c) every appeal from any decision or order of the Appellate Board under sub-section (3) or sub-section (4) of section 52 of the repealed Act shall, if not filed before the commencement of this Act, be filed before the High

Court within a period of sixty days of such commencement :

Provided that the High Court may entertain such appeal after the expiry of the said period of sixty days if it is satisfied that the appellant was prevented by sufficient cause from filing the appeal within the said period.

(6) Save as otherwise provided in sub-section (3), the mention of particular matters in sub-sections (2), (4) and (5) shall not be held to prejudice or affect the general application of section 6 of the General Clauses Act, 1897 (10 of 1897) with regard to the effect of repeal.

References

1. *Tourism: A New Perspective*. Burns, Peter, and Andrew Holden. 1995. London: Prentice Hall.
2. "A Conceptual Model for Facilitating Rural Tourism Development," Burr, Steven W. 1997. *Proceedings of the 1996 Northeastern Recreation Research Symposium*, March 31-April 2, 1996, Lake George in Bolton Landing, NY. U.S. Dept. of Agriculture, Forest Service, Northeastern Forest Experiment Station Report, General technical report NE; 232, pp. 15-18.
3. "The Potential for Tourism Development in Nonmetropolitan Areas," Gibson, Lay James. 1993. pp. 145-164, in David L. Barkley, ed., *Economic Adaptation*. Boulder, Colorado: Westview Press.
4. *Ethnic Variation in Leisure and Recreational Interests*. Jepson, Edward J., Jr., and David W. Marcouiller. 1994. Chicago: Council of Planning Librarians. CPL Bibliography No. 311.
5. *Q and A about Rural Tourism Development: Based on Questions from the Turn it Around with Tourism Teleconference*. Koth, Barbara, Glenn Kreag, and Matthew Robinson, comps. 1993. St. Paul, Minnesota: Minnesota Extension Service, University of Minnesota.
6. *A Training Guide for Rural Tourism Development*. Koth, Barbara, Glenn Kreag, and John Sem. 1995. St. Paul, Minnesota: Rural Tourism Center, Minnesota Extension Service.
7. "Organizing Resources for Rural Tourism Development: The Importance of Leadership, Planning and Technical Assistance,"

Long, Patrick T., and Jonelle S. Nuckolls. 1994. *Tourism Recreation Research*, Vol. 19, No. 2, pp. 19-34.

8. "Toward Integrative Tourism Planning in Rural America," Marcouiller, David W. 1997. *Journal of Planning Literature*, Vol. 11, No. 3: pp. 337-357.

9. *Tourism USA: Guidelines for Tourism Development*. U.S. Department of Commerce, United States Travel and Tourism Administration. 1991. 3rd ed. University of Missouri, Dept. of Recreation and Park Administration, University Extension.

7

FDI in Tourism Industry

Foreign Direct Investment: Concepts and Relevance

The potentialities of foreign direct investment (FDI) to both host and investor economies are commonly accepted, and there is a wide demand for reducing or eliminating barriers to global FDI integration. In the past few decades, continuous effort in multilateral trade negotiations, regional trade agreements, bilateral and multilateral investment accords have, to some extent, reduced obstacles to FDI. The World Trade Organisation (WTO) trade negotiations aim at continuing this trend. Thus, it is not concerning to observe that the FDI flows have increases obviously in the recent decades. The expansion in FDI was more pronounced during 1985-2000, when many host countries began to relax regulations to attract FDI, and during 1995-2000, when companies underwent mergers and acquisitions in the wake of the Asian financial crisis and privatisation programmes in Latin America. In fact, FDI flows grew from only USD55.3 billion in 1985 to a record high of USD1.4 trillion in 2000. The world FDI flows increased fivefold between 1993 and 2000 before starting to fall in 2001.

The growing internationalisation of both investment and trade has prompted some countries to call for increased cooperation through the establishment of international rules and commitments under the WTO. Concerning foreign capital is one of the top matters in Macao's economic agenda.

The SAR Government has deregulated key economic sectors like gaming and telecommunications. This policy has successfully drawn huge international capital into the territory and altered its macroeconomic conditions. This paper reviews major concepts of FDI as well as relevant developments in Macao.

Definition of Foreign Direct Investment

The Foreign Direct Investment defined the third edition of the OECD Benchmark Definition as a category of international investment that reflects the objective of obtaining a lasting interest by a resident in one economy (the direct investor) in an entity resident in an economy other than that of the investor (the direct investment enterprise). The lasting interest implies the existence of a long-term relationship between the direct investor and the direct investment enterprise, and a significant degree of influence by the investor on the management of the enterprise. It also stresses in the OCED guide that direct investment involves both the initial transaction between the two entities and all subsequent capital transactions between them and among affiliated enterprises, both incorporated and unincorporated.

The numerical guideline of direct investment ownership is made at a threshold of 10 percent. In other words, a direct investment relationship is established when the direct investor acquires 10 percent or more of the ordinary shares or voting power of an enterprise abroad. Once a direct investment relationship has been established, all subsequent capital transactions between the direct investor and the direct investment enterprise as well as capital transactions among affiliated enterprises resided in different economies are considered to be direct investment. The direct investment relationship is extended to certain other enterprises indirectly owned by the direct investor. Therefore, direct an investment enterprise consists of nonresident subsidiaries, associates, and branches either directly or indirectly owned by the direct investor. The inclusion of transactions with and between indirectly owned entities can greatly extend the number of entities involved in the direct investment relationship, and adds to the complexity of compiling the data.

As for the foreign direct investor, it is defined as an individual, an incorporated or unincorporated public or private enterprise, a government, a group of related individuals, or a group of related incorporated and/or unincorporated enterprises which has a direct investment enterprise – that is, a subsidiary, associate or branch 2–operating in a country other than the country or countries of residence of the foreign direct investor or investors. There are a number of common misconceptions about what FDI is, and hence it is worthy to be clarified as follows:

(i) FDI does not necessarily mean the control of the enterprise, as only a 10percent ownership is required to establish a direct investment relationship;

(ii) FDI does not comprise a group of "unrelated" investors domiciled in the same foreign country - FDI involves only one investor or a "related group" of investors;

(iii) FDI is not based on the nationality or citizenship of the direct investor, and is based only on residency; and

(iv) Borrowings from unrelated parties abroad that are guaranteed by direct investors are not FDI. As the world trade and FDI flourished in the 1990s, it has drawn attentions of some economists who like to analyse the behaviour of multinational enterprises (MNEs) on direct investment. Recent research points to the fact that the interdependence of trade and FDI derives from the decision by MNEs to export abroad by increasingly producing locally. Building on previous work of Dunning and Buckley and Casson, Markusen and Maskus suggest the "Knowledge-capital" theory of MNEs in which three types of firms exist in each country:

   (i) Purely domestic firms, which have headquarters and plants that produce only at home for local or export markets.

   (ii) Horizontal MNEs, which have headquarters at home and production plants both at home and abroad that produce the same goods. The objective of horizontal MNEs is to access foreign markets, as trading and investing abroad are two substituting activities. The decision either to trade or to invest depends on their relative returns, which depend on factors like cost of trade, cost of FDI and the firm-level economies of scale 3 they can enjoy by duplicating production plants in foreign countries; and (iii) Vertical MNEs, which divide production into different stages.

Headquarters are introduced at home but production plants are located indifferent foreign countries which produce different intermediate or final goods. Unlike horizontal MNEs, vertical MNEs are set up to take advantage of cross-country comparative advantage patterns by locating plants in different countries in order to specialise in different stages of production. Thus, trade and FDI are complementary activities. These enterprises very often export components to foreign affiliates and re-export processed articles to home or other markets. Recent studies show that MNEs in the OECD area are more inclined to horizontal strategy, possibly explained by the similarity of factor costs and endowments among member countries. Nevertheless, differences do exist between them with the United States dominating in horizontal strategies and Sweden and France in vertical strategies. There are two sets of factors jointly affecting the level of direct investment:

(i) Non-policy factors, for example, market size and potential, socio-geographical proximity and factor proportions (i.e. relative endowments of different inputs); and

(ii) Policy factors, including market openness and infrastructure. Non-policy factors are usually the characteristics of an economy which are relatively more difficult to be changed over a short period of time. Most studies are therefore focused on policy factors with which FDI can be hindered or encouraged at a faster pace:

(i) Market openness

The openness of Product-market of a country to FDI is evaluated in terms of policies that create or eliminate border barriers for direct investors, measured by tariff and non-tariff barriers, statutory restrictions to FDI and multilateral agreements that create areas of free trade among signatory countries. Tariff barriers usually have more dampening effect on vertical which needs to re-import goods to the home country or export to third-party countries in different stages of production. Costs of production will be driven up under tariff barriers. Statutory restrictions can be set upto encourage or discourage FDI.

Some of the favourable measures such as exemption of tax to direct investors in some particular sectors are not uncommon in many countries. However, in developing countries where FDI is utilised to help build up the local economy, limits on foreign ownership, screening requirements and restrictions on foreign personnel and operational freedom can easily be observed. As different countries adopt variable FDI restrictions that raise barriers to foreign investments, these policies are likely to influence choices among different investment locations.

(ii) Infrastructure

Those who are closely related to government policies on transportation, communications and energy often affects the FDI. Findlay opined that the provision of infrastructure affects both absolute and comparative advantages and, therefore, cross-country pattern of FDI. The availability and good quality of infrastructure create incentive for inward FDI by lowering transaction costs.

Impacts of Foreign Direct Investment

The strong global direct investment flows have influenced intensive debate and research on the impact of FDI on host economies. It is commonly accepted that FDI can inherently benefit domestic firms. Brooks suggests that apart from increasing output and income, host economies can benefit from FDI in five ways:

(i) Foreign firms bring in superior scientific or managerial technology. They will provide technological assistance to their local suppliers or customers, and train workers who may subsequently move to local firms. In addition, local firms could learn by simply watching foreign counterparts. The extent of benefits to host economies depends on if the technology could spill over to other firms in the local market.

(ii) Foreign investment steers up competition in the host economy. The entry of a new firm would tend to increase sectoral output and reduce the domestic price. In addition, the presence of foreign-owned firms may spur domestic firms to operate more efficiently and introduce new technologies earlier

(iii) Foreign investment typically results in increased domestic investment. Bosworth and Collins (1999) find out in a panel data study of 58developing countries that about half of each dollar of capital inflow translates into an increase in domestic investment. However, when capital inflows take the form of FDI, there is a near one-to-one relationship between FDI and domestic investment.

(iv) Foreign investment gives advantage in terms of export market access arising from economies of scale in marketing of foreign firms or from the ability to gain market access abroad.

(v) Foreign investment can aid in bridging a host country's foreign exchange gap. Investment often requires imported inputs. If domestic savings are insufficient to support capital accumulation to achieve a target growth, or barriers exist in converting domestic currencies into foreign exchange to acquire imports, foreign inflows can help ensure that foreign exchange will be available to purchase imports for investment. However, it should be noted that not all direct investments will lead to technological transfer or positive spillovers.

In case of the direct investors want to protect the technology, particularly a patented technology, production of foreign affiliates in host economies may be diverted to low value-added activities, limiting the benefit from technological learning. Sometimes, direct investors may also restrict or abandon completely vertical integration by importing inputs to the affiliates in host countries. Regarding competition, evidences have shown that direct investors, which have certain advantages like economies of scale and scope inherited in their global value chains, can even eliminate competition by crowding out relatively low-efficiency domestic firms. However, there are numerous effects of FDI on national economies and the international economy as a whole, due to differences in socio-economical and ideological conditions, the sheer size of FDI on the global level probably reflects that net effect of FDI is still positive.

The question as how to utilise beneficially FDI remains the policy decision for each government either through bilateral agreements or multilateral arrangements in the WTO framework 5 or other forums. As small open economies in the world, Macao is keen on attracting foreign capital to build up its own economy. There are a number of fiscal incentives like tax exemptions as well as financial incentives on interest subsidisation. In addition, the Macao Trade and Investment Promotion Institute (IPIM) established the Macao Business Support Centre (MBSC) in 2002 in order to reduce start-up costs for foreign investors, enabling them to familiarise themselves with Macao's business environment and the relevant administrative procedures in a relatively short time. The MBSC handles applications for business start up service, overseas trade fairs and business visits, as well as provides business information service and Mainland Chinese market advisory service.

In his policy address for the financial year 2002, the Macao SAR Chief Executive identified tourism and gaming as the leading or "dragon head" industry. Gaming, the most important sub-sector in the tourism industry, was liberalised when new casino licenses were awarded in February 2002. Ever since, the new perspective on economic prosperity has drawn attention of foreign direct investors, and foreign capital has found its ways into the SAR. In 2001, when the Census and Statistics Service of Macao (DSEC) began releasing its FDI statistics on a regular basis, the FDI inflow was valued at MOP1.3 billion. During the years between 2002 and 2004, due to the buoyant tourism sector following the relaxation of Hong Kong and Macao tour regulations and subsequently the Individual Traveller Scheme", the SAR's gross domestic product showed double-digit annual growth.

The economic growth rate slowed to a single-digit of 6.9% during 2005 before bouncing back to 16.6% in 2006. Meanwhile, the inward FDI flow picked up gradually to MOP3.9 billion in 2004 and further spurred to MOP10.6 billion in 2005 as foreign capital from the casino operators rushed in. Although the FDI stock rose generally in line with the GDP growth, it did not increase fast enough to catch up with the growth pace of GDP. Hence, the ratio dropped from approximately 48% in 2001 to 38% in 2004. Although, as the FDI, particularly those being poured into the gaming industry, started generating profits, FDI inflows rises to MOP10.6 billion during 2005, brought this ratio back to 44.5%. At the close of 2001 when the FDI had not yet heated up, the number of foreign direct investment enterprises stood only at 560. As the FDI picked up fast, this number surged rapidly to 723 in 2003, and jumped further to 1,024 in 2004 and 1,314 in 2005Although the number of persons employed by the FDI enterprises dipped from 31,210at the end of 2001 to 28,623 at the end of 2003, the buoyant economic conditions, led by the fast-growing tourism sector as a result of the relaxation of travelling policy by the Chinese Central Government, raised the labour demand again.

This number then rises with an average of 25.7% in 2004 and 2005, attaining 45,204 at the end of 2005. Equity capital, which is usually the paid-up capital, leaped from MOP2.7 billion at the end of 2001 to MOP10.0 billion one year later when the gaming liberalisation brought in two US operators. The equity capital gradually rose in the next three years to MOP12.3 billion at the end of 2005Regarding country origins of inward FDI, that the bulk of Macao's foreign direct investors is still from Hong Kong. FDI from Hong Kong reached MOP41.4 billion at the end of 2005, though its share in total FDI inflows fell from 70.7% in 2001 to 61.5%. FDI from the United States soared to MOP7.4 billion at the end of 2005 from MOP95 million four years ago, and its share in the total rose from 0.4% to 18.0%.

In Macao, Mainland China was the third largest direct investors having a share of 9.4%. It was followed by investors from Portugal and the United Kingdom, which had accumulated direct investment of MOP2.6 billion and MOP0.6 billion respectively In terms of sectoral distribution, it is clear that foreign capital did not flow into the manufacturing sector in the past few years. At the end of 2005, industrial production had an accumulative value of inward FDI at MOP2.9 billion which is virtually the same compared to that in 2001. Its share in the total stock of inward FDI fell from 12.2% in 2001 to 6.9% in 2005.

Since services, particularly tourism and gaming, represent the most important economic sector in Macao, it is not worthy to see that FDI to Macao mainly flowed into Cultural, Recreational, Gaming & Other Services, with an accumulated value of MOP25.6 billion. FDI to this sector had been growing by an annual average rate of 17.6% from 2002 to 2005. FDI to hotels and restaurants was also on the rise in the wake of the boom in the tourism sector, reaching MOP2.2 billion at the end of 2005, or 5.4% of the total inward FDI. In the financial sector, the stock of inward FDI rose from MOP5.4 billion at end-2001 to MOP8.3 billion at end-2005, of which MOP7.4 billion belonging to banks and securities companies.

In the last few decades, flows of direct investment have been increasing across national borders. Multilateral agreement on FDI has become an important issue in the WTO. It is widely believed that the setting-up of a multilateral framework on FDI can further boost world investment by creating a stable and transparent environment. As business confidence enhances, world FDI flows, especially those to developing countries, will be flourished. Meanwhile, the growing FDI flows have stimulated intense debate and research on the role of FDI. Recent studies do not only suggest that FDI serves as a mean to foster technological transfer, but also show that the entry of multinational enterprises into a host economy would have a significant bearing on spillover effects. Since the establishment of Macao SAR, the Government has designed strategically its policy to attract foreign capital to its leading or "dragon head" industry.

This policy has resulted in a spectacular economic performance with huge amount of FDI, and top-rated managerial expertise has poured in from abroad, strengthening the position of Macao as a regional tourism and gaming centre. According to the World Investment Report published by the United Nations Conference on Trade and Development, Macao ranked the third in developing Asia between 2001 and 2005 in terms of FDI inflows as a percentage of gross fixed capital formation, only after Hong Kong and Singapore.

However, it is noted that the majority of FDI inflows in the past few years has been concentrated in the gaming industry. In the policy address for the financial year 2007, the SAR Government proposed a strategy for proper diversification in a vertical manner. Looking into the overwhelming success of the gaming industry, it would be the right time to put more FDI policy focus on other sectors of the economy where benefits can be generated from foreign investment by another learning process.

The Nature and Role of FDI in Asia

The Foreign Direct Investment (FDI) is frequently considered as simultaneously being one of the results and drivers of globalisation. In the process of opening up economies to participate in some of the positive impacts of globalisation, countries position themselves in respect of attracting FDI. In addition, the ability to attract FDI and its positive impact on growing economies is valued as an integral part of the road to successful economic growth and development. The Asian economic crisis has highlighted the vulnerability and volatility of emerging economies especially in the financial sector and, in the case of Thailand, directly linked to FDI.

The question that prevails is to what extent FDI supports or sabotages globalization attempts by countries. This paper considers the role and impact that FDI has had in Thailand over the past decade. The first section identifies the nature and impact of FDI in general, followed by an explanation of the underlying reasons for the flow of funds. The nature and impact of FDI define the concept and summarize the consequences, both positive and negative, towards the recipient country. Different theories explaining why FDI takes place are also discussed here. The second section briefly considers FDI in Asia.

This chapter appears at tendencies in the flow of FDI in terms of target markets and industries. The role of FDI in Asia is analysed over the 1990 to 1998 period to show its behaviour before and during the Asian financial crisis. The third section reviews the impact of FDI in Thailand by pointing out its nature and origin in terms of the major sources of FDI and the industries most affected by them. Also included in this part is the relationship between FDI and the export performance of Thailand and the transfer of technology impact thereof. The last section discusses the current situation of FDI in Thailand and anticipates future trends. Assessing the impact on FDI of the recent change in political leadership and its redefining of priorities does this. A brief comparison to other countries in the region and possible future trends conclude the paper.

The Nature and impact of Foreign Direct Investment (FDI)

When one concerns about the cross border investment, it is important to distinguish between FDI, Foreign Portfolio Investment (FPI) and other types of foreign investment. The World Trade Organization (WTO) indicates that "FDI occurs when an investor based in one country (the home country) acquires an asset in another country (the host country) with the intent to manage that asset". Interpreting this definition from a more specific perspective means that ownership of 10 percent or more of ordinary shares or voting power represents a sufficient share to give the foreign investor a significant influence on the management of the enterprise.

Moreover, FDI is concerned to comprise three possible components; new equity from the parent company to the subsidiary; reinvested profits of the subsidiary; and long and short term net loans from the parent to the subsidiary. Foreign Portfolio Investment (FPI), in turn, entails passive holdings of securities and other financial assets, which do not reflect active management or control of the security's issuer. High rates of return and reduction of risk through geographic diversification positively influence FPI.

The management dimension is what distinguishes FDI from FPI in foreign stocks, bonds and other financial instruments. As a positive, FDI brings capital flows that improve the balance of payments, and other economic benefits such as employment, export markets, technology, management skill enhancement and spillover effects. The potentialities of negative consequences of FDI comprise of inappropriate technology transfer and a deteriorating balance of payments in the longer run. Within FDI, there are often trade-offs between different benefits and objectives. Countries may, for instance, have to choose between investments that offer short as opposed to long-term benefits; foreign firm involvement may lead to static gains but not necessarily to dynamic ones, such as infrastructure and living standards. A large inflow of FDI can add to investment resources in a host economy but it may deter the development of local firms.

The wants to generate employment may lead governments to favor labor intensive, low technology investments, while promotion of technology development may favor more sophisticated investors.

Similarly, the desire to upgrade technology may call for a heavy reliance on technology transfer by foreign investors, while to promote local innovation may require more emphasis on arm's length transfers to local firms. There can be many such trade-off, and there is no universal answer to how they should be made. Similarly, no ideal policy on FDI is there, which is applicable to all countries throughout the years. Rather than determining whether FDI is good or bad for economic development the focus should be on ensuring that it contributes in a balanced and sustainable way to the legitimate aspirations of host countries. Some foreign investors acknowledge that investment decisions and performance in host countries could have both positive and negative impacts on the local economy depending on policies of host countries.

Explaining Foreign Direct Investment flows

Various theories in explaining FDI assert that the basis for such investment lies in the transaction cost of transferring technical and other knowledge and market imperfections. Subsequently in a world of perfect markets, there would be no Multinational Enterprises (MNEs) and, thus no FDI as it is MNEs that make FDI.

Comparative cost advantage theory

As per the theory of comparative cost advantage (explaining the nature of imperfect markets), "a country should produce and export those goods and services for which it is relatively more productive than other countries and import those goods and services for which other countries are relatively more productive than it is". This is, however, "not a sufficient condition for FDI since the significance of investment flows concerns other conditions such as technology transfer, tax incentives and explanations of trade flows, rather than country-based theories".

Product life cycle theory

The outcomes of Life Cycle Theory describe about how MNEs undertake FDI at particular stages in the life cycle of a product they have pioneered. FDI will occur when the foreign market is large enough to support local production. However, the theory does not identify clearly when it is profitable to invest in activities, and it also fails to explain why companies choose FDI over other forms of market entry, such as direct exporting.

Internalization theory

The Internalization theory, or market imperfection theory, states that "when an in the market makes a transaction less efficient than it could be, a company will undertake FDI to internationalize the transaction and thereby remove the imperfection". The theory also explains why firms prefer FDI to licensing, as licensing has weaknesses, including exposing technological know-how to foreign competitors, absence of control over manufacturing, marketing, and strategy in a foreign country. In addition, a firm's uniqueness and competitive advantage may not be amenable for licensing.

The Eclectic paradigm theory

The Eclectic Paradigm theory describes both the ways in which enterprises of different nationalities and the industrial and geographical composition of such activities serve overseas markets. According to this theory, a firm will make a direct investment in a foreign country if the following three conditions are satisfied. "First, the firm must have a product or a production process such that the firm enjoys some market power advantage in foreign markets. Second, the firm must have a reason to locate production abroad rather than concentrate it in the home country, especially if there are scale economies at the plant level.

Third, the firm must have a reason to exploit its ownership advantage internally, rather than license or sell its process to a foreign firm". The theory furthermore suggests that all forms of international production can be explained by reference to these conditions. The country specific advantages have an important bearing on FDI often rendering the location preferable to other potential host countries, and to domestic investment.

Another determinant of FDI is the ability of the firm to generate ownership advantages, which are best exploited by the firm in a foreign rather than in a domestic location. In this way, the eclectic theory is able to provide an explanation for differences in the industrial pattern of outward FDI of different industrialized countries.

Market power theory

The Market Power Theory states that FDI will take place when a company tries to introduce a dominant market presence in an industry. In this theory, the firm will get more profit because it is far better able to dictate the cost of its inputs and the price of its output. Companies that are able to achieve a great deal of market power can integrate forward to increase control over output. As has been reviewed in this section, there are a number of theories that attempt to explain the flow of FDI. The Eclectic Paradigm theory is the most useful for analyzing the implication of FDI in economic development. The next section will discuss the flow of FDI to Asian countries.

Foreign direct investment in Asia

In Asian countries most affected by the Asian financial crisis have ranked high among developing host countries in the attractiveness of their economies to foreign investors. In particular, they have substantially liberalized their FDI policies and taken steps to facilitate business. However, the financial crisis and economic consequences will affect FDI flows to these countries. Thus, the tendencies and role of FDI will be discussed as following.

Tendencies

The tradition of FDI flows into and within Asian countries has had some structural changes since 1990. The change is assigned to two reasons; globalization and mergers and acquisitions. Firstly, increased globalization and lower trade barriers cause a growing number of international companies to undertake FDI, as companies realize they can produce in a more efficient and productive location in the world, and simply export to a worldwide market. This set off another round of FDI flows into low cost newly industrialized and emerging nations worldwide. Second, the number of M&A and their exploding values also underline the change in pattern of FDI flows.

Various cross-border M&A deals are driven by the desire of companies to get a foothold in a new geographic market, to increase a firm's global competitiveness, to fill gaps in companies' product lines in a global industry and to reduce costs in such areas as R&D, production, or distributions a result, FDI in the primary sector continues to experience a declining share with a greater distribution of FDI flows to the manufacturing and the tertiary sector.

FDI in finance and banking activities increased noticeably in the second half of the 1990s, particularly through M&A. The liberalization of financial sector processes taken up by countries in the region facilitates this development. These structural changes are partly due to the industrial development policies of the countries in the region, which aim to diversify economies from over reliance on agriculture. The developmental progress made in the manufacturing and financial sector further facilitates this process.

Role

FDI has shared significantly to the economic and industrial development of the Asian countries for the last many years and is expected to undergo for the same. Among the components of resource flows to Asian countries, FDI constitutes a considerable share, indicating the importance of FDI as a major source of finance for economic development. Moreover, most of the FDI flows played an important role in pushing the export sector of those countries. A large number of these, including Thailand, gave priority to export as a key mechanism for economic development. Nevertheless, Taiwan and South Korea did not resort to FDI as the impetus for exports and instead relied on the promotion of entrepreneurs to develop products for sales abroad.

Those countries which relied on FDI and consequently rose also experienced an increase in their trade deficits. Between 1990 and 1997, FDI represented about an annual average of 40% of the net resource flows to the Asian countries. A high ratio of FDI to net private capital flows in the 1990s is the norm for most developing countries, and particularly Asian countries. The Asian financial crisis has caused many countries to experience a severe shortage of funds and managing FDI has become a factor that governments have become more aware of. This is partly due to the role FDI played in bringing about an economic expansion in Asia.

Being a part of the increased awareness governments changed laws and regulations to attract FDI. Previously protected business sectors for local entrepreneurs were opened up to foreign investors, specially the financial institution sector FDI is expected to undergo to be a significant source of finance for development in the Asian countries, against the backdrop of the decline in official development assistance and difficult access to international debt markets and bank borrowing in recent times. An outstanding characteristic of FDI is that it is more stable than other kinds of international capital flows. This is confirmed by the flow of capital during the Asian financial crisis.

In countries affected by the financial crisis, portfolio flows and other investment flows have shifted from highly positive to strongly negative, while FDI flows remained positive. The size and the suddenness of the reversal in non-FDI flows in some countries has triggered and magnified the financial crisis in Asia. In addition, FDI has appeared to be an increasingly attractive alternative to long-term bank loans as a form of capital inflow for developing countries, and has been viewed by some as the remedy for declining domestic investment and higher costs of borrowing from abroad. Net Private Capital Flows to Five Affected Asian Countries (Thailand, Philippines, Malaysia, Korea, Indonesia).

Foreign direct investment in Thailand

FDI in Thailand has been a major contributor to the economic growth of the Thailand since the mid-1980s. In the late 1980s, about 50% of FDI inflow went to the manufacturing sector, especially in the area of labor intensive and export-oriented industries. Despite this Thai industry became less competitive during the 1990s, the real estate sector boomed and investment in private infrastructure increased in 1993.

This structural change shifted FDI from manufacturing to real estate and infrastructure. From 1993 to 1996, almost 40% of net FDI in Thailand went to real estate. In 1997, when the Thai financial crisis started, the composition of inward FDI shifted significantly to the industrial sector. This was derived largely from foreign partners contributing more capital to existing companies faced with financial difficulties. In addition to this, several Thai firms decided to sell off some of the non-core business activities to enhance their competitiveness, which in turn created opportunities for foreign partners to play a greater role.

The FDI flow in 1998 was influenced primarily by the acquisition of existing Thai and joint venture companies by foreign firms, especially in the banking sector. The high level of investment in financial institutions in 1998 was principally due to liberalization measures taken in late 1997, allowing foreigners to hold a majority of shares in Thai financial institutions for up to 10 years.

Source of Foreign Direct Investment in Thailand

FDI in Thailand is predominantly derived from five countries. The investment from some countries has remained relatively stable during the nineties while investment from Japan revealed some fluctuation. Japan has been the largest source of FDI since the late 1980s. High wages and a strong exchange rate forced many Japanese firms to relocate labor-intensive processes lower labour cost locations. This partly contributed to Japanese direct investment in Thailand, mostly involving joint ventures, being concentrated in the automotive and electronics industries.

Because of the economic recession in Japan in the early 1990s, the contribution of Japanese investment in Thailand fell to around 20% of total FDI. This decline resulted from the economic recession in Japan, and Japanese companies exploiting lower labor costs in China, India and Mexico. In 1997 and 1998, Japanese investment in Thailand recovered based on new foreign investment guidelines allowing the buy-out of local partners. In 1999, as this activity decreased, Japan's share of FDI decreased again The US direct investment in Thailand was encouraged in part by the US-Thai Treaty of Amity of 1966, which accorded national treatment to US investors.

Many of the investment involved fully foreign-owned affiliates in areas such as petroleum and chemicals. The level of FDI inflow from the United States was steady during 1990 - 1996. The increase of US investment during 1997-1998 was partly the result of the devaluation of Thai currency. Moreover, the restructuring of firms faced with large debt repayments, rising interest rates and urgent need for funds, combined with a more liberal policy towards M&A, provided opportunities for US firms to undertake direct investments in Thailand through M&As. The FDI flow from US peaked in late 1998 and started to decline in1999.

While FDI from Japan and the United States declined, FDI from Singapore increased to the value of US$ 1,151 million in 1999, up by 117% from the year before. This is attributed to the policy of the Singapore government to become the financial hub of the ASEAN region. The Government of Singapore Investment Corporation (GIC) made significant investment in Thailand, both in the financial institutions sector and the industry sector, particularly, in the fields of communications, electronics parts and equipment. In Thailand, exports have been the main engine of economic growth, particularly since the late 1980s.

Historically among the leading rice exporters of the world, it has become a major exporter of manufactured products, rising to over 80 percent of total export in 1999. This shafting exports is reflected in the structural transformation of the Thai economy from agriculture to industry in which FDI has played a leading role. FDI flows concentrated on manufacturing, (including automobiles, textiles and more recently electronics such as computers and parts), and have developed and diversified the economic structure, to the point where the manufacturing sector represented around two third of total Thai exports in the 1990s.

Nevertheless, the high export in percentage comes basically from foreign-owned firms. In 1997, the 125 most prominent Board of Investment (BOI) companies, which are mostly foreign-owned firms or Thai joint ventures, accounted for 90 per cent of total exports of electronic and electrical products. Foreign a affiliates in Thailand have become more export-oriented over time, in response to both export promotion policies and to favorable exchange rates. Over 80 percent of Thailand's total exports are now in manufacturing, including computers and parts, electrical appliances, integrated circuits and parts, automotive parts and accessories, mostly produced by foreign investors or joint-ventures. The basic impacts of foreign firms' activities on the Thai balance of payments go beyond the contribution to exports. Foreign affiliates also import goods and services, as well as attract capital and repatriate interest, income and royalties.

FDI in Thailand is frequently accompanied by an increase in imports representing a large share of inputs from abroad. It is estimated that foreign investment activities account for 90 per cent of all machinery equipment and over 50 per cent of raw materials imports. It is specially the case for export-oriented investment where investors must secure competitively priced and high quality inputs to compete effectively in global markets. In the period of the crisis, the importance of FDI as a potential source of net capital in flows has been emphasized. At the same time, however, it is important to point out that the impact of FDI on the export performance of the economy is limited to specific sectors, which are dominated by foreign firms, rather than the whole.

Foreign direct investment, technology transfer and industrial upgrading

The impact of the overall export of inward investment is itself a substitute for technology transfer and industrial upgrading, which are at the heart of FDI. Many developing countries, including Thailand, furnishes favorable investment incentives and even sometimes protection to attract FDI to high technology industries (electronics, automobile) with the expectation of mastering new technologies and skills eventually Various studies indicate that low value added product lines and downstream production technologies are located in Thailand. In some cases a large part of operational, maintenance and inspection activities of Japanese firms have been transferred to Thai affiliates.

However, highly sophisticated technologies, such as design and development of new products, have not been transferred. In general, the technology transfer process in Thailand is considered slow and inefficient by foreign investors, partly due to a lack of supply linkages and skilled labour force. To address the poor technology transfer, the Government has developed several schemes. An example of this is that BOI (Board of Investment) Unit for Industrial Linkages Development (BUILD) with the objective of enhancing local subcontracting through the provision of information and technical assistance. Moreover, new national initiatives have been launched to promote technology transfer as part of the goals of the 8th National Economic and Social Development Plan.

Support is granted to foreign investment in production requiring advanced technology, research and development. These efforts, however, are limited by the weak absorptive capacity of local management. Another way of capturing any potential beneficial effect of FDI is to assess whether inflows have been accompanied by industrial upgrading in the relevant sectors. In the case of Thailand, this is relevant in the electronics and automobile sectors, two of the most important recipients of FDI.

The continuation of new foreign investments has benefited the country in terms of industrial growth, including diversification and integration of the local industry. Although export growth was concentrated in high technology products such as computer components, automobile components and electrical goods, for most of these products Thailand was merely an assembly base. In Thailand, high-technology production is not associated with high value-added production. Moreover, the high-technology character of Thai exports is a reflection of high-technology imported inputs.

Assembly activities in the automobile industry may be seen as a first step to develop more advanced capabilities, but this has been a slow process given the lack of sufficient research and development (R&D) and relevant human capital. Problems of upgrading technology include the slow development of most capital goods industries (such as iron and steel, non-electrical machinery, metal products and transport equipment), as well as a heavy reliance on imports of both capital and intermediate goods.

The comparative advantage of Thailand in labor-intensive productions falls, the need to transform to production involving more skills and more capital becomes important. The Asian financial crisis raised fundamental questions relating to the political sustainability of programs of trade and investment liberalization and domestic economic reforms. While Thailand was one of the most open economies, the crisis has greatly extended the role and impact of FDI in several major industries. A weakened baht, high levels of local debt and bankruptcy eventuated in increased involvement of foreign firms. Thus, here in this context, legislative changes to permit 100% foreign equity in sectors previously reserved for Thais, enable foreign firms to participate more fully in the domestic economy. These legislative changes have raised public debate about the role of FDI in the Thai economy, and the degree to which domestic firms require and are entitled to special protection and support in a globalizing economy.

Aftermath

When acknowledging the need for liberalization development of FDI regimes, majority of the Asian countries felt that this process must continue to be adaptable to the individual host country's specific needs, level of economic development and resource base. The objectives of all government to achieve economic recovery through suitable policies toward FDI, included privatisation, export-led growth and technological capacities and the development of local business. As yet, there have been no comprehensive policy approaches, which are extremely beneficial, nor which have been counterproductive.

Lessons from other Asian countries

It has been a driving force for economic development of the FDI in Asian countries. Because of different attitudes towards FDI, the ultimate impact and permanency of FDI varies significantly among countries in the region. Countries like South Korea and Singapore were able to develop FDI policies that enabled them top benefit significantly and are pointed out as examples for the Thai situation. Before the Asian financial crisis, South Korean's policy toward economic growth relied heavily on borrowing from foreign countries, which largely was used to subsidize Korea's chaebol.

In spite of the fact that FDI could have been utilized to finance part of the South Korea's industrialization driven plan, the government preferred foreign borrowing to FDI because it wanted to maintain domestic ownership of its industries. Thus, many of the chaebol are protected by a number of entry-barriers, including restrictions on M&A.

However, after the crisis, internal reform is intended to attract FDI into both capital and management expertise. Major FDI reform initiatives to make foreign investment easier and more attractive include; foreigners being able to hold up to 55% equity in a company on the South Korean stock exchange; expanding tax exemptions to include high-tech, and value added service industries; and extending the tax concession period from the current 8 years to10 years. Cultural industries are those restricted business areas (foreign ownership of cable TV program procedures will be limited to 30%). What makes

South Korea distinct from Thailand is that it has a technologically up-to-date industrial base, efficient infrastructure and a large skilled workforce, thus South Korea has to satisfy a different set of needs by attracting FDI (Asia Pacific Foundation of Canada, 1998).

Singapore's greatest economic accomplishment is the integration and international orientation of its economy, which is mainly dependent on the performance of its electronic industry, all of whom are in one way or the other FDI. MNCs not only enabled Singapore to export but also to acquire technological knowledge by transferring technology to local subsidiaries, and training local employees. Singapore is an exceptional successful country in the way that it was able to attract MNCs in both manufacturing and services.

The Singaporean state has shaped an attractive investment environment by providing a range of facilities, infrastructure, subsidies, and complementary public investment. The current economic strategy aims to ensure that Singapore remains a highly attractive location for inward FDI and to continue assistance to local companies. The vision for the next phase of development is to encourage companies to continue undertaking innovation.

Current Thai foreign direct investment developments

Other than promoting domestic changes by grasping more foreign technology and managerial know-how through FDI, the recently elected government (Thaksin's government) is choosing to protect the Thai economy from global competitive forces. New policy approaches to economic recovery rely on SMEs utilizing locally embedded skills to create new products and services for consumers. According to Bide there are two main characteristics of the new development model. Firstly, since Thailand's comparative advantage does not lie in abundant cheap generic labour that caters for mass-industrialisation, the policy should accommodate a population and work force accomplished with an aesthetic culture and tradition in industries such as food processing, textiles, and ceramic products.

With this trend and its aesthetic skills, combined with a diverse geography, mean that Thailand's mass-tourism industry can also be transformed into a higher value-added sector. However, there are two major obstacles that restrict these industries from achieving full potential. First, the inability to blend fundamental local skills with international technology, such as knowledge on consumer tastes and marketing. Second, the lack of international brand names to secure pricing power.

The present government is addressing both impediments. The second characteristic of the model is that skill driven enterprises requires no large industrial base, as optimum size dictates they are SMEs. Such enterprises organize workers who excel in their local skills and other inputs in a flexible manner. This approach results in an ability to adjust to shifting global demand and supply and excess capacity is thus no longer an issue. It is expected that these SMEs will bring new products and services to the international market on improving terms of trade and pricing power.

This new scheme appears to have characteristics of being anti-FDI. Policy makers explained that this new policy would run parallel to MNC operations as long as these contribute to the Thai economy. The type of foreign investment that will be actively courted is those ensuring to forge synergies with local enterprises. Under this new policy, international food companies and foreign tour operators are more likely to be investors and partners. Thailand aims to reposition itself from supplying cheap labor to MNCs or industrial products at the lower end of global supply chains to capitalizing on sales of differentiated, branded products and services to global consumers.

Future Foreign Direct Investment prospects

The FDI outlook of Thailand depends on the successful implementation of domestic structural reforms, the external environment, including regional competition for foreign capital, the depth of future FDI regime liberalization and investment promotion restructuring. Apart from the economic recovery, the pace of deregulation and corporate and financial restructuring, three key factors will determine the level of foreign investor interest in Thailand. First, the speed with which remaining constraints to FDI is removed. Second, the tempo of state enterprise privatization and government regulatory streamlining. Third, the change of FDI promotion measures.

With the comparison to regional competitors like the Republic of Korea, China and Malaysia, Thailand's FDI regime reform has been very slow and restrictions remain considerable. Moreover, after an election in January2001 and under the new government, public, media and political support given to nationalistic elements oppose further FDI reform and imply slow future liberalization. As Prime Minister Thaksin announced "his government would not beg foreign investors to come to Thailand because the main economic development strategy under his government was based on the concept of self-reliance. He also taken much consideration that once the country's internal economic situation had improved, FDI would quickly follow without the need for attracting foreign investors". A practical example is where the Internal Trade Department in Thailand has initiated anti-competitive investigations against foreign owned retail stores by restricting operating times and tough new zoning laws.

Further limitations to FDI in many sectors are heavily regulated domestic markets, including the insurance, non banking financial sector and steel industry. Moreover, the government announced recently that it would dramatically reduce the tax and other privileges that were granted in the past under the Board of Investment and the Industrial Estate Authority laws and regulations to limit the dependency on FDI for domestic economic growth.

Because of the impact of the Asian financial crisis, Thailand is undergoing in the process of economic recovery. During the crisis, non-FDI investments were shifted largely from the Thai economy although FDI flows into Thailand were higher after the crisis. FDI is deemed to play an important role in the recovery of the economy. Key drivers of the FDI increase include an increased focus on FDI resulting from fiscal pressure, a reduction in foreign investment restrictions, and the devaluation of asset prices. The majority of FDI into Thailand originates in Japan, the US and Singapore and is concentrated in export-oriented sectors such as electronics and automobile. The transfers of technology and industrial upgrading from FDI have been disappointing in Thailand.

Moreover, export performances are generally limited to sectors that are dominated by foreign firms and based heavily on import inputs, questioning the real role and contribution of FDI in the Thai economy. Before the January 2001 election, the government adopted a flexible policy approach toward FDI, in line with the economic recovery program agreed with the International Monetary Fund (IMF). The program also aimed to promote local enterprises through attracting FDI. However, the current government, lead by Prime Minister Thaksin, has a vision of increased self-reliance.

The FDI policies are also revised in terms of privileges given in the past and conversely, it is expected that more benefits are to be given to local businesses. In reality, national resources are insufficient to restore economic health and Thailand needs FDI to bridge its saving gap. Thai policy makers may need to look at other Asian economies to assess how they used FDI as an instrument to economic recovery and to sustain long-term economic development. Foreign Direct Investment, Services Trade Negotiations and Development

Commitments in Services Negotiations and Inward FDI in Tourism

Theory and Evidence so far

Theory: GATS and inward FDI Trade in services rules are an important, but hitherto largely neglected in the empirical literature, way in which WTO membership may enhance trade performance through their potential effects on inward FDI. The GATT/WTO included for the first time in 1995 commitments on treatment of foreign providers of services in the General Agreement of Trade in Services (GATS). Countries can commit any of around 160sub-sectors and four modes. Mode 3 in particular relates to the conditions under which foreign firms have access to particular services sectors, and which conditions apply after their establishment. 5 In theory there are three types of effects. First, countries can offer market access to foreign providers of services, though in practice GATS commitments have gone little beyond existing liberalisation. Hence, GATS is scarcely used as a liberalising tool. Second, the set of trade rules contained in GATS (especially mode 3 on investment) provides for a transparent framework conducive to private sector activities, reducing uncertainty and encouraging investment.

A country's obligations under GATS can be divided under two headings: (1) General obligations and (2) Specific Commitments. General obligations apply directly and automatically to all members and services sectors. Under these members are required to accord (a) Most Favoured Nation Treatment (Art II) to all the WTO members (a country has to extend immediately and unconditionally to services or service suppliers of all members treatment no less favourable than that accorded to like services and suppliers of any other country) and maintain (b)Transparency which requires members to publish all measures of general application and respond to other members' queries. Specific commitments are commitments laid down in individual country schedules and concern specifically designated sectors. The scope of these commitments may vary across countries and sectors.

Specific commitments concern (a) Market Access (Art XVI) which states that 'members give no less favourable treatment to the services and service suppliers of other members than is provided in its schedule of commitments' and (b) National Treatment (Art XVII) which implies that members do not discriminate between foreign and domestic services or suppliers.

Art XVI specifies the following six measures affecting free market access that may not be applied to foreign services or suppliers unless they are clearly specified in the schedule – limitations on (1) the number of service suppliers (2) the total value of services transactions or assets (3) the number of services operations or the total quantity of service output (4) the number of persons that may be employed in a particular sector or by a particular sector (5) measures that restrictor require supply of the service through specific types of legal entity or joint venture (6) percentage of participation of foreign capital or total value of foreign investment effects on investment, when investment involves large sunk and irreversible costs and there is the option to delay the decision to make the investment until further information becomes available.

This is also the sentiment of firms. Signalling is the third effect. Countries that make offers and requests to GATS are willing to seriously consider development of the services sectors, sending positive signals to potential investors. Singh contrasts negotiation capacities and commitments in Costa Rica with those in Belize and finds that Costa Rica has started much earlier in prioritising and developing services sectors and taking commitments with obvious success, Belize took much longer.

Effects of GATS on inward FDI: Empirical studies have considered only to a limited extent whether WTO rules can affect inward FDI and trade in services. This seems to be a significant gap in the literature. WTO rules that lead to a more predictable investment climate should lead to more private finance and this may affect trade in goods and services. Te Velde and Bezemer show that regional trade and investment rules may lead to more inward FDI from outside the region.

Halward-Driemeier and Tobin and Rose-Ackerman shows that bilateral investment treaties (BITs) raise FDI slightly but only act as a complement rather than as a substitute for weak political and legal institutions. Salacuse and Sullivan find a strong correlation between BITs and FDI flows. Most studies assume that there is a link between mode 3 commitments and increased inward FDI, and some are cautious suggesting that GATS is but one factor in the host of factors explaining FDI. One study for Turkey suggested that GATS commitments did raise inward FDI. This paper aims to provide evidence for the Caribbean.

Current patterns of GATS commitments: The appendix reviews domestic regulation and GATS commitments and current offers in the tourism sector in most Caribbean countries. Most of the Caribbean countries have specific laws regulating the tourism sector in general and the hotels industry in particular, with the exception of Suriname and St Kitts and Nevis. Although the latter countries do not have specific laws, they have alternative systems in place governing the sector with variable success. There is evidence emerging on the effects of WTO rules on trade in goods. Rose uses a gravity model of bilateral merchandise trade over 50 years and for 175 countries and finds that membership of GATT/WTO has not significantly affected trade patterns.

Rose argues that this may be because WTO members may not have more liberal trade policies estimate the effects of WTO membership in a gravity model of imports and find a positive impact when they distinguish between developing and developed countries, and amongst sectors. There is little econometric evidence on the effects of WTO rules on services trade. Mattoo et al. construct an index of financial services and telecommunications openness on the basis of GATS commitments and liberalisation, which has a positive sign in an equation explaining GDP per capita growth ownership of hotels in terms of foreigners or domestic nationals with restrictions on foreign participation in hotels depending on the number of hotel rooms.

Suriname has an integral Tourism Development Programme and is considering a new tourism law. In terms of treatment of foreign investors in hotels, the only country that discriminates against foreigners and places limitations on their investment in terms of minimum number of hotel rooms is Antigua and Barbuda. St Kitts and Nevis also places limitations on foreign ownership for hotels having less than a certain minimum number of rooms. All the other countries such as Barbados, Belize, Dominican Republic, Guyana, Haiti, Jamaica, Suriname, Saint Vincent and the Grenadines, Saint Lucia, Grenada and Dominica grant national treatment to foreign investors in their domestic laws. Several countries have recently stepped up their efforts at reforming regulation of the Tourism sector. Belize has introduced two new acts since 1995.

The National Tourism Council Act in 1999 and the Hotels and Tourist Accommodation Act in1997. Other countries such as Barbados, Dominican Republic, Guyana, Antigua and Barbuda, and Saint Lucia have introduced a single new tourism act in the period

1995–2003. But countries such as Haiti, Jamaica, Suriname, Saint Vincent and the Grenadines, Saint Kitts and Nevis, Granada and Dominica have not introduced any new laws in the tourism sector since 1995. GATS commitments in the tourism sector (sector 9 out of the 12 main GATS sectors) can be divided into four sub sectors (A–D) as indicated below: A. Hotels and Restaurants (incl. Catering) B. Travel Operators and Tour Operators C. Tourist Guide Services D. Other In terms of existing GATS commitments Barbados and Belize have not included any commitments in the tourism sector. All the other countries such as Dominican Republic, Guyana, Haiti, Jamaica, Mauritius, Suriname, Antigua and Barbuda, Saint Vincent and the Grenadines, Saint Lucia, Saint Kitts and Nevis, Grenada and Dominica have made GATS commitments in the tourism sector but they vary by mode, and national treatment and market access conditions. Guyana, Suriname and Jamaica have commitments in the sub sectors 9A and 9B with Guyana and Suriname placing no restrictions and Jamaica having some limitations in place. All the other countries have commitments only in the sub sector 9A with some limitations except in the case of Haiti and Dominican Republic who have placed no limitations.

There are several observations. First, several barriers to market access and national treatment of foreign firms remain possible because they are not enshrined in international trade commitments, so countries have not even committed the statusquo. Second, because there are still trade barriers (in GATS) in all countries (maxscore is 4 out of 8), there is scope for progress for all countries. Third, because the scope of commitments varies considerably by country (ranging from 0–4), this presents a good basis for testing the effects this might have on inward FDI. St Vincent and the Grenadines is the only Caribbean country with new GATS offers in the tourism sector. St Vincent has liberalised market access in some sub-sectors.

While we focus on the tourism services sector (9) in GATS, it should be borne in mind that tourism is not a separate GATS category. Outside GATS, tourism comprises several services such as travel and transportation services, while the cruiseships industry does not fall under GATS tourism services. It is also related to e.g. health services exports (health tourism). The importance of health tourism is well documented in the case of the Caribbean. It is also interlinked with cultural services. An important issue for health tourism is the extension of portability of national health insurance to the Caribbean; for example, the UK does not seem to have an agreement on this with St Lucia.

Empirical Strategy

Dunning and Carr et al. provide a rationale for including variables such as infrastructure, human capital and market size. This paper limits the choice of key determinants of FDI to avoid over parameterisation, but acknowledges that there could be additional factors that we cannot deal with. DOMREG includes measures of domestic regulation, while GATS includes a measure of GATS commitments, the main variable that this paper is interested in. (GATS) Rules that are expected to raise FDI would appear in the regression with a significant and positive regression coefficient.

Measurement of variables

The dependent variable is the flow of inward FDI in the Tourism sector and uses a variety of detailed sources on sectoral FDI flows: ECCB, UNCTAD and domestic sources. Chart 1 plots the average annual inflow of FDI over the most recent 5 years for the 9 Caribbean countries that we are interested in: Antigua and Barbuda, Belize, Dominica, Dominican Republic, Grenada, Jamaica, St Kitts, St Vincent and St Lucia. The other data we include is market size. Normally, national income (real GDP) is used as the market size variable in regressions explaining FDI.

However, this is not always clear in the case of investment in tourism which may not only depend on the general market but also the potential for the tourism market, such as tourism arrivals or real exports of services. We will experiment with all three measures; but need to acknowledge measurement of 'market size' is more difficult than for say market-seeking manufacturing FDI. The data comes from the World Development Indicators 2005, and from UNCTAD on exports of travel services.

The deflators used to make the market size and FDI variables constant is the GDP deflator. We introduce a one-year lag for all market size variables, thus avoiding a possible endogeneity between market size and FDI. We use the sum of Tourism FDI in all Caribbean countries as regional tourism FDI. New Evidence First look at the evidence Casual observation of the data is informative on how GATS commitments might be related to inward FDI. The countries that attract most inward FDI also have a higher score on the GATS commitments variable (Dominican Republic, and Mexico and Costa Rica for countries outside CARIFORUM), while a country such as Belize with relatively little in FDI has not made any commitments so far. Furthermore, St Vincent has made a recent GATS offer in tourism and is also receiving relatively large FDI inflows.

These are signs of a positive relationship between GATS and FDI. Implications for negotiation strategies The main findings of the analysis in the previous section suggest that being actively involved in services negotiations (in the form of commitments or offers in GATS) is a good thing for attracting more FDI into tourism, but it is easy to overestimate the results: they are not always significant or clear, and other determinants may still be much more important. We also pointed out the limited sample size. There is a further issue: services negotiations need to be a tool for development, and an increase in FDI may be welcome but its positive impact on development is not always secured.

This has led to a set of recommendations, 7a set of possible offers in trade negotiations: a) liberalise services sectors that help tourism (utilities, insurance); b) reduce tariffs on goods used by tourism; c) facilitate movement of visitors and tourism professionals; and a set of requests: a) access to developed markets for tourism students, and for tourism professionals, who should be included in the category professionals, and whose qualifications should be recognised fully; b) extend portability of developed country health insurance to the Caribbean, and a set of other demands. The Caribbean Hotel Association (CHA), representing more than 800 hotel members, responded and among others confirmed to a) use trade negotiations to attract FDI in tourism, and remove services limitations to hotels with more than 75 rooms (different from 100 rooms common in some countries); b) secure mutual recognition agreements for tourism qualifications; c) enhance mode 4 market access (for tourism professionals and hospitality students) and d) examine schemes to extend insurance cover to Caribbean Hotels.

The European Services Association also highlights the lists of GATS commitments as one (but only the most important) of the factors on list of determinants affecting inward FDI in the Caribbean. Thus, it seems that, on the available evidence and policy statements, removing additional trade and investment barriers through negotiations in GATS should help to Encourage public/private dialogue and trade/tourism ministries dialogue; Develop encompassing definition of tourism Develop regional policy on cruise tourism; Introduce Tourism Satellite Accounts (TSAs) to measure impact.

The Review health and safety standards used by developed country tour operators, and compensate Caribbean Hotels when the tour operators become insolvent; Encourage conferences to be held in Caribbean through tax incentives and reduce taxes on travellers to Caribbean, and increase their duty-free allowances; Build regional hospitality services programmes; Introduce market access points for Caribbean Tourism Services providers; Introduce Caribbean airlines in global reservation systems; Establish internet marketing strategies for small business/hotels, introduce TSAs; Facilitate Caribbean commercial presence abroad; Encourage partnership programmes in hospitality institutes; Increase air services to small countries. increase more FDI and exports of services in the tourism sector.

GATS appears specially appropriate because it can be used to signal openness to FDI through effective offers in mode 3 (in the Caribbean) and it can be used to get more credible access in export markets through requests in mode 4. The credibility of GATS commitments comes in part from an effective dispute settlement mechanism. While GATS flexibility can itself be used as a means of special and differential treatment (SDT), some would argue that GATS provisions (or indeed Regional Services Trade Agreements) could be made more directly development friendly.

A Dominican Republic's proposal for a new Tourism Annex to the GATS includes three such provisions: need for multilateral competitive safeguards to counter anti-competitive practices in the international tourism sector; the need to promote sustainable tourism development in the GATS, and the need to expand the definition of tourism under the GATS agreement. Thus, one possibility is to include provisions on competition policy so that the Caribbean can make a case when large tour operators operating from developed country markets behave uncompetitively.

There is possibility to attach certain conditions to increase market access offers in GATS. For instance, for political economy reasons countries can commit the hotels sector subject to an economic needs test (e.g. minimum occupancy rates). This is unlikely to go down well with investors, as it can be a way to protect an inefficient local industry. Current GATS negotiations are not only about sectoral commitments, but also about GATS rules, including rules on subsidies.

Unlike in the case of goods, where the Agreement on Subsidies and Countervailing Measures makes discriminatory subsidies that affect export performance illegal, subsidies (e.g. tax free concessions) are still permitted, and they are being used by the Caribbean. While little is known about the effects of subsidies on investment as the effects are not properly monitored, the Caribbean may want to consider whether it wants to keep the possibility of using discriminatory subsidies (general subsidies are possible) for services development.

EPAs Potential negotiations on services EPAs are different for at least three reasons. First, these are Regional Trade Agreements (RTAs) and are therefore not the most efficient way of liberalisation: opening up the tourism sector for the EU investors alone would leave out potentially more efficient investors. It is said RTAs are well placed to deal with liberalising sensitive services sectors such as Mode 4 which would get too little attention at multilateral level. Second, EPAs are less credible because they are not backed up by effective dispute settlement mechanisms. EU agreements have so far not included any rules on investment in relation to protection.

Its investment agreements are in essence investment promotion agreements. Thirdly, the EU sees EPAs as WTO compatible trade parts of the Cotonou agreement with the inclusion of Special and Differential Treatment for ACP (African, Caribbean and Pacific) suppliers. SDT can include trade options (which may economically not be the most efficient) and aid options. The Cotonou agreement (CPA), and before it successive Lomé conventions, has coincided with aid funds.

These aid funds can also be used for the development of services sectors (when they are part of the EU indicative programmes) and hence can be used to improve the effects of liberalization of the services sector. CPA Article 24 deals with tourism: 'Cooperation will aim at the sustainable development of the tourism industry in ACP countries and sub-regions, recognizing its increasing importance to the growth of the services sector in ACP countries and to the expansion of their global trade, its ability to stimulate other sectors of economic activity, and the role it can play in poverty eradication.

Many cooperative programmes and projects will support the efforts of ACP countries to establish and improve the countries' legal and institutional framework and resources for the development and implementation of sustainable tourism policies and programmes, as well as inter alia, improving the competitive position of the sector, especially small and medium-sized enterprises (SMEs), investment support and promotion, product development including the development of indigenous cultures in ACP countries, and strengthening linkages between tourism and other sectors of economic activity. Concrete examples that address CPA. Art. 24 to promote sustainable tourism, i.e. tourism that contributes to the local economy, include support for a heritage trail in St Lucia and an integrated tourism programme in Suriname.

There is a debate regarding the way of contribution of tourism to the local economy. One part of this debate is the extent to which local suppliers are connected to big (foreign-owned) hotels whose numbers may increase after more commitments in GATS. The extent of such linkages usually depends on good quality and timely supplies. However, access to finance is another factor. From the discussions in St Lucia recommended that big hotels usually do not pay small local suppliers of flowers on time, so that access to credit is one of the constraints to further profitable tourism.

Another example would be to ask for measures to support an integrated tourism policy to make tourism work for development. While attracting large hotels or being linked in with large tourism operators seems desirable to expand the market, there are also problems. Tourists tend to go to all-inclusive resorts with little linkages with the local economy and the possibility of profit repatriation.

Another way of treatment with this is to maintain local economic activities (e.g. cultural services, restaurants) which require support for human resource development that can deliver a change in the mind-set of many Caribbeans away from seeing commodities as a career towards seeing the hospitality sector as a career path. The CPA may be helpful. This paper examined whether and how developing countries can use services trade negotiations to increase the amount of inward FDI conducive to development, with a focus on the tourism sector in the Caribbean.

The paper reviewed the evidence and views on whether and how services trade rules (supply of services mode 3 relates to cross border investment) can affect inward FDI, with specific attention to inward FDI (mainly in hotels and restaurants) and the regulatory framework in the tourism sector in the Caribbean. There were many observations.

First, many barriers to market access and national treatment of foreign firms in the Caribbean remain possible because they are not enshrined in international trade commitments, so countries have not even committed the status quo. Second, because there are still trade barriers (in GATS) in all countries (maximum score is 4out of 8), there is scope for progress for all countries. Third, because the scope of commitments varies considerably by country (ranging from

0–4), this presents a good basis for testing the effects this might have on inward FDI. The paper then performed a simple statistical analysis, presenting panel data on inward FDI in the tourism sector in 9 Caribbean countries and correlated these with data describing the regulatory framework committed in for a such as the WTO General Agreement of Trade in Services, and controlling for other factors affecting inward FDI.

It is evidenced from the total aspects (statistical, theory and statements) we inferred that GATS negotiations are likely to interest inward FDI. The final section discussed options in current trade negotiations on trade in services to attract tourism FDI. In multilateral trade negotiations (GATS), Caribbean countries may want to signal openness to inward FDI while maintaining a degree of flexibility in the use of policy measures; in current negotiations on Economic Partnership Agreements with the EU, the focus could be on liberalising sensitive services sectors (e.g. mode 4) as well as on making use of the development dimension of EPAs such as the inclusion of support measures for investment in tourism conducive to the competitiveness of local economic players.

References

1. Travel Industry Association of America.
2. Forrester Research.
3. ICM for The Guardian.
4. "Tourism: A Potential Source of Rural Employment," in *Rural Employment: An International Perspective*, Ray D. Bontron, Jean-Claude, and Nadine Lasnier. 1997. Bollman and John M. Bryden, eds. New York: CAB International, pp. 427-446.
5. "Leaders' Perspectives on Rural Tourism: Case Studies in Pennsylvania," Bourke, Lisa, A. E. Luloff. 1995. *Journal of the Community Development Society*, Vol. 26, No. 2, pp. 224-39.
6. *Community Tourism Assessment Handbook*. Brass, Jane L., ed. 1996. Corvallis, Oregon: Western Rural Development Center, Oregon State University.
7. *Tourism Strategies for Rural Development*. Bruce, David, and Margaret Whitla, eds. 1993. Sackville, New Brunswick: Rural and Small Town Programme.
8. "The Rural Action Class's Perceptions of Tourism and its Potential for Economic Development: Case Studies from Four Rural

Pennsylvania Counties," Burr, Steven W. 1995. *General Technical Report*, Report No. INT-323: pp. 82-89.

9. *Tourism and Recreation in Rural Areas*.Butler, Richard W., C. Michael Hall, and John Jenkins, eds. 1998. Chichester, U.K.: John Wiley.

10. Tourism. *Proceedings of a Regional Conference*, Sem, John H. 1992. October 16-18, 1991, Jackson, Mississippi. Southern Rural Development Center, Mississippi State University.

8

The Performance of Tourism Firms

The neoclassical analysis of market structure proved useful for identifying different types of markets and giving a number of valuable insights into aspects of firm's conduct and performance. However, such phenomena as imperfect competition, particularly oligopoly, and uncertainty, as well as the need to explain market dynamics, are inadequately explained by traditional analysis. The development of industrial economics and other schools of thought have attempted to fill the gaps left by traditional approaches and illustrate the theme of this book not only by indicating recent theoretical developments and advanced economic analysis but also by helping to explain tourism supply. Within industrial economics, two main approaches have been used to examine the conduct and performance of firms in different types of markets. The first is the structure, conduct and performance (SCP) paradigm which has played a major role within empirically oriented studies of firm's within manufacturing industries. Although it has been subject to some criticism, particularly in more theoretically based analysis, the paradigm remains a useful framework and appears to be relevant to a complex service industry such as tourism. The second, more recent approach is game theory which is used to analyze the strategies which firms adopt in relation to the actions and probable reactions of their competitors.

Game theory has been applied extensively in oligopolistic situations and has vastly improved the comprehension of firms' interactions and their outcomes in dynamic situations. It seems particularly important for understanding the behavior, and strategies of tourism suppliers. Before considering these analytical developments, it is instructive to review briefly the approaches which have been adopted in economics with regard to central issues concerning the market environment in which firms exist and the way in which it can influence their structure and behaviour. First, the main schools of thought which are relevant to industrial economics and which can assist the explanation, as opposed to the description, of tourism supply and changes in it are discussed. Therefore, elements of the Austrian school and behavioral, evolutionary, institutional and psychological economics are outlined. Although they are not applied to tourism supply owing to constraints of space and the absence of tourism literature on the subject, they are useful in providing the context for the ensuing discussion and a basis for future research. The paradigm is then explained, and its application to services, using the case of tourism intermediaries, is indicated. The contribution and limitations of the approach will be evaluated. The role which game theory can play in explaining the strategies of tourism firms in a dynamic context and the associated changes in the structure of tourism markets will be examined subsequently. An overall assessment of the two approaches is provided in the conclusion.

This paradigm dominated industrial economics until the 1980s. According to the paradigm, it is the type of market structure within which firms operate, which is the ultimate determinant of their conduct and performance, measured by such criteria as profitability. Market structure variables such as the number of buyers and sellers and degree of market concentration are assumed to be relatively stable. As an empirically based analytical framework, the SCP approach accepts that market structures usually differ from the benchmark of perfect competition, so that if firms set prices in excess of marginal cost, there is a prima facie case for government intervention and the implementation of measures to bring about increased competition. The SCP approach is, thus, policy-oriented.

In contrast to the more empirically oriented SCP model, the Chicago School continued to adhere to and propagate an approach based on the conventional neoclassical model of long-run equilibrium within competitive markets. Its thesis is that resources are allocated optimally by competitive forces within the market and that market power and pricing in excess of marginal cost are eliminated by free entry into the industry. A notable contribution, partially modifying the somewhat restrictive conventional position, was that of Baumol who, reflecting concern that traditional models failed to explain competitive structures fully, promoted the theory of contestable markets. The Chicago School views perfectly competitive, or at least contestable, markets as the dominant market structure which emerges over the long run so that consumer's benefit and government intervention is regarded as unnecessary. The Chicago stance was adopted by some economists in Europe, as indicated in the reviews by De Jong and Shepherd and Hay and Morris.

There has been a long-running controversy between the Chicago economists and proponents of the SCP paradigm, broadly supported by the behavioral, evolutionary and institutional schools of thought, who do not adhere to the view that markets are generally competitive over the long run (S. Martin).Research on the economics of industry undertaken outside mainstream analysis has moved the debate on the competitive structure of the market into a different arena. There are two distinct but related strands to this work. One has concerned the accommodation of the dynamic nature of markets while the other has concentrated on the representation of the characteristics and circumstances of firms, industries and markets. The Austrian school, associated with scholars such as Hayek, Menger, Mises and, initially, Schumpeter, is notable for its concentration on the process of competition as opposed to the static equilibrium analysis embodied in much conventional market structure analysis. These scholars acknowledge that change and uncertainty are endemic and that those involved in industry have to make decisions within this context.

However, they argue that over time, with experience and the benefit of increased knowledge of processes and opportunities, better decisions are made in succeeding periods, thus tending to produce more competitive market conditions. In this sense there is a degree of what Hayek calls emerging 'order' but not necessarily equilibrium. Latter-day researchers who can be viewed as constituting the neo-Austrian school are Kirzner, Reekie and Little Child. This view of industrial activity is paralleled by what R.R. Nelson and Winter refer to as 'Evolutionary Economies' in which procedures for carrying out required actions evolve with the accumulation of knowledge. The development of evolutionary economics has run in parallel with that of institutional economics and, in part, the thinking of the Austrian school. It has been concerned primarily with treating endogenously the way the beliefs, norms and customs of society might lead to the formation of institutions which facilitate corporate behavior. Theories of the evolution of institutions are based on those employed in biology and mathematics involving natural selection.

Hirshleifer reviewed these when modeling social and institutional change, arguing that game theory can indicate the outcome of co-operative and non-cooperative behavior to show the desired human traits which would be required to devise effective institutions. The relevance of these notions to economic organizations such as the firm is to underpin the importance of the attitudes and objectives of entrepreneurs, managers and workers in determining the operation of industries and markets. Tourism supply is an interesting case because it displays, through the instability in some sectors, a measure of immaturity with respect to the evolution of its business organizations .In emphasizing the dynamic nature of the market system and its institutions, the Austrian and Evolutionary Economics schools echo Marx. In his analysis of competition, Marx was concerned not only to reveal its process but also to ascertain the outcome in terms of the impact on the distribution of income and wealth and the allocation of resources. Followers of Marx have tended to underplay his perception of competition and accentuate his view that industrial production would become more concentrated, thus focusing on the potential for exploitive behavior, particularly concerning labour.

While mainstream economics has been a formidable tool with much empirical relevance, it has been subject to criticism because it does not explain the rationale for different forms of economic organization and the effects of social rules on behavior and outcomes. Institutional economics, although essentially adhering to the basic tenets of neoclassical theory, introduces information, time and transaction costs and property rights as constraints on the attainment of business objectives. It also emphasizes the need for empirical testing of hypotheses concerning such constraints. To this extent, the stance of institutional economics is fairly close to that adopted by much of industrial economics. The institutional perspective on business activity is a relatively new one and for this reason there is, as yet, no clear agreement on its principles. Because it is still at the exploratory stage, there are differences of opinion as to its postulates. For example, some institutional economists reject the profit maximizing and rationality principles, replacing them with Simon's satisfying concept. The danger is that abandonment of too many principles leaves industrial economics with no theory so that any investigation is merely descriptive.

Notwithstanding its infancy and the problems of the choice of theoretical foundation to adopt, institutional economics offers insights into the impact of variables hitherto ignored and it also underlines the need for economic analysis to consider market dynamics and the uncertainties encountered in the business environment. In this respect, it is consistent with game theory analysis. It also links conventional analysis with behavioral approaches, which attempt to relate human activity within business organizations to economic outcomes. Furthermore, it contributes to explanations of why market failure occurs, a factor of importance when environmental issues are examined, regarding property rights. R. Coase, O.E. Williamson and North have made important contributions to the analysis of market imperfections in the form of information and transaction costs, and are reviewed by Stiglitz and O.D. Williamson. These are the costs incurred in searching for and procuring information, which helps to reduce uncertainty, and in executing transactions. They are likely to be substantial in some spheres, such as where a firm assembles a product from many sources, a feature of tour operators marketing package holidays. Such imperfections provide an incentive for economic integration between firms, as in the case of the Thomson Corporation, as a means by which firms can internalize the costs, which they would incur by operating as separate units.

A principal-agent relationship exists where one party's welfare depends upon the actions of the another. The principal is normally affected by the actions of the agent. It is possible for this kind of relationship to occur within a firm, such as between an employer and employee or shareholders and management. Transaction costs are relevant in the principal-agent link as it may be necessary for the principal to monitor the agent's behavior to ensure that the former's objectives are attained. Within the tourism industry there is a principal-agent relationship between tour operators and travel agents. Commission rates offered by tour operators are conventionally 10 per cent in the UK, but if agents reach target numbers of holidays sold, override commissions are paid. Incentives are also provided for devoting a certain proportion of racking space for the principal's brochures and direct reservation links which cut costs.

Another important development of a specific nature, related to both transaction costs and uncertainty, has been the investigation of innovation, especially the role of research and development, for example, Scherer, Stoneman, Davies and Reinganum. Clearly not all research and development yields marketable products or usable processes, such as 'just-in-time' and 'total quality control' systems, and the costs of their discovery and adoption are subjected to much uncertainty. There is the additional problem of the extent, to which a particular firm can safeguard any discovery in order to reap the rewards of its cost of development. Attempts to model innovation and growth have been made within the neoclassical framework. An interesting feature of the evolutionary and institutional branches of industrial economics and the associated concepts of transaction costs, principal-agency analysis and the innovation process is that they identify market phenomena which are external to individual businesses and industries. The issue which is emerging in these area of investigation, which is relevant to the development of industrial economics, is the extent to which the problems can be internalized to minimize their adverse impact, in terms of costs, on a firm's or industry's operation. This raises a matter of fundamental importance in economic supply analysis, namely the organizational arrangements which are necessary. In short, it poses the question as to why firms exist. Are they merely entities for transforming inputs into outputs or are they production—distribution units which, in order to operate efficiently, requires organizational structures by which their objectives are attained? Moreover, is it possible that managers and employees set their own objectives which the organizational structure also facilitates? The latter notion acknowledges the force of the longer-established behavioral analysis of firms and individuals within them. Such issues cannot be pursued here, but a not implausible inference to draw is that although the theoretical development of evolutionary and institutional economics, transaction costs, principal-agency and innovation concepts, is in its infancy, a degree of consensus, if not convergence in economic thinking, is occurring. This might suggest that a more dynamic and unified theory of organizations will emerge.

Research in industrial economics, does indeed demonstrate a concern with firmly rooted theoretical base. This is the justification for using such terms as New Industrial Economics and New Industrial Organization. It is not entirely coincidental that these movements were reinforced by the emergence of game theory as a means of analyzing business strategies. The applications of game theory not only allow for the incorporation of uncertainty and asymmetric information, but it also made it possible to construct more dynamic models, thus increasing their explanatory power. Game theory has reawakened interest in the long-established duopoly form of oligopoly models such as those constructed by Bertrand, Cournot, Stackelberg and S. Martin, 1993, included in mainstream microeconomic texts, so that the development of oligopoly theory is now a dominant element in industrial economics. This analysis has generated research into a number of issues, such as in entry and exit conditions, price wars, predatory pricing, the role of advertising, co-operative contractual arrangements between the different elements of supply and demand and collusion. The re-emphasis on theory, however, has been criticized for failing to provide empirically testable models of industrial behavior. Nevertheless; there has been renewed interest in specific case studies, relative to the earlier bias towards more generalized econometric analysis. Moreover, greater attention is being paid to the scope and impact of intervention, for example, anti-monopoly legislation, market regulation, taxation and subsidies.

Despite the apparent conflict between, the desire by theorists to develop general models of supply and the insistence by empiricists on establishing how firms actually behave, industrial economics, and with it the comprehension of what determines the pattern of supply, has made great advances. There is a better understanding of the inter-relationships of suppliers within particular industries, as such between intermediate and consumer goods producers and between principals and agents. Models now provide better reflections and explanations of reality. However, most progress has been made in developing the market behavior models out of their duopoly origins, again incorporating the application of game theory and accommodating such notions as product differentiation, market segmentation, price discrimination and the reactions by firms to their rival's price and non-price competitive strategies. It is useful to consider briefly the behavioral theories of the firm which have been developed outside mainstream economic analysis, before proceeding to examine the ways in which the different approaches can shed light on behavior in tourism markets.

Models of The Firm

Concurrent with the development of new industrial economics, but hardly acknowledged by it was the growth of behavioral models of the firm, studied within the sub-discipline of economic psychology. Behaviorally oriented theories do not rely as heavily on two major assumptions of conventional analysis, first, that business decisions are identical to those of individuals within firms, and second, that theoretically derived optimizing positions are representative of actual behavior. The main thrust of such studies of the firm is that analysis of business behavior produces observations which generate, through replication, broad generalizations which aid the construction of theories, through an inductive process. Business behavioral researchers argue that decision-makers may not apply clear choice models when they lack knowledge of possible alternative courses of action and are not certain of their outcome. Preferences may be inconsistent and they may not possess firm guidelines or rules by which to make decisions. In this sense, the assumptions of conventional economic theory are challenged, as is apparent in the observations of pioneers in business behavioral theories such as Simon, March and Simon, March, Cyert and March, Simon, and Cyert and Simon.

It is hypothesized that business people lack the information and time to optimize their activities. They are, therefore, aware of only a small number of options to choose. Thus, a predominant issue which behavioural researchers have investigated is the institutional structure and process of decision-making. The interest has been the ways in which problems are identified, the process of learning by experience, perceptions of probable outcomes, attitudes to risk, and the allocation of attention to multiple problems and activities, and organizational adaptation. Economic psychology, is not in direct conflict with neoclassical optimizing theory, but has modified the theory by relaxing the more abstract assumptions. Its principal contributions, however, have been to widen the scope of analysis by including the human behavioral element and to strengthen the links between theoretical and empirical studies. To an extent, therefore, industrial economics and the economic psychology of the firm have grown out of traditional theory and run in parallel with each other. Recent developments in these two areas of economic analysis, with the greater emphasis on the testing of theoretical models in an empirical context, have increased their potential for explaining the structure and operation of tourism supply.

Many of the issues examined by the theoretical approaches are manifested within tourism markets. Furthermore, some aspects of the structure and operation of tourism markets, especially the persistence in some markets of overcapacity and disequilibrium, question the explanations, predictions and relevance of some industrial economic and economic psychology models. Thus, it would be informative to examine the rich empirical evidence which a study of tourism supply could yield. Hitherto with the exception of the transport sector, and some examination of accommodation, tourism markets have not been analyzed by mainstream industrial economics, despite the major contribution which tourism is making to the economies of many countries. Accordingly, the remainder is devoted to an examination of the contribution, which economic thinking on industrial issues can make to understanding the behavior of tourism firms and their market conditions using the limited empirical evidence which is available.

Performance of tourism intermediaries

The SCP paradigm is a feasible means of analyzing complex markets comprising firms of differing sizes, in which varying degrees of concentration or integration occur and market power can be exercised. The approach has the advantage of providing a clear framework, which avoids unstructured descriptions but instead permits the examination of markets in terms of the analytical categories of market structure, firm's conduct and performance. The ability of the SCP approach to encompass many of the elements of tourism supply is based on Scherer and derived from Mason. The principal modification to the conventional SCP diagram, for the purpose of applying the analytical framework to tourism, is the omission of elements concerning the supply of tangible products, only peripherally relevant to a service sector, and decreased emphasis on the welfare considerations of performance which are not the focus.

The commonly used market structure variables in industrial economics analysis were introduced. The two key measures key measures of competitive conditions are the number and size of firms and indices of concentration. Additional variables which can be considered are the number of buyers, entry and exit conditions, cost conditions product differentiation and diversification and inter-firm integration. Firm's conduct relates to pricing behavior, advertising, marketing, research and development and innovation, sometimes in the context of tacit collusion or more formal cartels. Although innovation is partly seen as the result of exogenous technological change, it is also driven by competitive conditions in markets, for instance, in tourism, the pressure on suppliers to install central reservation systems or electronic means of advertising products or payments transmission in order to reduce costs. To protect an innovation or to control the sale of products, companies resort to such strategies as licenses and contracts organized through the legal system, and such arrangements often reinforce entry barriers and, the structural characteristics of markets.

Performance can be considered in terms of consumer satisfaction, efficiency of operations, the growth rates of firms and industries, firm's market shares and profitability. Short-term performance measures have sometimes been paramount, such as in the UK package holiday sector where the concern has been for the growth of sales and market shares, often at the expense of efficiency and profitability. Performance is affected by public policy, with special changes in regulation, international trading arrangements and competition laws which have played an important role in tourism. Furthermore, the promotion of tourism by public sector bodies and the provision of subsidies or tax incentives have had a marked impact on production, for example in relation to the supply of tourist accommodation. The interrelationships between structure and the conduct and performance of firms within particular markets, as well as the basic conditions of demand and supply and public policy show the causal links as originally posited in the economics literature, running from structure to conduct and performance.

However, the more recent formulation of the model does not deny the possible influence of conduct and performance on structure, thereby allowing its endogenous determination. In this respect conduct, where it embodies the actions of managers and employers in firms, reflects the importance which institutional economics attaches to the influence of human behavior on outcomes. Therefore, later considerations of SCP analysis suggest, that not only performance and conduct, but also public policy, affect market structure.

The Tour Operations Sector

A wide range of tourism supply issues can be examined in the context of the SCP framework. The insights which the SCP model can provide will be illustrated using the tour operator sector because of the sector's central position in tourism supply and the availability of evidence on its structure and performance. An overview of structure, conduct and performance characteristics based on available data for tour operations. Although barriers to entry and exit are generally low, the concentration ratio is high in terms of market share and there is a little empirical evidence concerning the extent of economies and diseconomies of scale and economies of scope, capital indivisibilities, fixed capacity and fixed costs.

The larger operators in the top tier, which have invested in charter airlines and some travel agents, appear to enjoy economies of scale and scope, although such investment has entailed the problems of indivisibility and high fixed costs with the concomitant fixed capacity which needs to be filled. Average load factors on aircraft and occupancy rates in hotels are measures which indicate the extent to which such problems are overcome. However, the majority of tour operators are relatively small and these structural characteristics tend to be less important. Operators which organize the more specialized forms of tourism where the market is not extensive do not require high investment in fixed capacity and, indeed, would be likely to suffer diseconomies of scale if the more personal bespoke service were undermined. Tour operator's conduct involves recurrent price wars and high volume sales by the largest operators in the absence of collusion between them. Firms have differentiated their products in the context of segmented markets.

Performance outcomes include moderate consumer satisfaction and moderate efficiency of firms' operations, with low profit margins and some bankruptcies. The sector has been subject to regulation although anti-competitive conduct has not been deemed a significant problem to date. In addition to providing a framework for the examination of market and firm characteristics, the SCP model predicts that structural features affect firms' conduct and performance. Owing to the important role which the structural base is hypothesized to play, two structural features which are of particular relevance to tour operations will now be examined. First, the role of entry and exit conditions for the sector will be discussed and measures & changes in concentration will be considered subsequently.

Conditions for tour operations

The high growth rate in the number of tour operators is indicative of low entry barriers. Capital costs are low and the identification of a niche and expenditure on promotion to bring the product to the attention of the potential tourist do not constitute major obstacles to entry into the market. It is necessary to convince purchasers of the viability of the company in terms of guaranteeing the security of payments made in advance. A significant cost of entry is therefore the bonding requirements. Additional entry barriers may also occur. Salop distinguishes between innocent barriers and strategic barriers with incumbent firms erect. Even if perfect information is assumed, economic theory can show that there are advantages to incumbent firms. For example, incumbent firms may have erected pre-entry barriers by having established licensing and franchise schemes, created a differentiated branded product, secured consumer and supplier loyalty and contracted with hoteliers and facilities in the most desirable locations. These kinds of asymmetries between the positions of entrants and incumbents were originally seen by SCP advocates, such as Bain, as entry barriers but more recently they have been interpreted as first mover advantages.

Strategic entry barriers are a conscious effort by established firms to deter new firms. Typical ploys are to adopt limit pricing, perhaps of a predatory nature, to differentiate products, increase advertising expenditure in a counteractive manner, and seek improvements in efficiency or capacity to lower unit costs of production. Firms have also reinforced the strategic core of the business. The strategic core is the principal activity of a business enabling it to achieve its aims and objectives, taking account of the prevailing opportunities and threats and its strengths and weaknesses. In economic terms, the core activity facilitates the attainment of increased economies of scale, or extended product differentiation and multi-market targeting to exploit economies of scope. In some cases, incumbents maintain spare capacity so that they can increase output and decrease their price rapidly if a new firm enters the market, making its position unprofitable and forcing it out of the market.

The maintenance of spare capacity is, therefore, a strategy which involves a credible threat to potential entrants, backed by the "punishment strategy" of a price war. Vertical integration involving investment in sunk costs, i.e. those which are large and not recoverable in the short run without involving the business in considerable expense, such as the purchase of aircraft or a chain of hotels, can also constitute a 'pre-commitment' which acts as a deterrent to entry and exit, especially where substantial cost savings are achieved. Entry deterrence strategies and their likelihood of being successful are examined within a game theory context. Tour operators have not vigorously pursued such strategies to deter entry per se. They have tended to be more concerned with increasing market share, accepting that they have insufficient power to exclude new entrants. In this respect, economic theory would suggest that sunk costs are low and similar for newcomers and incumbents alike. Baumol argued that low or recoverable sunk costs make markets contestable, concluding that if prices are competitive and not far above marginal cost, then monopoly and oligopoly structures are largely benign. Such a view, prima facie, appears to apply to the UK tour operations sector up to the mid-1990s. It is clearly dominated, in terms of market share, by a few firms which do not always earn supernormal profits.

However, an assumption of low sunk costs in all sectors of a market is an over simplification. It is more likely that the level of sunk costs varies, depending on the market segment into which entry is sought and also on the strategic group into which a particular firm falls. Entry and exit conditions do not necessarily relate to an entire industry or market but may be specific to sectors or segments within them. An example serves to illustrate not only entry and exit conditions but also their interrelationship with sunk costs and economies of scale and scope. Suppose a tour operator in a specialist segment with a limited market, say activity holidays, contemplates expanding into the mass package market. Exploitation of economies of scale and scope and so the reduction of unit costs may act as an entry condition which must be met. To achieve such economies the operator may be compelled to operate its own airlines and hotels, thus incurring substantial sunk costs which act as a deterrent to entry.

The strategic group argument is that in a comparatively diversified market in terms of firm size, importance and products, there are marked similarities in the characteristics of a number of companies and their products, which suggests common interests, and that they can be classified into identifiable and distinct groups. In tour operations it has been posited that there are three tiers of companies distinguished by size, capitalization, market share and range of products offered. It is useful to re-examine this feature in order to illustrate the concept of the strategic group. The first tier, consisting of around ten operators, is more integrated and heavily capitalized and serves several market segments and enjoys economies of scale and scope and wields considerable market power. The second tier, of around twenty to thirty firms, is more specialized but still has a significant share of the market. The remainders, in the third tier, are numerous, small and are often unincorporated, with low sunk costs. The apparent absence of barriers and deterrent action to entry, bear out the contestability thesis, even in the top tier of the market, of the top five operators trading in 1994, only two were in existence in the early 1970s.

Concentration

Much effort has been devoted to determining the best method of ascertaining the extent of concentration as a measure of the competitiveness of the markets in the SCP framework. High concentration would suggest an oligopolistic structure, while a low incidence would indicate a highly competitive market. However, there is a problem in using relatively crude measures, such as the number of firms. It is conceivable for a few firms to be engaged in fierce competition with each other, because they are spatially separated or serving different segments of a market, and might be relatively uncompetitive, representing the Chamberlinian's notion of monopolistic competition. Tour operators, particularly in the package sector, normally require a license in order to gain access to means of travel so that it is possible to estimate reasonably accurately the number of firms. On the other hand, size may be defined in several ways. Simple concentration measures, relying on size in terms of market share by number of holidays authorized by license or actually sold, and number of firms, can easily be applied to tour operators.

In the inclusive package holiday supply sector which dominates the international tourism market, a key measure used to indicate concentration is market share, derived from the number of holidays sold. Information about such variables as capitalization, the number employed and turnover is not readily available for small firms. Taking the UK and US tour operations sector as examples, in the USA in 1993/94 the top forty companies controlled 30 per cent of all holidays sold. In the case of UK tour operations, the degree of concentration has been more dramatic, increasing markedly over time as the share of package holidays sold by the top five companies has risen to 62.5

per cent of the total of 15.5 million sales compared with 49.5 per cent in 1983. Another example of concentration in tourism is the airline sector. Data for three variables can be used to measure market share as an indicator of concentration: sales revenues, profits and passenger numbers or passenger kilometres.

However, because of the extent of both regulation and state support for national flag-carriers, the use of statistics for revenues and profits in the international market are not always feasible indicators. Indeed, in the early 1990s profits would not be an appropriate measure as, with the exception of British Airways, the largest ten airlines, in terms of passenger kilometers, all made losses. As suitable data for tour operations are not available, data for the largely unregulated US domestic air travel sector have been used to illustrate concentration. A concentration curve for this sector depicts the size of firms by using the number of passengers carried as a proportion of total numbers traveling with the top twenty-five US airlines. Thus, for example, American Airlines carried 18 per cent of all air travelers in 1993-94; the top eight airlines accounted for over 90 per cent of traffic in the same year.

Conduct in Tour Operations

Inter-relationships between tour operators have tended to be antagonistic, as witnessed by periodic price wars, heavy discounting and commission rate incentives offered to travel agents retailing holidays. Low entry costs, into not only tour operations as a sector but also specific segments within it, indicate the possible recurrence of price wars, as tour operators attempt to maintain or increase market share and gain scale economies by means other than formal cartels or collusion. Large companies have pursued expansion in growth and market share, more to secure their own positions in an unstable and volatile market than to oust rivals. The largest tour operators experience legislative constraints on anti-competitive strategies and also face competition from second tier tour operators. However, although the 'second tier' operators showed the highest growth in the early 1990s and some of these operators can provide the element of choice that customers demand, by the mid 1990s they were losing ground in both the mass and specialist holiday markets. This was unanticipated since they appeared to be well placed to serve the needs of both the multiple and independent travel agents (East).

Strategies undertaken by the top tier to consolidate its share of the mass market and break into the specialist segments indicate that a large number of the second tier tour operators, together with many operators in the third tier, face a high level of risk. Some companies are badly exposed, since they sell standardized mass market package products in a market that is, to a large extent, controlled by the largest vertically integrated companies which can undercut them on bed prices negotiated in bulk. Kirker argues that they are destined to fail without clear product differentiation and a clearly defined market segment. However, the 'new' and more affluent tourist is demanding more innovative, flexible and tailored products and small to medium-sized operators can meet these requirements. The chase for market share and for the 'old' mass market tourist is no longer a viable strategic option except, perhaps, for the five to ten largest tour operators and even they are likely to continue to experience cycles involving low or negative profits.

In terms of performance, there is little evidence that the leading tour operators have earned high rates of profit up to the mid-1990s. Within the tour operator sector, profits have been relatively low in the face of variability in demand, low entry costs, the high birth-death rate of firms and a high level of price competition. Therefore, tour operators may do to stabilize the market and ensure long-run profitability? Devices such as incentives to persuade agents to be sole distributors, restricting universal information technology systems, franchises, licensing and reciprocal agreements may be considered but some measures are difficult to enforce and others are regarded as anti-competitive by the regulatory authorities.

Product differentiation, niche marketing and price discrimination are alternative strategies which may be more effective. Tour operators may attempt to deter entry into the sector, by convincing potential competitors that entry will be unprofitable. Entry deterrence tends to increase concentration, with all the advantages of scale economies and market power it can confer. However, tour operators are likely to be constrained by a number of countervailing forces. Ryan, using a Delphi technique to assess the views of twenty-eight leading industry practitioners, identified three main constraints on further increases in concentration: first, if competition is based on quality of product rather than price, small tour operators can still compete; second, the threat of anti-monopoly legislation may act as a deterrent to strategies aimed at curtailing competition; third, large tour operators may be insufficiently adaptable and flexible to maintain quality for clients. Notwithstanding these constraints, Ryan also found that the major tour operators can establish subsidiary companies to offer specialist products and these companies can reap the benefits of economies of scale in administration and transport. In such a situation, even though the market may be shifting towards niche marketing, smaller specialist companies and greater customer awareness, there is little to inhibit growing concentration ratios.

Large tour operators may adopt other strategies to expand or safeguard their businesses on the other hand they can look for overseas expansion to fuel growth. Thomson, for instance, held talks with Scandinavian Airlines System (SAS) regarding the acquisition of Sweden's largest tour operator, SAS Leisure (Outbound Travel Industry Digest), before the company was sold to Airtours in June 1994. Airtours increased its capital by sales of shares to Carnival Corporation, the largest US cruise line. Ultimate Holidays raised £3 million in venture capital to create a pan-European company (Travel Trade Gazette). The characteristics of price competitive conduct and relatively low profits performance imply that tour operators have been operating in consumer's interests. This outcome has persisted over time and appears to be at odds with the implications of the SCP model, that increasing structural concentration would result in higher prices and increased profits. One possible explanation is that supply characteristics should be considered within an international context.

Thus, although tour operations may be construed as oligopolistic in domestic markets, such as those of the UK, USA, Germany and the Netherlands (Fitch, Sheldon), internationally no single firm or group of companies is dominant (Monopolies and Mergers Commission). Economic integration between firms will be considered, in the international context of tourism supply. However, it is clear that firm's conduct, such as their strategies towards inter-firm integration and expansion, can affect the market structure.

The Context of tourism markets

The SCP framework is well suited to examining the characteristics of market structure and firm's conduct and performance, and allows for considerable flexibility in terms of the wide variety of variables which it can accommodate and also provides a useful framework, to describe industries and markets as a basis for analysis. Major criticisms of the paradigm are that market structure is assumed and that it is set too firmly within a neoclassical static equilibrium framework, resulting in limited ability to accommodate market processes. It is certainly true that having grown out of conventional market analysis, the approach has been used to ascertain the conditions for highly competitive, oligopolistic and monopoly markets to exist and its application has sometimes been restricted to focus on these objectives. The SCP paradigm in its original form does not claim to show the process of change in markets so that it is not well placed to explain, in particular, how certain market structures come about, the impact of entry barriers, the size and number of firms and the effects of firm's growth rates on market structures.

To this extent it reflects the origins from which it has developed. The problem of identifying causal linkages largely flows from the model's static equilibrium analysis and assumption of an exogenously determined market structure which determines firm's conduct and performance. This has inhibited consideration of the impact of conduct and performance on structure, so determining it endogenously. More recent investigations, which attempt to take account of the dynamic nature and uncertainty of markets, have emphasized the cost structures of individual firms, including those associated with acquiring information and conducting transactions. In particular, the impact on the firm of the nature of the fixed assets required the timing of the purchase of variable inputs, the linkages between inputs and outputs, scale and scope and the range of outputs have been investigated. Such studies have departed from the traditional SCP framework, which tends to concentrate on an entire industry and to focus on product as opposed to factor markets.

The SCP paradigm should not be viewed as a fully adequate analytical framework, but as a starting point for examining key economic issues. Its strength is that it is an appropriate method for providing a market perspective in contrast to one based on industry alone. It has the merit of giving a holistic view and identifies the wide range of variables which require examination. It highlights the importance of certain characteristics, for example entry conditions, which have a bearing on the number and size of firms and thus the likely contestability of the market, firm's conduct in terms of pricing behavior and strategies and profitability. None the less if, as posited, tourism markets are not only complex but also in disequilibrium, then more recent developments in the economic analysis of industry which accommodate their dynamic nature should also be employed. Indeed, economic explanations of the tourism industry and the strategies of businesses within it need not be confined to a specific framework of analysis, such as the SCP paradigm. It is likely that the range of schools of thought, can offer valuable insights into the operation of tourism markets. The dynamic processes according to which firms behave, changes in market structures and a number of the insights provided by diverse schools of thought can be taken into account by game theory, whose relevance to tourism will now be discussed.

Tourism and Game theory

Conventional analysis of supply and market structures has proved inadequate for explaining strategic inter-relationships between firms, particularly within the context of oligopoly which is an increasingly prevalent form of competition. In contrast, game theory lends itself to many circumstances which arise in oligopolistic markets, particularly where uncertainty prevails, and can be used to examine many of the strategies which are employed by tourism firms. There are many situations in which decisions are interdependent and firms may gain by engaging in co-operative strategies, such as those which previously characterized the airline sector, or they may decide that competitive strategies are required, as in travel agent operations where a firm may gain an advantage by continually changing strategies. What is not in dispute, however, is that many firms in tourism supply sectors take account of the behavior of other firms in the market when deciding upon their own strategies. The crucial question is when it pays to collude as opposed to competing.

Game theory can be used both to explain behavior and to predict the outcome of strategies regarding price-setting, product choice and differentiation, advertising, capital investment, mergers and takeovers, and entry deterrence. In observing firm's behavior and interaction, it is also possible to understand how markets operate and evolve an important attribute in analyzing some tourism sectors which are newly emergent and unstable. It is of value not only to distinguish co-operative and non-cooperative games but also to vary the initial assumptions concerning participant's behavior, objectives and knowledge of their rival's reactions.

Normally, in simple explanatory simulations, rational behavior by competitors, profit maximization as an objective and, initially, perfect information and symmetry are assumed, so that firms have full knowledge of their rival's cost structures, production levels, prices and so on, as well as the market conditions under which they operate. Such restrictive assumptions can be relaxed in more complex situations and game analyses. In addition to co-operative and non-cooperative games, it is possible to consider either "one-shot" or repeated games and, furthermore, distinguishes between those played simultaneously and others which are sequential. In some circumstances, firms mindful of the illegality of collusion in some countries may initially conduct non-cooperative strategies but in the light of the experience of rival's reactions establish stable patterns of behavior which may result in tacit collusion.

For example, maintaining high prices in the knowledge that rivals will do the same would confer advantages on all firms. One-shot games reflect situations where once and for all decisions need to be made, for instance whether to invest in capital to produce a new product or to deter entry. Conversely, repeated games are indicative of circumstances where continual jockeying to gain short-term advantages would be appropriate. For example, pricing and product differentiation strategies may be changed frequently, so that rival firms periodically engage in non-cooperative games. There are a number of instances in tourism where this occurs, such as airlines, ferry and tour operators, engaging in price wars to increase market share, while product differentiation is attempted in order to extend a firm's total market or serve a new segment.

A distinction is made between simultaneous and sequential games because they represent different market situations calling for changes in strategies. In some circumstances, for example the "Cournot Duopoly Model", firms decide on their levels of output at the same time, whereas in "Stackelberg Analysis", one firm makes a decision independently, to which the rival reacts. This is an important factor in situations where the first mover may gain an advantage. In the context of tourism, simultaneous decisions are often made in the light of short-run changes in demand levels and patterns in the airline, ferry and hospitality sectors, especially where there is excess capacity. Sequential or reactive strategies occur in these sectors and in the tour operator market where lead times are rather longer. For example, in the summer sun package holiday sector, the offer of discounts for early booking by one operator is almost certain to lead to retaliation by rivals if it appears that their market share will be lost.

It has already been shown that some sub-sectors of tourism supply are oligopolistic and therefore strategies concerning price setting, level of supply, product differentiation and branding, market segmentation, advertising, innovation and entry deterrence are common. In addition, it is possible to consider circumstances where a key firm can exercise a dominant strategy, perhaps because of a particular attribute the firm has such as a brand name commanding a degree of loyalty, which might give it an optimal strategy independent of its rivals.

In order to illustrate the application of game theory to tourism, the cases of advertising, the pricing decision and entry deterrence are considered, using examples of strategic decisions which those in the tour operator sector of tourism supply might face. The first shows a non-cooperative, simultaneous game in which the impact of advertising on market size and share is demonstrated; the second, on pricing, is an example of a non-cooperative repeated game, while the third is a one-shot case which is non-cooperative. The second and third, however, show the possible outcomes of co-operative behaviour. The simplest condition to examine is where firms have a dominant strategy, i.e. an optimal position can be achieved by an enterprise, irrespective of what its rivals choose to do. This basic notion in game theory is illustrated by the case of a tour operator deciding whether to advertise. The example pre-supposes that advertising is both competitive by each tour operator to capture a larger market share as well as informative to extend the market and increase the pay-off for both firms. A typical 2×2 matrix in a two person game, which represents the duopoly form of oligopoly, in which the pay-offs to tour operator X with respect to advertising or not advertising (rows) are given in bold while those for tour operator Y (columns) are in italics and in parentheses.

Tour operator X will advertise, as this is the best strategy (best net pay-off) which can be adopted irrespective of what Y does. If Y does not advertise the pay-off for X is 25, whereas if Y does advertise X will achieve a pay-off of 20. Likewise for Y, the pay-off is respectively 10 if both advertise and 15 if X does not advertise. It can be seen, therefore, that both will advertise where the total market pay-off is 30 (20X, 10Y) in the top left cell. This position is a stable one. If X does not have a dominant strategy then the optimal decision depends on what Y does. For example, if the pay-off to X is 40 if neither advertises (bottom right cell) then X's strategy is determined by what Y does. If Y advertises then so must X but if Y does not advertise, neither should X because the pay-off is much greater in adopting this strategy. Therefore, X must guess what Y will do. As Y has the same dominant strategy as before it will obviously advertise because whatever X does this is its best action. If X correctly guesses Y's action, which it should given the assumptions of the model, then a stable equilibrium can still be attained.

Where a dominant strategy does not exist, perhaps where advertising would extend the market rather than increase market share for individual tour operators, the question as to whether a stable equilibrium can be reached is raised. This is especially, so if the assumptions of rational behavior and correct interpretation of rival's strategies and actions are relaxed. Game theory can show that there might be several equilibrium or that there are none. Thus, it is possible to explain why instability may occur in certain industries in which particular circumstances prevail. The example of the dilemma facing firms in deciding on price in each trading period can be employed to illustrate the point. At about the turn of the year, tour operators launch brochures for the mass summer sun market for the coming season. Given the extent of the market and the fixed capacity of airline seat and accommodation capacity, individual tour operators recognize that consumers not only are price-sensitive but also may withhold purchase in the hope of late-availability bargains.

Therefore the tour operators may consider, offering holidays at low prices to induce consumers to book early and so fill the capacity. However, given the tight margins within which tour operator's trade, such a strategy may result in low profits or even losses. The preferred strategy would be for all to charge a high price but there is no certainty that rivals would adhere to an implicit understanding either at the beginning of or throughout the season. Repeated games can represent this real-life situation and feasibly predict what the outcome is likely to be, the main objective of simulating the market in this way being to identify the most robust strategy. It includes negative as well as positive pay-offs and is akin to the "prisoner's dilemma", a case where each participant has a dominant strategy which, if pursued, produces a joint profit which is less than, that obtained if both collude.

If both charge a high price each gains a pay-off of 10 (20 in total) whereas if both charge a low price each obtains 2, giving a total of 4 (the top left and bottom right cells respectively). The matrix also shows that if X charges a high price and Y a low one X suffers minus 10 while Y gains 20 (a net total of 10). Conversely if X charges a low price and Y a high one the positions are reversed. Obviously the preferred strategy for both is to charge a high price but the issue is whether one or the other will 'break ranks' and charge a low price in the hopes of a greater gain. As long as implicit co-operation occurs both will charge a high price. If one charges a low price, then the other will follow until such time as one goes back to a high price. Provided each act rationally, can ascertain the other's strategy and believes any threats are real, a consistent pattern is likely to emerge so that tacit co-operation occurs. However, this outcome seems to be at odds with what is being observed in the tour operator sector, where price wars continue to occur, i.e. non-cooperative behavior persists. The likely reason is that other factors, such as variations in demand and costs, low entry barriers, excess capacity and the presence of many firms preclude the establishment of co-operative strategies. Uncertainties introduced by such phenomena make it difficult to create the required stability. However, game theory can also accommodate other market conditions and situations, such as first-mover advantages, threats, including those referred to above regarding entry and the consequent change in numbers of firms, which are factors which if stabilized might, in turn, stabilize markets and therefore prices. It is not possible to examine these cases in detail but some further exposition of the implications of relaxing the assumption of simultaneous action by firms is of value. The "Cournot Model of Duopoly" considers the case where firms decide how much output to produce simultaneously while Bertrand's approach examines a context in which firms engage in simultaneous price-setting. In contrast, the Stackelberg Model posits that one firm sets output before the other. The Stackelberg approach facilitates the analysis of first-mover advantage. Sequential games, as they are called, make game theory dynamic as it is possible to trace the processes which are initiated once a strategy is implemented.

Examining product choice as an example, if two specialist tour operators, each unaware of the other's intentions, decide to introduce one of two new types of holiday, either an activity or cultural holiday with a limited market, then it is likely that both will lose money if they market the same product simultaneously. However, if firm X is able to market the activity holiday first, then Y will introduce the cultural holiday and so both will gain. This is essentially what the Stackelberg model posits, where the size of output can be determined by the first-mover, leaving the remainder of the market to the rival.

Firms can ensure that they can obtain an advantage as first movers by preemptive strategic moves, i.e. by influencing rivals' choices. This can be done only if the firm has a reputation for doing what it states it will do; lack of commitment to a strategy suggests to rivals that subsequent announcements or threats as to a particular course of action are empty. Entry deterrence is another key strategy because, if successful, it confers greater monopoly powers and the potential to increase profits. Therefore, the incumbent firm has to convince potential entrants that it would be unprofitable to enter. If the potential rival decides to enter the high-priced market, the incumbent firm will gain more by maintaining a high price. However, the incumbent firm should threaten a price war which would bankrupt the new entrant or expand capacity to exploit economies of scale to sustain the possible price war, the deterrence commitment is substantiated.

Scenario 1, the first row indicates the pay-offs at both high and low prices to the potential new entrant, X, shown in bold, and incumbent Y, shown in italics in parentheses, should X decide to enter the industry, incurring sunk costs of £20 million, it being assumed that the market is shared equally. The second row, in italics, indicates the pay-offs to incumbent firm Y if it takes action in response to X's intended entry and successfully deters it without having to incur increased costs. Suppose firm X predicts that Y will maintain a high price in order to gain the most it can of the current £50 million total market pay-off, then X will get £5 million (£25 million half-market share minus £20 million sunk costs) and Y will retain £25 million (top left cell of the matrix). However, should Y decide to engage in a price war, i.e. charge a low price, then assuming a total market pay-off of £30 million, X will suffer a loss of £5 million (£15 million minus £20 million sunk costs) and Y will receive £15 million (top right cell of the matrix). If Y successfully deters entry by X then, at a high price, it gains all the pay-off available of £50 million (bottom left cell). Should Y threaten a price war and lower price to signify its commitment to deterring entry, then it gains the total market pay-off of £30 million (bottom right cell).

In Scenario 2, it is assumed that Y, in order to substantiate its threat to deter entry, is obliged to undertake a £15 million investment programme to increase its capacity. This may allow it to exploit economies of scale so reducing unit costs, thereby enabling it to sustain a price war should it be necessary to charge a low price. If X nevertheless decides to enter the industry and Y elects to charge a high price but is unable to extend its market or increase profits, the result is shown in the top left cell where X is in the same position as before but Y obtains a £10 million pay-off (£25 million minus the £15 million investment cost). If Y predicts that by charging a low price it will sell more and at least recoup the investment cost, the result will be as shown in the top right cell where X loses £5 million and Y retains the same pay-off as before of £15 million. Of course if Y has completely misjudged the market and fails to sell more, then a zero pay-off is suffered, i.e. the £15 million share is wiped out by the £15 million investment cost; Scenario 2. Clearly, if X decides not to enter the industry, Y suffers a reduced pay-off of £35 million (bottom left cell) if a high price is charged and the market is unchanged so that the £15 million investment cost reduces the total pay-off (£50 million minus £15 million). In the bottom right cell the pay-off for Y is shown as £30 million if the investment pays for itself whereas if Y has misjudged the market the net pay-off will be £15 million.

The example serves to show that many uncertainties arise when a would-be entrant attempts to break into a market dominated by an incumbent firm. The outcome for both entrant and incumbent largely depends on the extent to which deterrent threats are credible, the cost of gaining entry or deterring it and the changes in sales and profits with changes in prices. Within tourism supply, as argued earlier, entry costs are often relatively low and the opportunities for pre-emptive investment are limited, so that deterrence strategies are unlikely to be successful. Nevertheless, the example given here serves to illustrate one important aspect of tourism development in an international context. Investment supported or subsidized by the state, can give an advantage to a country.

For example, airline, ferry and train operations and, to an extent, the serviced accommodation sector, are characterized by substantial economies of scale. By subsidizing these, more rapid expansion can be encouraged. This might prevent foreign firms from entering the market, thereby allowing the domestic sectors to charge higher prices or obtain larger sales. This notion is significant in the case of developing countries which choose tourism as the engine of economic development. This relatively brief and simple exposition of game theory, using a few illustrative examples, indicates the direction in which economic analysis of industrial operations and market behavior is moving. Attention has tended to concentrate on competitive interaction between firms because this reflects the current position in most tourism markets. Game theory can accommodate many other circumstances, for example collusion where firms produce a low output and sells for a high price, akin to the outcome under a monopolized market structure, or instances where greater uncertainty prevails and there are a considerable number of possible outcomes. In more complex cases, the analysis involves determining the probability of specific pay-offs which accords much more closely with dynamic real-life situations.

Game theory can also accommodate different theories concerning the process by which firms reach a decision about the strategies which they adopt, put forward by the schools of thought. A range of modes of behavior is feasible and the Chicago school neoclassical tenet of optimizing behavior in competitive markets is a specific case within this range. The Behavioral school's hypothesis that decisions are made according to established norms and rules and the Evolutionary Economics school's view that behavior evolves in accordance with past practice can also be incorporated within the range of possible modes of decision-making.

The concept of updating can be used to describe consistent decision-making based on learning about other firms' behavior (S. Martin) and economic psychology can help to explain the process of expectations formation. Principal-agent models shed light on behavior by owners and managers respectively, permitting them to have different expectations and reactions. Hence, game theory is capable of analyzing a variety of modes of decision-making and behavior by firms in different sectors of tourism, in different countries and contexts. This has examined tourism supply using the SCP paradigm and game theory and has also endeavored to examine in greater depth, a number of the economic issues in tourism. Recent developments in the industrial economics field were introduced in order to provide additional insights into the operation of tourism markets. Underpinning the discussion is acceptance of the need to perceive tourism markets as dynamic and frequently in disequilibrium.

The SCP paradigm can be used to describe tourism markets and to highlight key features as a necessary first step towards the analysis of market structures, behaviour and performance. The advantage of the SCP paradigm is that it gives an overview showing the interrelationship of many elements. These can be added to or adapted to reflect the circumstances in different markets, as was indicated by the application of the framework to tourism intermediaries. However, the approach is not well suited to examining the process of firms' decision-making and behavior, for which recent developments in game theory are more appropriate. Game theory has the ability to encompass insights from various schools of thought and to provide a dynamic analysis of tourism firms, industries and markets. Thus, it can incorporate the Austrian and Evolutionary schools' critiques of static equilibrium analysis of markets. It can also consider the role of technological change, which Schumpeter highlighted as of key importance in the growth process, by showing how firms use research and development and the associated changes in technology as a competitive strategy vis-à-vis other firms. Such strategies can alter the structure of the market over the long run.

The theory acknowledges that, when making business decisions, most firms consider the likely responses of competitors. Inter-firm differences in the extent of knowledge, the degree of co-operation or non-cooperation can be taken into account and simple one-off strategies or sequential adjustment to different moves by competitors can be examined. The approach can indicate the credibility of signaled intentions and the probability that threat strategies will be successful. The theory also incorporates the most recent developments in industrial economics and, because of its widely encompassing framework and ability to analyze the processes of change, is clearly appropriate for examining tourism market structures, conduct and performance.

The discussions of supply in this have not taken explicit account of the international context of tourism markets, despite the importance of cross-country links between firms at different stages of the supply chain. The globalization of tourism supply, involving a variety of forms of economic integration, has implications for specialization in production and trade between different countries. Such issues as the contribution of tourism to income, employment and foreign currency earnings and the relationship between tourism and economic growth are relevant. Attention is now turned to these issues, prior to investigation of the wider environmental effects of both domestic and international tourism.

References

1. Tourist Flows and the Spatial Distribution of Tourists: Bob McKercher and Alan A. Lew (Hong Kong Polytechnic University; Northern Arizona University)
2. Behavioral Approaches in Tourism Research: D. Jim Walmsley (University of New England, Armidale)
3. Spiti: Adventures in the Trans-Himalaya / Kapadia, Harish
4. Cultural Geographies of Tourism: Mike Crang (Durham University)
5. Tourist Practices and Performances: David Crouch (University of Derby).
6. "Rural Tourism: Small Towns and Villages Appeal to U.S. Travelers." Travel Industry Association of America. 2001a.
7. The Tourism/Rural Economic Development Link, Woods, Mike D. 1992. " *Blueprints for Economic Development*, Cooperative Extension Service, Oklahoma State University, Vol. 2, No. 2: p. 2.

9

Principles of Tourism Marketing

Tourism Supply and Its Market Structure

Tourism supply is a complex phenomenon because of both the nature of the product and the process of delivery. It cannot be stored, cannot be examined prior to purchase, it is necessary to travel to consume it, heavy reliance is placed on both natural and human-made resources and a number of components are required, which may be separately or jointly purchased and which are consumed in sequence. It is a composite product involving transport, accommodation, catering, natural resources, entertainments and other facilities and services, such as shops and banks, travel agents and tour operators. Many businesses also serve other industrial sectors and consumer demands.

Some modifications to the standard assumptions are then introduced using the concept of contestable markets. This is followed by an analysis of monopoly, the limiting case of an uncompetitive market. The discussion proceeds to the less restrictive cases of monopolistic competition and oligopoly which more closely represent the conditions found in most industries. The value of the theoretical constructs is that they impart rigor to the analysis of real life situations. The characteristics of tourism sectors and markets are then outlined and related to the economic theories of competition already examined. Attention is concentrated largely on the types of market structure which apply to three main components of tourism supply, namely accommodation, transport and intermediaries.

A number of key features of tourism supply are identified, reflecting issues which are investigated in industrial economics, almost all of which act as indicators of market structure. Each feature is examined and illustrated by reference to conditions in tourism sectors and markets. The extent to which the economic models can explain and predict the operation of firms in the different tourism sectors is then appraised.

The discussion acts as a link in which the interrelationships between tourism firms and sectors, especially the strategies adopted in dynamic situations in which uncertainty prevails, are examined in the light of developments in industrial economics. In further issues relating to market strategies and structural changes occurring in tourism supply are considered in an international context.

Tourism Theory

The model of perfect competition provides a benchmark, illustrating the limiting case of a market involving a very high level of competition. It is assumed that there is a large number of firms and consumers so that neither producers nor consumers can affect the price of the posited undifferentiated product. An example which might approach these conditions is the existence of the numerous producers of snacks, meals and drinks which are sold in streets and on the beaches of tourist destination areas in relatively poor countries, although there may be a spatial separation of such sellers which affects the degree of competitiveness, thus raising the question of the extent to which suppliers can be considered as primarily suppliers of tourism.

The many components of the product, supplied by a variety of businesses operating in a number of markets, create problems in analyzing tourism supply. It is, therefore, convenient to consider it as a collection of industries and markets and to examine it using not only the neoclassical paradigm but also other schools of thought. This approach allows the analysis not only to cope with the complexities of the tourism product but also to take account of developments in economic concepts, theories and methods, especially the orientation of supply analysis towards industrial economics and the issues with which it has been concerned.

The main objective in this is to provide a wider and more advanced exposition and application of economic principles to tourism supply. Initially, the basic tenets of the theory of the firm concerning output, costs, pricing decisions, revenues, profits and losses are explained within the traditional analytical framework of economic models which consider the competitive structures of the markets within which consumers and producers interact.

Economic models of different types of market structure provide explanations of the operation of firms under well-defined conditions, each type of market structure being distinctly identifiable. First, the extreme case of a highly competitive structure, perfect competition, is examined. Some modifications to the standard assumptions are then introduced using the concept of contestable markets.

This is followed by an analysis of monopoly, the limiting case of an uncompetitive market. The discussion proceeds to the less restrictive cases of monopolistic competition and oligopoly which more closely represent the conditions found in most industries. The value of the theoretical constructs is that they impart rigor to the analysis of real life situations. The characteristics of tourism sectors and markets are then outlined and related to the economic theories of competition already examined.

Attention is concentrated largely on the types of market structure which apply to three main components of tourism supply, namely accommodation, transport and intermediaries. A number of key features of tourism supply are identified, reflecting issues which are investigated in industrial economics, almost all of which act as indicators of market structure.

The extent to which the economic models can explain and predict the operation of firms in the different tourism sectors is then appraised. The discussion acts as a link in which the inter-relationships between tourism firms and sectors, especially the strategies adopted in dynamic situations in which uncertainty prevails, are examined in the light of developments in industrial economics. In further issues relating to market strategies and structural changes occurring in tourism supply are considered in an international context.

Perfect competition

As much as the seller wishes can be sold at the price P. Each additional unit of output (such as a snack or drink) is sold for the same price. Therefore the extra revenue which the producer obtains from selling every additional unit of output, the marginal revenue, is equal to the price and is also equal to the average revenue from selling each unit of output. A cost structure is assumed where both the marginal cost of producing each additional unit and average cost per unit first decrease as output rises and then increase owing, initially, to increasing returns to scale and subsequently to decreasing returns.

For example, snack and meal producers purchase a certain amount of fuel for cooking, and if they were to produce only one meal, the cost of the meal would be relatively high. Since a given amount of fuel can be used to produce more than one meal, the marginal cost of producing each additional meal declines and the average cost of producing the meals also declines. At some point, more fuel, or even another appliance or cook, is necessary to produce more meals, so that the marginal and average cost rise.

Producers are unwilling to produce for a price less than the prevailing market price, P, as they would make a loss. Hence, the section of the marginal cost curve to the right of Q is the producer's supply curve, since it shows the quantity of output which the producer would like to supply at each price in the short run. Effectively, this means that the quantity supplied will be increased only if prices rise.

The optimal point of production from the supplier's viewpoint occurs where the marginal cost is equal to the marginal revenue, corresponding to an output, Q. This is the point at which profits are maximized, as can easily be demonstrated numerically. Output below Q is associated with marginal revenue in excess of marginal cost, so that producers wish to increase production because they can increase profits.

Conversely, at levels of output above Q, marginal revenue is less than marginal cost so that producers experience reduced profit and would seek to decrease production to the profit maximizing level of output. Hence, the supply curve for the industry is horizontal at the price, P, over the long run. If costs were to increase, for example, fuel became more expensive, producers with higher average costs would go out of business if they are just breaking even at output Q, i.e. earning only normal profits.

An overall decrease in costs would result in a short-run outcome of supernormal profits which would attract more producers into the industry until profits returned to their normal level. Thus, within a perfectly competitive market, the prevailing price may result in supernormal profits or losses in the short run. However, there is a tendency towards a break-even price, equal to marginal cost where average cost is at a minimum, and consumers appear to benefit.

This raises the issue of whether tourism markets which involve low levels of competition whereby supernormal profits are earned should be rendered more competitive and whether this would increase consumers' welfare. There is no unequivocal answer because, in the context of economies of scale where an increase in the firm's output is accompanied by a fall in the average cost of each unit of production, it is possible for imperfectly competitive markets to be more efficient than those under perfect competition. This issue is taken up below.

Contestable markets

It has been argued that although most real world markets are not perfectly competitive, a significant number give rise to similar economic outcomes. Baumol (1982) introduced the concept of contestability to take account of this outcome. A contestable market is characterized by insignificant entry and exit costs, so that there are negligible entry and exit barriers.

Sunk costs, which a firm incurs in order to produce and which would not be recuperable, if the firm left the industry, are not significant. Because of reasonably efficient information flows, the same supply conditions and technology are available to all producers. It is posited that producers are unable to change prices instantaneously but consumers react to them immediately.

The key insight of contestability is that new and existing firms, find it possible to challenge the position of rivals through pricing strategies. Thus, firms in contestable markets operate similarly to those in perfectly competitive markets in that they charge approximately the same price for a given product.

Although economies of scale and scope may arise, incumbent firms are unable to charge a price exceeding average cost because this would attract competitors into the market. Rivals would not be averse to entry because of the low sunk costs and low entry and exit barriers.

Hence, contestable markets may be beneficial to consumers. For example, independent tour operators who are not vertically integrated with an airline, accommodation chain or other facilities are governed by many of the conditions prevailing in this type of market, especially ease of entry and exit and minimal economies of scale. N. Evans and Stabler, in considering the air inclusive tour market, discuss such behavior using the categories of 'second tier' and 'third tier' tour operations.

Fitch's and Sheldon's earlier work also pointed to tiers of tour operations. The same kinds of conditions apply in travel agencies where, notwithstanding the presence of multiples in the sector, at the outlet level operational costs are not markedly below those of independent firms.

Monopoly

Monopoly represents the opposite extreme of perfect competition. Unlike producers in a perfectly competitive market, the monopolist has considerable control over the product price and level of output. Given normal demand conditions, in order to sell additional output, the product price must be lowered so that average revenue falls and consequently the marginal revenue per additional unit of output sold decreases as the amount sold rises.

The relationship between the two forms of revenue is such that marginal revenue decreases by twice as much as the average revenue and hence the marginal revenue curve lies below the average revenue curve. Following economic suppositions regarding cost structures, returns increase and then decrease; therefore the marginal and average cost curves initially decline and subsequently rise.

Profits are maximized at a level of output where the marginal cost of production equals the marginal revenue and marginal cost is rising (or in cases where increasing returns prevail, marginal cost is falling less rapidly than marginal revenue). The average cost of production is lower than the price charged giving rise to supernormal profits, above the minimum required to keep the firm in the industry. Thus, consumers are paying a price in excess of that which might emerge in a more competitive market. This raises the issue of whether the monopoly should be allowed to trade unhindered or be regulated or reorganized as a competitive industry.

Various components of tourism supply in different countries are deliberately organized as monopolies. For example, domestic air flights may be monopolized by the state airline and railway networks sometimes operate as a single industry. This may appear paradoxical as it would appear to counter the interests of consumers. However, two interesting outcomes may occur under monopoly as opposed to competition, which illustrate the debate concerning the relative advantages and disadvantages of each type of market structure.

The first case involves a comparison of the equilibrium price, and output combinations under competition and monopoly respectively, in which is assumed that a competitive industry is monopolized without any change in production conditions. The outcome assumes that each competitive firm has the same costs and therefore, for simplicity, the average cost curve can be excluded. It is clear that the price, P1, is lower and the quantity produced, Q1, higher under competition than under monopoly. If the industry were monopolized, profit maximization would occur where the short-run marginal cost, SMC, is equal to the marginal revenue, MR, resulting in a higher price, P2, and lower output, Q2.

In the long run, the monopolist could close some production units, decreasing output to Q3 and increasing the price to P3. Thus, consumers would be worse off under monopoly than under competitive conditions. This could occur in the tourism accommodation or intermediaries sectors, but more particularly in the transport industry where small independent airlines, bus, coach or ferry operators are amalgamated as, to an extent, has occurred with deregulation; after an initial influx of new entrants, larger enterprises have taken over many of the smaller firms and exercised monopoly powers.

In the second case, production conditions differ according to whether the industry is operated as a monopoly, or under competition as large economies of scale can apply when production is undertaken by a single firm. This applies in the case of a so-called natural monopoly in which both the marginal and average costs are lower over the range of output which could be purchased in comparison with competition. In these circumstances, consumers could benefit in terms of a lower price and higher quantity of production even if the monopolist made supernormal profits.

These shows the price and quantity combinations under an unregulated monopoly, P1 and Q1. If the monopoly were regulated so that the price charged was equal to the marginal cost of production at P2, consumer's welfare would increase owing to the lower price and higher output, Q2. However, a government would need to subsidize production since the price would be lower than the average cost of production, so that the supplier makes a loss.

Even if the monopoly were not regulated consumers might benefit, in the long run, from product and process innovations resulting from the reinvestment of some of the profits gained by the monopolist, including the necessary research and development.

The availability of funding for research and development is sometimes problematic under competitive conditions. Therefore the issue of whether monopolies in tourism supply, as well as in other sectors of the economy, should be allowed to exist or be regulated is complex and varies according to the differing circumstances of particular industries. The absence of a general conclusion concerning the relative merits of the different market structures, strengthens the case for specific empirical investigations of the tourism sectors in question.

The difficulty of predicting a determined outcome can be aptly illustrated by reconsidering the examples of state-sanctioned monopoly rail and airline markets. Many governments have partially or totally privatized a number of services, which were hitherto perceived as natural monopolies. The rationale has often been that, not-withstanding economies of scale, they could be operated more efficiently as private sector industries.

Privatization has often been accompanied by de-regulation to encourage new entrants and increase competition. However, paradoxically, the eventual effect has often been to bring about greater concentration. One important reason is that, smaller new entrants are unable to fully exploit economies of scale and therefore fail. It is still too early to establish empirically what the structure of the airline, bus, ferry or rail sectors will be.

Effective regulation may be needed to prevent abuses of monopoly power in the form of high prices, and the extraction of super-normal profits or restraint of competition. In practice, governments usually define monopoly as occurring when a single producer accounts for a specific, relatively high percentage of production of a particular product and monitor the operations of the firm in question in an attempt to ensure that consumers are not disadvantaged.

Monopolistic competition

Monopolistic competition is a type of market structure, often associated with retailing, which is intermediate between perfect competition and monopoly. It is similar to that of perfect competition and contestable markets in that there is ease of entry and exit in the long run. In tourism monopolistic competition applies, in many respects, to the hotel accommodation sector which is characterized by many suppliers who provide products which are close but not exact substitutes, so that there is some degree of product differentiation reinforced, as in retailing, by the spatial separation and location of businesses.

In the short run, suppliers within a monopolistically competitive market can charge a price, which provides them with supernormal profit. Firms produce where their short-run marginal revenue, SMR, is equal to their marginal cost and charge a price which exceeds their average cost, as illustrated by the price and output combination, P1 and Q1. However, in the long run, supernormal profits, combined with the virtual absence of entry and exit barriers for the industry, attract new competitors so that existing firms experience a decline in the demand for their products. This is illustrated by a shift to the left of the average revenue (demand) curve, SAR, and the short-run marginal revenue curve, SMR, until they attain their long-run positions, given by LAR and LMR with an equilibrium price P2 and output Q2.

Over the long run, demand decreases until the break-even point where average revenue, shown as the price P2, is equal to the average cost of production so that there is no further entry into (or exit from) the industry. Although output has contracted and supernormal profits have disappeared, the price charged is still greater than the marginal cost of production. Hence this form of competition appears less efficient than perfect competition although the wide variety of products provides consumers with greater variety of choice.

There are a number of examples of tourism businesses in this position such as the smaller firms in the contestable segments of the accommodation and transport sectors, where the extent of their market limits the possibilities of operating at a level which reduces their costs. This might explain why smaller airlines, bus and ferry operators eventually.

Oligopoly

An oligopolistic market structure occurs, when a small number of producers dominate the industry, the international airline industry being a case in point. The key characteristic of oligopoly is the interdependence between producers, so that each firm's price and output decisions depend, in part, on those of its competitors. One well-known example of such interdependence, which has become a standard case in economics, is that of the oligopolist's perceived kinked demand curve, which shows the likely outcome for a firm, should it contemplate a change in its price in the absence of changes in cost or demand conditions which affect the whole of the industry.

It knows that, if it decreases its price, competitors will follow suit, demand for its own product becoming more inelastic, so that it will not increase its market share by doing so. Conversely, if it increases its price they will maintain their own prices so its demand is more elastic and it will lose market share. Thus, the prevailing market price is the profit-maximizing price for the firm.

The equilibrium price and quantity of the oligopolist are P and Q. If the firm increases its price above P, it experiences a large decrease in demand as its competitors fail to decrease their prices in line, so that the average revenue (demand) curve for the oligopolist is relatively elastic (flatter) between A and B. If, in contrast, it decreases its price below P, it increases its sales only marginally because its competitors also tend to decrease their prices, so that its demand curve is relatively inelastic (steeper) between B and C. The firm's marginal revenue curve is, similarly, relatively elastic up to the quantity Q and relatively inelastic for quantities in excess of Q. Thus, the prevailing pr

Ideally, individual oligopolists prefer prices to be set at a level which maximizes the joint profits of all producers in the industry. In effect, if all the firms in the industry could act together, the result would be similar to a monopolist, leading to an increase in price and a decrease in the quantity sold, in contrast to the outcome that would occur under competitive conditions. For example, inter-airline pricing and route-sharing agreements have been one example of a strategy which has been used to increase joint profits. On the other hand, there is an incentive for an individual firm to cheat as, if it could do so successfully, it would increase its profits and market share relative to those of its competitors.

The stability of a number of pricing and output-sharing arrangements may be accounted for, by the fact that should all firms cheat, all would be likely to be worse off. Oligopolists can alter their output as well as the prices charged and take account of their competitors' possible reactions when they make their price and output decisions, as was shown in the case of the Bermuda resort hotels market.

However, to consider more fully not only the relevance of these basic constructs but also their limitations, it is necessary to delineate morphology of tourism sectors and markets and describe their principal characteristics.

Market Structures in Tourism Supply

The approach adopted in this section is to outline the sectors which have been recognized in the tourism literature. Those which appear representative of the market structures in tourism are described concisely and the key factors indicating their competitive status are identified, such as the degree of concentration, entry and exit conditions, pricing strategies, profit levels, product differentiation, cost structures and capacity and interaction between firms.

The problem with any classification of the supply components of tourism is how broad or narrow they should be. Such categories as transport and accommodation are very broad and benefit from disaggregation into submarkets with different structures and modes of operation. The classification of tourism markets adopted here largely follows the convention adopted in the tourism literature, with some modifications to the nomenclature employed.

Major tourism markets

Discussion of tourism supply has been conducted largely outside economics, with the result that coverage of economic issues is patchy and there is no coherent overview. Many texts directed at practitioners, particularly in the hospitality sector, touch on supply and associated issues in discussing financial structures, management, marketing, quality and training. At a very specific and applied level, studies of the planning, development, operation and performance of such enterprises as hotels, guesthouses, holiday villages, ski and timeshare resorts and theme parks have been undertaken.

At a more general level, attempts have been made to model tourism locations, for example by geographers who aim to identify key factors determining growth or decline. Economists' tendency to neglect the service sector in general and tourism, in particular, creates difficulties because there are large gaps in the empirical evaluation of parts of the industry. While some reference is made to the other sectors, in order to keep the examination within bounds attention will be concentrated on accommodation, transport and intermediaries as illustrative cases.

Some fundamental economic factors characterize the accommodation sector, notwithstanding its complicated structure. It is subjected to fixed capacity with all its attendant problems in the face of periodicity, perishability and seasonality.

Allied to this, particularly in larger units offering a wide range of services, high fixed costs drive operators to attain high occupancy rates through such devices, as product differentiation and market segmentation. Many seek flexibility by targeting the business market during the working week and the leisure sector at weekends. In holiday resorts, the needs of different groups can be met over the year, for instance catering for skiers in winter and walkers in the summer, as occurs in Austria, France and Switzerland. Despite these attempts to exploit market potential, in the early 1990s hoteliers who bought at the peak of the property boom in the UK were put under extreme pressure as they had made an over-priced purchase which could not be serviced by revenue. The property market collapse exacerbated the problem as the fall in property values reduced the collateral security.

There is evidence (Horwath Consulting), that some forms of accommodation can exploit economies of sale not only within individual establishments, but also by the management of a large number of hotels. This partially explains the existence of chains which control many hotels, such as Choice, Accor, Bass and Forte/Granada. To an extent it also accounts for concentration in the sector, the nature of ownership and location being other explanatory variables.

For example, in the USA with a much higher proportion of corporate ownership, the concentration ratio is over 30 per cent while in eastern Mediterranean holiday resort destinations, comprised of family-owned businesses, it is less than 2 per cent. Economic integration between firms may result in reduced fixed costs and entry barriers and may make it possible to increase occupancy rates by tapping new segments of the market. Independent and smaller operators sometimes try to combat the power of the large firms by forming co-operative consortia to reduce overheads, for instance by setting-up referral or reservations systems.

Large corporate-run hotels, mainly serving business travelers, tend to cluster in and around large urban areas, airports and on land transport routes. Holiday hotels are more likely to be independent and more widely dispersed, although clustering still occurs, such as in resorts or locations which are principal tourist attractions. In this sense the accommodation sector is akin to monopolistic competition in the retail market, in which accessibility and complementarity's, central tenets of urban economics, are characteristics (Balchin). Urban economic theory shows that key locations confer benefits which give a commercial advantage and therefore a higher turnover and profits, explaining why large firms can outbid smaller ones in high cost areas.

In effect, a market monopoly can arise because of location monopoly of specific sites. It also helps to account for the pattern of accommodation in holiday areas like sea-side resorts where smaller, lower quality hotels are pushed into secondary locations away from the sea-front. This is explained in terms of spatial rent and property price gradients whereby, for individual businesses, location is determined by the property and land costs.

Thus, businesses with lower revenue and profits are forced into areas with lower rents and prices. Even though, the intensity of competition is lower in particular destinations outside locations subject to such clustering, it is still significant in terms of the total market, given the number of holiday choices open to consumers and the size and quality range of accommodation available.

The self-catering sector is an interesting area of the accommodation market which has shown both high growth rates and great diversity. It has complemented the service sector by providing additional rooms whose clients are allowed to use the facilities provided. Holiday centres and villages and timeshare come into this category. There are a number of large players in the field, for example in the UK, Butlins, Haven, Holimarine, Pontins and Warners, formerly low-cost concerns which have upgraded their product, while the Center Pares organization is an innovative market leader. Disney Vacation, Hapimag, Vacation International, Villa Owners Club and timeshare are similar in terms of the holiday centre concept but differ in that they involve capital investment by consumers.

However, none of these control the market which displays two principal economic features. The first is the wide range of standards of quality and therefore segments of the market targeted. The second is its relative infancy, making it difficult to predict its eventual characteristics and competitive structure.

The picture which emerges of the holiday accommodation is of a fragmented sector, dominated numerically by small and medium-sized businesses, even if not in terms of the value of total market transactions. This is largely the result of its relatively low entry barriers, and generally labour-intensive nature, where the emphasis is on customer service within a small market area, owing to the spatial separation of both demand and supply. Thus, the market exhibits characteristics which reflect more than one form of economic classification, ranging from highly competitive conditions in the small unit sector in clustered locations, to a virtual monopoly of specific locations by large hotels.

However, the appropriateness of neoclassical analysis of tourism accommodation is put to the test by its segmentation, and by its temporal and spatial dimensions. Consequently, two branches of economic analysis appear to be pertinent to understanding and explaining the accommodation market. Industrial economies concern with market structure, entry conditions and concentration, product differentiation, segmentation and spatial competition is certainly relevant. Urban and regional economics, with its focus on the determinants of location and spatial distribution of activity, can also make a contribution.

The market structure of tourism accommodation tends to accord with the contestable—monopolistic competition positions taking into overall, taking account of the significance of spatial factors in moderating market conditions. In business and resort centres, large hotels experience oligopolistic conditions but outside these areas the structure is closer to monopolistic competition. The picture is clouded somewhat by the intra-sectoral choice of type and quality of accommodation with some segments, for example self-catering, being more contestable than others. The lack of empirical evidence precludes making further inferences.

The Intermediary sector

The role of tour operators is to supply holiday packages and to facilitate the link between the suppliers of travel, accommodation, facilities and services, both in origins and destinations, and the tourist. They procure the components of the product, usually by negotiating discounted prices, and retailing it through travel agents or directly to the customer. Tour operations are conducted in a number of ways: by an independent firm specializing solely in holiday assembly and marketing; as a subsidiary of a conglomerate business with diverse interests; as a division of an airline; or linked with a travel agency.

Tour Operators

The structure of the intermediary market, for example, in Europe and the USA, raises other interesting questions apart from their principal- agent relationship. There are some large players in the market in terms of both ownership and control and market share. In the USA, there were approximately 1,500 in total in the early 1990s, of which forty tour operators (3 per cent) controlled almost a third of the market. In the UK, the top ten tour operators accounted for over 70 per cent of the 17 million seats of ATOL (Air Travel Organizers' License) licenses granted in 1993-94. Four companies—Thomson, Airtours, Owners Abroad (First Choice from 1994) and Cosmos—took almost 60 per cent of the air holidays licenses (Civil Aviation

Authority (CAA), N. Evans and Stabler). In addition to this marked concentration, there is also extensive vertical integration with respect to travel, accommodation, and travel agency and holiday services.

Other features of tour operation of note are the rate of increase in and the total number of firms. In the USA nearly 600 companies were operating in the late 1970s, but this number increased to over 1,000 by 1985 (Sheldon). Similar is the case in UK where, there were around 500 firms in 1985 which, by 1993-94, had nearly doubled when 1,000 companies were licensed. Of more significance, however, is the birth and death of tour operators, mostly of smaller firms. It has been estimated that only a third of those in business in the late 1970s were still extant in the middle to late 1980s in both the USA and Europe (Sheldon).

The performance of tour operators is very sensitive to market conditions, particularly variations in demand arising from such factors as changes in exchange rates, economic recession in origin countries and inflation and perceived political instability in destinations. In the face of tourism development and the continuing extension of possible destinations, capacity has sometimes out-run demand. Furthermore, as in the hospitality market, seasonality is significant.

Large firms rely on a high volume of sales with low margins, a significant proportion of profit being generated by investing receipts from advanced bookings. A high rate of sales makes it possible, to achieve substantial economies of scale and scope through operating efficiencies, a wide knowledge of an extensive market and market power to gain large discounts from carriers and hoteliers, where past performance is the key. Provided fixed investment is low, as in the case of smaller and more specialized tour operators, the return on fixed investment can be relatively high. Nevertheless, many firms suffer losses over a run of years and when net profits are made they are modest, the return often being less than 4 per cent in the UK, although there is considerable variability.

Overall, taking account of the significance of spatial factors in moderating market conditions, on a continuum of perfect competition to monopoly, the market structure of tourism accommodation tends to accord with the con testable—monopolistic competition positions. In business and resort centres, large hotels experience oligopolistic conditions but outside these areas the structure is closer to monopolistic competition. The picture is clouded somewhat by the intra-sectoral choice of type and quality of accommodation with some segments, for example self-catering, being more contestable than others. The lack of empirical evidence precludes making further inferences.

Travel Agents

Travel agents function as brokers in arranging all aspects of business travel and holidays but act as agents in that they represent principals, whether they be tour operators or the ultimate suppliers such as carriers, hoteliers, car hirers and insurance companies. The travel agency component of tourism supply is concentrated in that a limited number of firms with multiple outlets, some integrated with tour operators or carriers, dominate the market, particularly in the USA.

There is a need to generate a high turnover in the face of low margins; commissions average less than 10 per cent, representing the gross margin which has to cover all operating costs and yield a net profit. This sector of the intermediary market has also experienced a rapid growth in numbers. In the USA, there has been an almost fivefold increase in agency outlets since the early 1970s.

This is in contrast with Europe where single outlets number no more than a third of the total, the major multiples (100 or more branches) owning just over a quarter. In comparison with tour operators, the death rate record of travel agents is somewhat lower. Half of the agents currently in business have existed for ten years or more. By the early 1990s, twenty agency firms had captured approaching half of the market, five alone controlling almost a third.

As in tour operations, economies of scale and scope characterize the travel agency sector but to exploit these fully in the UK, a company needs to own 150–200 branches. The principal economies are gained in the provision of central, mainly back-office, services such as accounting and computing. However, the experiences of multiples in the UK in the late 1980s do not verify that scale economies are actually achieved, where other smaller multiples were taken over. Because these struggling chains were not always profitable, the large multiples did not always increase their market share.

What has become apparent is that the selective opening of new branches, sometimes in new forms such as in large stores or through franchising, has often been a better strategy than absorbing smaller enterprises (Liston). Evidence provided by Liston indicates that travel agency, like tour operations in the UK, appears to be polarizing into the extremely large and the very small, although independent travel agents may co-operate to counter the dominance of the larger chains (Daneshkhu). The low entry costs contribute to explaining the large number of independently owned travel agencies but another important reason is that travel agency, as a retail activity, normally involves face-to-face contact with customers so that a more personal service is possible.

Well-trained and skilled staff and close management control can be an asset to a business and engender a loyal clientele. The single independent travel agent or small local chain with a sound knowledge of the local market can perform better than the branch of a multiple, especially where specialization in certain services or types of tourism is required. In this sense, the large multiples with a uniform approach to selling holidays suffer diseconomies of scale.

An advantageous location is an important determinant of success, but this is offset by the costs of prime sites because of the competition to occupy these from not only other travel agents but also other forms of retailing. Nevertheless, spatial separation of travel agency lessens this competition and makes it possible for a firm to earn an adequate return on its investment. Though not conclusive, it partially explains the high proportion of independent agents in the USA, 60 per cent of which are located in sub-urban or small- urban areas. Opinion is divided, both among academics and practitioners as to the competitive structure of travel agents. Innovation, especially the introduction of information technology in the area of computer reservation systems, may prove to have a mixed effect (Bennett).

Principals can potentially increase travel agency dependency and reduce competitor's impact by affecting the businesses that serve them, and the terms on which they do so, by utilizing a system specific to their own operations, as the only means of communicating with the company, for example Thomson's TOPS (Thomson Online Program System). Such practices not only constitute a restraint on trade, so acting against consumer's interests, but also increase agency costs because of the need to set up the means of accessing a number of systems. They also inhibit the long-run achievement of economies of scale by the agencies.

The issue of whether trade associations perpetuate restrictive practices or promote greater efficiency in the intermediary sector is problematic. Those associated with travel agents have been able to secure as members a high proportion of those trading, largely because of the need to subscribe to schemes, such as bonds as a guard against the failure of tour operators, as a pre-requisite for the procurement of a license or to reassure customers. The American Society of Travel Agents (ASTA) and the Association of British Travel Agents (ABTA) are cases in point.

Smaller businesses have also considered that these associations have given them a measure of protection, often by representing their interests to larger and powerful principals and public bodies. Of late, the function of these associations has been called in question as the cost of membership and protective schemes has risen sharply. Thus, many facets of the intermediary market are of current interest in economics, in particular, the study of company strategies and operations in what would appear to be both oligopolistic and competitive situations.

An oligopolistic structure prevails in the intermediary sector of the UK in that fewer than ten tour operators dominate the inclusive tour holiday market and determine the terms on which travel agents operate. This is particularly the case where tour operators have the potential to sell directly to the customer. Travel agents, therefore, are in the peculiar position of obtaining their inputs from an imperfectly competitive market but selling in one which is highly contestable. This peculiar structure again puts the theory of the firm to a severe test and the issue is one of the need for empirical investigation to establish the nature of the competitive structure of the travel agency sector, perhaps more in the context of an industrial economic analytical framework.

Transport

Transportation is best examined as a number of sub-markets, given the wide range of transport modes, each possessing its own particular features and competitive characteristics and structure. As for instance the main commercial modes of air, bus, coach, ferries and rail suffer problems arising from indivisibility and associated fixed capacity and high fixed costs, periodicity and seasonality. None the less, there are considerable differences in their respective market structures and conditions. For international travel, air far outstrips bus, coach, sea and rail.

Air travel has shown extremely high rates of growth since the 1960s, fed by technological change, with potential for continued growth in the future. Car ferry operations have benefited from the introduction of the roll-on roll-off vessels whereas bus, coach and rail traffic have experienced relative decline in the face of the growth of private motoring.

The competitive conditions of transport sub-markets and the structures are strongly influenced by the inter-relationship between certain modes and the severity of the constraints imposed by regulation. There is also competition within modes, such as in the airline sector, where there is fierce competition on many short- and long-haul routes. Similar circumstances apply in the bus and coach market. In the ferry market, high volume routes tend to be subject to keen competition. For instance, air travel depends on both bus and coach and rail for transfers to and fro from the airports. Likewise sea crossings rely on road and rail transport for a large proportion of their traffic while the cruise-liner market is now largely based on air travel to and from the point of departure of the vessel.

However this complementarity, is an important feature of the transport market, does not suggest that there is not intense competition within and between modes. With respect to competition between modes, the opening of the Channel Tunnel linking the UK and France has demonstrated the fierce competition of ferry and rail although the merging of some ferry operations raises the possibility of an oligopolistic market structure. In some European countries, on domestic routes, air and rail travel are in competition, especially where rail systems have been updated for high speed trains. Bus and coach travel and rail also compete, the former offering a low cost alternative to the latter's shorter travel times.

Regulation of transport has occurred for two main reasons, safety and the preservation of a market for a national or state-owned or supported mode. Interest in the impact of regulation has centered more on de-regulation with the aim of fostering greater competition. However, it has become apparent, as will be shown, that such an action often has unintended and opposite effects, as has been manifested in air and bus/coach transport. Moreover, the extent of regulation varies even within a specific mode. Again, in air transport, part of the market is more strictly controlled than others, creating considerable variations in competitive situations.

Air Travel

The operation and regulation of air transport has been widely investigated in the context of both business and holiday travel. Useful reviews of the situation in the early 1990s are given in Ferguson and Ferguson and Lundberg and Melville has provided a thorough review and evaluation of economic studies of the sector, including econometric modeling approaches. Evidence of its conditions and structure illustrate a number of tourism and economic issues arising in other transport markets, especially the economic environment created by regulation and deregulation and the resulting level of competition.

An allied factor is the process of the privatization of a number of airlines. The cost structure of airlines is quite complex and operating costs and efficiency are related to technical factors relating to the distance to be traveled, the size and type of aircraft and the payload, as well as the support services such as marketing and the reservations system, whereas capital costs are likely to be affected by whether aircraft are bought outright or leased, new or secondhand.

Direct and indirect costs, such as airport charges and ground handling, are outside the control of the airline. Prima facie, airlines are high fixed cost enterprises with fixed capacity so that they need to attain high payloads and even break. Short-haul flights, involving fewer hours in the air and more take-offs and landings are relatively more expensive than long-haul carriage. Furthermore, aircraft are designed to fly specific distances as efficiently as possible so, for example, employing a Jumbo jet on European routes of up to 2,500 km is un-economic.

In general there are economies of scale, stemming from technical efficiencies in operating large aircraft provided the routes operated on warrant it. In addition they depreciate less quickly. Uncertainty is a significant factor because of the rate of technical development of aircraft, for example with respect to aerodynamics and engine efficiency.

The market served influences the economics of airline operations in a number of ways. For scheduled services, to maximize the payload and revenues, demand has to be ascertained in advance to discover its composition with regard to the numbers of business and economy customers, for example. The approach being adopted by airlines is termed 'yield management' which in its most developed form is akin to perfectly discriminating monopoly pricing. Pricing policy also needs to take account of the route, destination and stage stops, the pressure of competition and longer-term level of demand.

Chartered services reduce market uncertainty because it is possible to ascertain the payload well in advance. However, the distinction between these two main types of services has become more difficult to discern, as charter airlines have moved into the scheduled market and vice versa. This has occurred because travel on what were holiday charter routes has become so regular as to warrant scheduled services. Conversely, some under-used scheduled services, perhaps operated as a social service when airlines were state-owned, may be served more irregularly by special charters.

The advent of de-regulation and privatization has dramatically changed airline operations and has had some interesting economic consequences. The US experience, where de-regulation occurred in 1978, holds implications for what might happen elsewhere, such as in the European Union, where moves to relax controls have been initiated.

Competition has certainly intensified as new companies moved into the market, entry having been made easier. This tends to suggest that entry costs, particularly the capital costs, are lower than casual observation indicates. Chartering, leasing or buying aircraft second-hand facilitates ease of entry, as does negotiating reservation, ground handling services and maintenance agreements with specialist contract firms or established and larger airlines. In the short run the increased competition has brought fares down and extended the market, also forcing airlines to be more sensitive to their customers' needs.

Recent developments have thrown up the negative effects of deregulation, with some former major airlines having such severe financial problems as to be forced out of business, Pan Am in the USA being a well-known example. Also some major national airlines in Europe, such as Air France, Iberia, Sabena and SAS, have had problems in adapting to severe competition, especially on key routes, mainly because of inflexible structures, engendered by highly restrictive international fare policies and state support as national flag carriers. The benefits to consumers may be short-lived as the number of airlines will almost certainly decrease in the long run through mergers and reciprocal agreements and the failure of smaller, newer entrants.

This concentration and consolidation is likely to lead to higher fares as the larger companies take control of key routes and gain the market power to dictate price levels and limit choice. The development of the hub and spoke pattern of air travel where long-haul flights are concentrated on major airports gives opportunities for smaller feeder airlines to create a market niche, although the larger airlines may determine the terms on which spoke routes will be served. There are additional concerns where airlines cut costs in order to remain competitive as the quality of the service may be lowered, less attention being paid to maintenance and safety margins.

The pattern of air travel is evolving given the differences in the rate of growth in sub-markets, and the fact that de-regulation has not yet had a full effect on the airline structure and the market. However, there are signs that market power is likely to be concentrated in a few international giants, especially as state support for national airlines declines under privatization programmes and agreements, such as that in the European Union, which generally forbids subsidization of unprofitable airlines. A case in point was the proposed agreement between British Airways and American Airlines, two of the largest airlines in the world, which control around 60 per cent of the UK-US routes.

The evidence from this brief description of what is the best researched tourism sector is that although a domestic monopoly or oligopoly structure has been common, with a single state-supported airline or a small number of competing airlines; de-regulation has made some markets competitive in the short run. In the international market some routes are competitive, being served by many carriers.

Most of the others are served by at least two carriers, indicating an oligopolistic market, although a few routes are served by a single carrier which may be tempted to exercise monopoly powers. This does not undermine the ability of the theory of the firm to explain the market structure; it signifies a need to divide the sector into sub-markets and to consider each separately. The sector, in common with the others reviewed, is in a fluid state, reflecting deregulation and the changing demand for foreign air travel.

Other transport sectors

The structures of the bus, coach, ferry and rail sectors are similar to that of air travel. They also experience the problems of high capital costs, fixed capacity, peaked demand, the need for feeder routes to sustain profitable ones. Some state support and regulation characterize these modes. On the other hand, there are opportunities to exploit economies of scale and exercise price discrimination to maximize revenues and fill any excess capacity. For example, the principal problem of the rail sector is the high fixed costs associated with the track, signaling system and stations. In the UK, the privatization process has been facilitated by separating this basic infrastructure from the rolling stock, making it possible to reduce entry costs and to perceive it as resembling air travel where airports and services, navigational and air traffic control systems are operated by bodies on behalf of the airlines.

The crucial difficulty in deregulating and privatizing rail markets and operating them commercially is that uneconomic lines may be closed, although they have the potential to support the principal inter-city services on the same basis as the evolving hub and spoke structure in air travel. Another similarity with air travel is the endeavor to fill excess capacity by a complex pricing system resembling a crude form of yield management.

A number of elements of the bus and coach market resemble the air and rail sectors. The main issues in the market in the mid-1990s are the standard of service, safety and reliability, with de-regulation in creating uncertainty for both long-established and new entrant operators. The aim of deregulation, as in the air travel market, is to engender greater competition. A large number of new operators has given rise to substantial overcapacity. Although this initially lowered prices on key routes, the entry of many small companies has been accompanied by greater concentration at the national and regional level of operations.

Large companies not only offer a more comprehensive coverage but also are able to exploit economies of scale in such factors as reservations, repairs and maintenance, administration and advertising, as well as more fully utilizing vehicles with respect to payloads and operational hours and operating only the most lucrative routes at higher fares, endangering the long-run existence of the smaller companies. Consequently, market power may be vested in few hands.

The ferry market clearly serves the private road, coach and rail transport modes and has grown strongly with the increase in surface holiday travel, particularly in Europe. New forms of conveyance, such as hovercraft, hydrofoil and catamaran craft, have reduced travel times and extended the market, increasing both intra- and inter-mode competition. Short routes involve high entry and operating costs, somewhat resembling short-haul air travel. There are economies of scale in increased vessel size and speed but these can be offset by the danger of increasing loading and unloading turn-round times and excess capacity in off-peak and off-season periods, akin to those in the air, bus, coach and rail market, giving rise to a complex fare structure and travel conditions.

The existence of the cruise-liner sector as a sea-based form of tourism needs to be acknowledged if only because it is a growth sector, especially in the USA, which accounts for over three-quarters of the global market. It is not considered here, except to note that from an economic standpoint it has many of the same characteristics as air travel, being capital-intensive with high fixed costs for operators who own rather than charter ships and depending on high volume and repeat bookings to fill the fixed capacity. Technically there is a parallel between the type of vessel and aircraft which can operate at optimum efficiency so high payloads are essential.

Key features

The structure of tourism supply and the degree and type of competition between firms, described in the preceding overviews of tourism sectors, is facilitated by reference to the theoretical models presented at the beginning. The models identified a number of criteria which indicate the competitive structure of markets; for example, the number and size of firms and level of entry and exit barriers indicate the degree to which oligopoly or monopoly powers may be exercised by tourism firms.

Similarly, the extent of market concentration or of price leadership signifies potential limitations on the level of inter-firm competition. These criteria can be examined in the context of specific tourism sectors in different countries, providing insights into the types of market structure which prevail and the nature of inter-firm competition. This is useful because of the implications of different market structures for the extraction of profits above the break-even level and, hence, for consumer welfare. Key criteria which were identified within both the theoretical models and the overviews of tourism sectors are

- number and size of firms
- degree of market concentration and level of entry/exit barriers
- economies and diseconomies of scale and economies of scope
- capital indivisibilities, fixed capacity and associated fixed costs of operations
- price discrimination and product differentiation
- pricing policies—leadership, wars and market-share strategies.

The first four indicate market structure, while the last two also relate to the strategies which firms pursue within imperfectly competitive markets. They will now be discussed in more detail, linking the theoretical and empirical discussions, as well as acting as a bridge to the more industrial economics-oriented analysis.

Number and size of firms

A small number of firms, in contrast indicate an oligopolistic structure, with monopoly being the limiting case of dominance by a single firm. Evidence on the numbers and sizes of firms in the transport and intermediary sectors is relatively easily ascertained, where there are requirements regarding registration and regulation and trade associations exist. For example, the International Air Transport Association (LATA) and International Civil Aviation Organization (ICAO) publish statistics on airlines while in the UK and many other countries, there are intermediary trade associations representing tour operators and travel agents which allow estimates of the numbers of intermediaries to be made. However, the size, diversity and fragmentation of the accommodation sector mean that except for hotels of an international level, ascertaining the number of establishments is extremely difficult.

The size of firms can be measured by a number of variables, ranging from number of employees, sales revenue, number of unit sales to capital employed. In the accommodation sector, the number of rooms offered by each establishment or the total number of bed nights achieved are useful measures. The number of holidays sold is a feasible measure for intermediaries.

In the case of air transport, IATA statistics reveal that in the early 1990s, for international travel, British Airways carried by far the largest number of passengers and had the greatest passenger kilometers, followed by Lufthansa, Air France and Japan Airways. In the UK intermediary sector, Civil Aviation Authority (CAA) data showed that in the mid-1990s, the largest tour operator in the air inclusive tour (AIT) market was Thomson, accounting for nearly a quarter of the total number of holidays sold.

Tourism sector's composition differs between countries, in terms of the number and size of firms. A domestic monopoly exists in the airline sector in some countries, as in the case of Aloha Airlines in the Hawaiian Islands, while in others an oligopolistic structure prevails; for example, in Australasia, the air transport sector has been dominated by two to three airlines operating reciprocal agreements. Within the accommodation sector, the large number of establishments selling differentiated products is suggestive of monopolistic competition, while some bus and coach sectors have been highly competitive.

However, it is also clear that although in some sectors a few large firms command a substantial market share, the remainder of the market consists of many highly competitive small firms. Hence, it is possible to conceive of a spectrum of competition with strongly competitive conditions coexisting with oligopoly in some tourism markets, with a degree of interaction between them. For example, innovations by small companies may subsequently be taken up by larger entities, as in the case of the timeshare concept or activity holidays. Thus, tourism markets are complex and may consist of different sub-sectors characterized by alternative competitive structures.

Level of entry and exit barriers

The competitiveness of markets is a further indicator of the degree of competitiveness High concentration is suggestive of oligopoly or monopoly while a low incidence implies a high level of competition. Measures of concentration can be broadly divided into those which focus on the number and size of firms and those which consider the implications of variations in size. Size may be defined in several ways, as mentioned above, the indicator used depending partly on the availability of data and partly on the nature of the business. The Lorenz curve can be used to rank, in cumulative form, the smallest to the largest firms as a percentage of the total number of firms trading in the market.

The Gini coefficient represents the magnitude of the divergence from exact equality in size of firms, so that a value of zero denotes that all firms are of equal size and, ostensibly, highly competitive conditions prevail, whereas a value of unity equates to pure monopoly. The concentration ratio ranks firms from largest to smallest, so that a high percentage score indicates a market in which monopoly prevails, while a low score suggests that many firms serve the market. More sophisticated measures attempt to take account of the greater impact of larger firms, on the market by weighting their market share more heavily.

Well-known examples of such measures, widely applied in the industrial economics field, are the indices proposed by Herfindahl and Hirschman, Hannah and Kay, evaluated by Davies. The degree of market power can be measured by the Lerner index which considers the discrepancy between market price and marginal cost, where zero denotes equality and a highly competitive market and a value approaching unity indicates high profits and a highly concentrated market.

The degree of market concentration in different sectors of tourism varies between, countries and regions and key tourist locations of a given country. In Spain, the five main charter airlines were responsible for over 80 per cent of all passenger kilometers flown by Spanish charter airlines at the end of the 1980s while in the UK, the top five firms carried approximately 70 per cent of all charter passengers (Bote Gomez and Sinclair). At the same time, the top five UK travel agents had a market share of 47 per cent compared with a share of 77 per cent for the top five tour operators.

The extent to which a higher degree of market concentration is accompanied by profits in excess of the break-even level is determined, in part, by ease of entry into and exit from the sector and the level of sunk costs involved in operating the firm. Traditionally, attention has concentrated on 'innocent' entry and exit barriers determined primarily by technological requirements, principally the scale at which firms can operate efficiently. However, firms may also engage in strategic entry deterrence in an attempt to maintain relatively high prices and supernormal profits over the long run.

Scale and economies of scope

In order to relate economies and diseconomies of scale to models of market structure, it is necessary to look into the economic theory. The essence of economies of scale is that supply costs per unit of production decline as inputs are increased and output expands. Clearly, as long as average unit costs are falling, there is an incentive for a firm to go on enlarging. The point where unit costs start to rise again, i.e. the lowest point on the average cost curve, is where diseconomies set in and the firm would no longer expand. In economic theory the issue is whether diseconomies are reached at a relatively small or large size of firm. The former implies many small firms operating in a highly competitive market, trading at prices which equate with lowest average cost, while the latter suggests the converse.

Thus, in conjunction with the number of firms, their size and the level of barriers to entry, evidence of the extent of economies or diseconomies of scale can indicate market structure (Lyons). In order to establish whether this exist in tourism, it is necessary to look at the cost structures of firms of differing sizes. In some markets, particularly air and sea travel, there are technical reasons which explain why larger aircraft and ships are more efficient, in terms of both operation and maintenance, therefore reducing per unit passenger costs.

Furthermore, there are economies of scale in production through specialization. Increasing size in the accommodation sector also yields some economies of scale with respect to the management, staffing and servicing of a greater number of rooms and in the travel agency sector overhead costs can be spread over additional outlets. Economies of scope occur, where additional products share common inputs. For example, in advertising and marketing new products, suppliers can draw on existing resources. Thus, airlines, bus, coach and ferry companies may add new routes, more fully utilizing the means of conveyance.

Travel agents and tour operators can serve new market segments using existing reservation systems and staff, while in the accommodation sector, the market may be extended via the supply of self-catering in addition to serviced holidays or access to the establishment's facilities by non-residents. To an extent, therefore, opportunities for economies of scope are possible where there are capital indivisibilities or spare capacity. These are considered in the fourth feature of tourism supply examined below.

Evidence of unexploited economies of scale or scope, or potential for them to occur in the future through technical change, would indicate the likelihood of increased firm size and greater market power, and so rendering the less competitive market. Diseconomies of scale, or supply where widely differing input proportions are possible, would enhance the long-term viability of smaller firms and create a structure which is more competitive.

The discussion of tourism supply sectors indicated that although large firms can incur economies of scale and dominates some markets; this does not preclude many small firms from being successful in the same market. The latter can often serve specialized segments which are not susceptible to large-scale operations and some activities remain small scale because the markets are local or national rather than international; enlargement of their activities would generate diseconomies of scale. In general, the principal transport sectors are characterized by the possibilities of economies of scope. It is in the accommodation and intermediary sectors where greater polarization has occurred.

Associated fixed costs of operations

Many tourism sectors utilize capital equipment which is indivisible, aircraft being an obvious example. The firm often possesses a set amount of equipment, and thus fixed capacity over the short run and incurs fixed costs in maintaining it and can be altered only in the long run when re-capitalization occurs. As capital is used, variable costs arise, for example, in the form of fuel and staff costs in the case of air transport. In the short run, economics argues that a firm, even if it does not cover its total costs, should continue to trade as long as it covers its variable costs.

However, in the long run the firm must generate sufficient revenue to cover both its fixed and variable costs, if it is to remain in business. There may also be sunk costs which are not recoverable if the firm leaves the sector and normally relate to indivisible inputs and can affect the contestability of the market as they deter entry into a sector if wholly irrecoverable. For example, if an airline, bus or ferry operator finds a route uneconomic or a hotelier in a particular location finds demand to be lower than the break-even level, each would, ideally, wish to execute a costless withdrawal. This depends on whether assets can easily be redeployed or, through marketing and pricing strategies, market demand increased to fill space capacity.

It is useful to analyze the structure of costs to ascertain both the absolute level of costs and the proportion which is fixed, as opposed to variable. In the airline sector in the early 1990s, International Civil Aviation Organization statistics indicated that fixed costs were high in absolute value and were of the order of two-thirds of the cost of running an airline, if skilled aircrews are taken as a fixed input and aircraft need to be stored and maintained if not operational.

The variable costs are those which would be avoided if the aircraft were withdrawn from service, mainly fuel and landing charges and some on-board consumables and aircrew costs. They account for around one-fifth of the total costs although there is obviously some variability between airlines and routes. For rail systems, the infrastructure and rolling stock create high fixed costs and relatively low variable costs. However bus and coach services are not characterized by high fixed costs but in relative terms, particularly for the smaller operator, they are significant.

In the accommodation sector, the fixed costs as a proportion of total costs are much lower than in the transport field (Horwath Consulting) and the value of fixed costs associated with small accommodation establishments are often low. Capital and recurrent costs related to hotels in the UK account for about one-third of total costs. Overall, with items such as insurance and other capital inputs included, fixed costs are between half and three-fifths of total costs in the UK. Evidence of high fixed costs coupled with fixed capacity in some sectors is indicative of the emergence of large firms which can exploit economies of scale, increasing the degree of concentration.

Operations subject to high fixed capacity and fixed costs require relatively high occupancy rates or load factors in order to meet both fixed and variable costs; the distinction between profits and losses occurs at occupancy rates around such break-even points. Cyclical and seasonal variations in tourism demand exacerbate profits volatility, especially where aggregate fixed capacity is a feature of independent decisions made by many suppliers such as in the accommodation sector. Strategies in the short run are aimed primarily at covering fixed costs, involving attempts to capture trade from rivals whereas in the long run, consideration is given to means of raising demand in order to increase load factors or occupancy rates, particularly in off-peak periods. The characteristic of high sensitivity of profits to occupancy rates and load factors engenders various responses by suppliers.

Product differentiation

The pricing and output policies practiced by tourism firms provide some indication of market structure. A large number of firms producing relatively homogeneous products must be sold at the prevailing price in highly competitive markets approximate to the model of perfect competition. Taxi services in many tourist destinations are a case in point. In imperfectly competitive situations, where firms have a degree of control over the market, pricing and output strategies can be implemented.

There is considerable interdependence in the pricing and output policies of oligopolists as they have to take account of their rivals' actions when determining their own strategy. However, given the appropriate conditions, firms operating under all types of imperfect competition can benefit from price discrimination, which involves targeting specific groups of consumers. Thus, its existence indicates an imperfectly competitive market. Price discrimination is based on the idea that many consumers, who purchase goods and services in markets where a single price prevails, enjoy a welfare gain known as consumer's surplus.

Suppliers who recognize this can discriminate between purchasers and charge higher prices to those with higher reservation prices, and vice versa. There are various degrees of discrimination depending on how many groups of customers can be identified. In the extreme case it is hypothetically possible to exercise perfect, or first degree discrimination where every consumer pays a different price. Firms gain increased profits provided that the price at which additional units are sold is greater than the cost. The most likely situation in which price discrimination can be employed is where different consumers have distinct price elasticity's of demand, permitting the supplier to charge higher prices to those whose demand is inelastic while others, whose demand is more elastic, are charged lower prices. The supplier wishes to divide the total units of the product available between the different groups of consumers so that marginal revenues for each group are equal.

Consumers with an inelastic demand change their demand for the product by only a small proportion in response to a proportionate change in price and their demand. The corresponding additional revenue which the firm receives for each extra unit of the product sold is shown by the marginal revenue curve, MR1. The average and marginal revenue curves for a consumer with more elastic demand are flatter and are given by AR2 =D2a and MR2. The marginal revenue curve for all consumers is indicated by the broken line as MR1 =MR1 +MR2 and is obtained by adding horizontally the marginal revenue gained from each group of consumers. The marginal cost curve, MC, shows the additional cost incurred by the firm for producing each extra unit of production. The total profit-maximizing output occurs where MC = MRT, giving rise to output QT =Q1 +Q2 and a marginal cost MCT. The firm divides its total output between the two groups of consumers, selling a quantity Q1, determined where MR 1 =MC T, at a relatively high price, P1, to consumers with an inelastic demand. A higher quantity, Q2, determined where MR2 =MCT, is sold at a lower price, P2, to consumers with a relatively elastic demand.

In tourism, there are numerous examples of discriminatory pricing and there are price discrimination in air, ferry and train travel and in the accommodation sector. For example, airlines perceive their passengers as falling into three broad groups—first class, club and economy—in which first and club class seats are filled mostly by business travelers. In ferry operations, commercial demand is generally more price inelastic than holiday demand.

For rail travel, the division between commuting and pleasure demand is particularly significant, so that low prices are offered at times of low weekday and weekend demand in an attempt to attract travelers with a relatively high price elasticity of demand, while business people who often need to travel in peak periods are charged relatively high prices. In the accommodation sector, the larger hotels which have spare capacity offer weekend bargain breaks, charging guests with inelastic demand higher prices during the working week. Airlines, bus, coach and ferry companies also follow this practice in the off-season. Market segmentation and product differentiation are also common practices under imperfect competition. Product differentiation can take the form of vertical differentiation between different quality products so that, for example, some tour operators attempt to specialize in providing luxury holidays in expensive locations. It may also involve horizontal differentiation via the supply of a range of product types, such as the provision of holidays for mass market demand as well as for the upper segment of the market, young people, elderly people and a wide range of special interest groups.

The strategy of branding aims to raise consumer awareness of and demand for particular product types and advertising performs a similar function. Few smaller firms have either the capacity, or the market power to exercise significant control over prices so that serving a specific segment or differentiating their product is the only option open to them. Their concern is often to create rather than extend a market. Effectively they look for an unfilled niche and attempt to meet a specific demand in what may be a relatively small market segment. To this extent the product is automatically differentiated. It is large firms, enjoying economies of scale and scope and spare capacity, which attempt to differentiate their products through branding in addition to engaging in price discrimination. In the accommodation sector many inter national hotels serve the top end of the market, very often for business travelers, while budget hotels, for example Travelodge and Budget, cater for families. In some cases, such as the Accor group, both markets are targeted under different brand names.

Pricing Policies

Pricing strategies are central to oligopoly and may be used in attempts to maintain or increase market share or to eliminate excess capacity. The strategies of Laker Air in the 1970s and Virgin in the 1990s are prime examples and the advent of deregulation has engendered further price competition among airlines on key routes. As the economics of oligopoly predicts, price-cutting by one airline provokes a response from others. This occurred in the case of Trans World Airline (TWA) when it cut fares within the United States in 1991. The matching of these fare cuts by rivals with a lower operating cost base partially explains the airline's bankruptcy. The air transport sector also contains small airlines which are relatively efficient over particular routes. Thus, British West Indian Airlines (BWIA) is cost-effective on a number of Caribbean routes and British Midland is able to compete on domestic and European inter-city routes despite the domination of the market by British Airways.

Price-cutting has also occurred within other transport sectors, such as bus, coach and ferry services. In the first it is very much the outcome of deregulation, while on heavily used routes in the last, although there is intra-sectoral competition between companies, the price 'war' has been driven more by inter-sectoral competition. A feature of some interest is that many air, bus and coach sectors have experienced significant volatility because of structural changes which have destabilized trading conditions and prices. Ferry services are in a slightly different position because the entry of new companies is uncommon and there has often been tacit or overt collusion between the main ferry companies, giving reasonable stability in fares. This was also the case prior to deregulation in air travel where air fares were more formally controlled by IATA, resulting in a virtual cartel. In the accommodation sector, price wars have been less evident because there is greater separation of establishments in the market in terms of type, quality and location. Where establishments are clustered, such as the larger hotels in holiday resorts, near airports or in city centres, there may be implicit price-fixing because operators have easy access to information on competitor's charges and can set their own prices accordingly.

The almost classic demonstration of the oligopoly case in tourism supply is package market tour operations. Here price leadership and wars and attempts to increase market share by the larger players are strategies which have been adopted since the advent of mass tourism in the 1960s. The evidence for the UK, including an historical review, can be found in N. Evans and Stabler, following the studies of competitive structure and strategies by Sheldon and Fitch. Evans and Stabler suggest that structural changes are occurring, such as the entrance of corporate tour operators, often part of a conglomerate, which emphasize the gaining of profits rather than market share. There are also discernible trends in demand towards more specialized holidays. The mass package market is dominated by the top tier of approximately ten tour operators, who have increasingly diversified into specialized types of holidays to exploit economies of scope. At the other end of the firm size spectrum are small specialist operators which can survive through niche marketing, although there has been a high birth and death rate of companies. It is the second tier of thirty, the firms which has lost part of its share of the mass market to the top ten operators and the more specialized segments to the smaller firms.

Price leadership and pursuit of increased market share is predominantly undertaken by large groups through longer-term strategies such as mergers or takeovers. Increased integration between firms appears to be a logical outcome of tourism markets where, there is a long chain of supply. Large tour operators in the UK are vertically integrated, particularly with travel agencies and airlines, while in the USA there are strong linkages between travel agencies, the accommodation sector and transport modes, with the initiator tending to be the transport company. The relevance of integration to competitive structure is that, its existence suggests information advantages, cost savings and higher profits affected by enlargement of the firm and the possibilities of increased market power, associated with oligopoly and even duopoly or monopoly. At an international level, integration has ramifications much wider than those appertaining to the suppliers and tourists themselves, particularly in developing countries.

The outlines of the structure of the accommodation, intermediary and transport sectors and the discussions of their key features reveal that market structures can be quite heterogeneous within each sector. They possess such characteristics as a wide range of competitive forms, market segmentation, product differentiation, high rates of entry and exit, some scale economies and significant variations in the degree of regulation. In the intermediary sector, there appear to be considerable changes in the structure of tourism supply in terms of the number of firms, their size and market share. These characteristics raise two questions. First, how far does the neoclassical theory of the firm and the competitive structures it has identified explain what is observed in tourism supply? Second, does heterogeneity within a specific sector suggest that the theory of the firm is inadequate or does it merely signify that the categorization of tourism sectors and markets adopted currently is too broad? As regard to the first question, the test of the appropriateness of the theoretical concepts is whether they can explain actual market structures, and predict the outcome of changes occurring in the industry or its markets.

It appears that in each of the three main sectors considered, there are elements of contestability, alongside the dominant market forms of monopolistic competition and oligopoly. This contestability aspect is not easily encompassed within the conventional theory of the firm because its static equilibrium analytical framework is not well suited to accommodating what is effectively a dynamic situation. Thus, while it is possible to explain the conditions of tourism supply sectors as being indicative of particular theoretical competitive structures, it is more difficult to predict the outcome of changes in the conditions. In the transport sector for instance, the possibilities of exploiting economies of scale should give rise to increasing concentration and few firms, therefore denoting an oligopolistic structure, as appears to be the case in the air, bus, coach and ferry sectors. Furthermore, the theory would indicate reasonably stable prices, given the constraints which individual firms face in raising or lowering them because of possible reactions by rivals. Deregulation has effectively reduced entry barriers which have an impact running counter to that of economies of scale. It has created greater volatility in prices and led to an influx of smaller companies and greater competition in the short run.

Although, after initially successful trading, there are signs of a decline in the number of firms because of failures by new entrants, particularly in the bus and coach sector. Thus, the predictive power of conventional theory is called into question. In the intermediary sector, particularly tour operations, increasing concentration is occurring in what conventional theory would posit to be a highly competitive market because of low entry-exit barriers and limited economies of scale. Paradoxically, the largest tour operators in what might be termed the oligopolistic segment of the UK holiday market have been engaged in fierce price competition and, over many years, margins and profits have been low or even losses sustained. Conversely, the many smaller specialized tour operators have avoided such competitive conditions. A similar scenario applies in the UK travel agency sector. The long-running pursuit of increased market share in the intermediary sector appears to be at odds with theory which assumes profit-maximizing behavior. The second question as to the observed competitive heterogeneity of most tourism supply sectors, and the relation to the theory of the firm is problematic.

Analysis within the conventional framework tends to compartmentalize markets into clearly defined competitive structures, seldom acknowledging that sub-markets may be subject to different conditions. Does this matter? Is the theory undermined by recognition that in particular markets different competitive forms coexist? The response by mainstream economists might be that the various segments should be treated as separate markets. This may not be appropriate since there is an interrelationship between the differing competitive segments within a single sector. For instance the largest firms within the transport sector do react to the behavior of smaller and newer rivals. Accordingly, the further sub-division of tourism markets to meet traditional analytical requirements may not be appropriate.

The illustrative examples indicate the limitations of its explanatory and predictive power, in the context of tourism supply while acknowledging that a full exploration of the applicability of the theory of the firm has not been undertaken. The theory aids identification of the key variables determining individual firm's and industries behavior within each of the competitive forms and it acts as a rigorous foundation on which to develop more complex and differentiated models. Increasingly, the economic analysis of industry is recognizing the role of institutional structures and their possible evolution, together with the need to examine the dynamic nature of markets where information availability uncertainty and transaction costs are significant. Attention, therefore, is now turned to a more industrial economics-oriented perspective where a number of features of tourism supply, perceived as important to its structure and operation, are identified and examined.

References

1. Towards a Political Economy of Tourism: Allan M. Williams (University of Exeter).
2. The Cultural Turn, Towards a More Critical Economic Geography of Tourism: Keith G. Debbage and Dimitri Ioannides (University of North Carolina at Greensboro; Southwest Missouri State University).
3. Entrepreneurial Cultures and Small Business Enterprises in Tourism: Gareth Shaw (University of Exeter).
4. Sustainability Profitability and Successful Tourism, 2 Vols. / Raj, Aparna.
5. *Rural Tourism and Sustainable Rural Development: Proceedings of the Second International School on Rural Development*, Bramwell, Bill, and Bernard Lane, eds. 1994. 28 June-9 July 1993, University College, Galway, Ireland. Clevedon, U.K: Channel View Publications.
6. "Toward a Definition of Sustainable Development in the Yampa Valley of Colorado,"Culbertson, K., D. Turner, and J. Kolberg. 1993. *Mountain Research and Development*, Vol. 13, No. 4: pp. 359-369.

10

Tourism Destinations and Tour Packages

Tourist Attraction

The place of interest and enjoyment where tourists visit is called a tourist attraction. Historical places, monuments, zoological garden, museums, art galleries, botanical gardens, buildings and structures, national parks and forests are some examples of Tourist attraction. A tourist attraction is one of the main sources to capitalize an economy. Some examples of Ethnic communities becoming tourist attractions are Chinatowns, the Vietnamese community of Little Saigon in southern California in the United States and the black British neighborhood of Brixton borough of London. Especially in remote areas and along the side of highways and roadways, owners and marketers of tourist attractions usually advertise on billboards. Some tourist attractions have free promotional booklets and flyers in information centres, fast food restaurants, and hotels. Some owners of tourist attractions provide visitors, a very low and reasonable rental charge in order to catch up more customers and to gain hugely. Such places are commonly known as tourist traps.

Package Holiday

A package holiday comprises of transport and accommodation publicized and marketed by a tour operator. Some other accessories may be provided like a rental car, swimming pool, amusement activities etc. Package holidays are organized by a tour operator and sold to a consumer by a travel agent. Some travel agents are owned by tour operators, others are independent private firms.

Organised tours

The first ever organized tours dated back to 5 July 1841. Thomas Cook hired a train to take a group of campaigners from Leicester to a rally in Loughborough, twenty miles away. Thomas Cook - the company - grew to become one of the largest and most well known travel agents before being nationalised in 1948. With the gradual decline of visits to British seaside resorts after the Second World War, Thomas Cook began promoting foreign holidays (particularly Italy, Spain and Switzerland) in the early 1950s. Information films were shown at town halls throughout Britain. However they made a costly decision by not going into the new form of cheap holidays which combined the transport and accommodation arrangements into a single 'package'. The company run down and was only liberated by a take over on 26 May 1972.

Package Tours

Vladimir Raitz initiated the first mass package holidays abroad with charter flights between Gatwick airport and Corsica in 1950, and organised the first package holiday to Palma in 1952, Lourdes in 1953, and the Costa Brava and Sardinia in 1954. In addition, the amendments made in Montreal to the Convention on International Civil Aviation on June 14, 1954 were very liberal to Spain, giving a momentum for mass tourism by means of charter planes. During the late 1950s and 1960s, these low-priced package holidays, which included flight, transfers and accommodation, provided the first chance for most people in the United Kingdom to afford a travel abroad. Despite opening up mass tourism to Crete and the Algarve in 1970, the package tour industry declined during the 1970s. On 15 August 1974, the industry was shaken when the second-largest tour operator, Court Line which operated under the brand names of Horizon and Clarksons, collapsed. Nearly 50,000 tourists were stranded overseas and a further 100,000 faced the loss of booking deposits. As a new trend, recently many travelers are traveling with budget airlines and booking their own accommodation, avoiding package holidays. In the UK, the downturn in the package holiday market led to the consolidation of the tour operator market, which is now dominated by a few large tour operators. The major operators are Thomson Holidays, part of the TUI AG, Thomas Cook AG, My Travel, and First Choice. There exists a whole range of different holiday operators catering to different markets, such as Club 18-30 or Simply Travel, under these umbrella brands.

Passport

A passport is a must to carry while going abroad. It identifies the bearer's nationality of the person Passports are linked with the right of legal protection abroad and the right to enter one's country of nationality. Passports usually contain the holder's photograph, signature, date of birth, nationality, and sometimes other means of individual identification. Many countries are in the process of developing biometric properties for their passports in order to further confirm that the person presenting the passport is the legitimate possessor.

Types

There are many types of passport viz., Ordinary Passports, Diplomatic Passports, Official or Service Passports, Alien's passports, collective passport, Internal passports, Emergency or Temporary Passports, Business Passports, Laisser Passer,Family Passports.

- Ordinary Passports are the normal passports issued to most citizens and have no special connotations.
- Diplomatic Passports are issued to Diplomats and diplomatic representatives of a home country, or can be issued for any state employees who serve on long-term (resident) duty, and in other cases official passport holders may be granted visa-free entry, while normal passport holders are required to get a visa.
- Official or Service Passports are issued to employees of a government traveling for work related reasons that either do not qualify as Diplomats or are not entitled to Diplomatic Status under the Vienna Convention.
- Alien's passports are documents issued by some countries to non-citizen residents.
- Collective passport may be issued, for example, for a study tour or a school trip. All children on the trip would be covered by the group passport for the duration of the trip.
- Internal passports have been issued by some countries, as a means of controlling the movement of the population. Examples include the Soviet internal passport system and the hukou residency registration system used in the People's Republic of China.
- Emergency or Temporary Passports are issued to persons whose original passport has been lost or stolen and who need to urgently travel.
- Business Passports are passports with extra pages issued to frequent travellers.
- Laisser Passer are the documents issued by organizations

such as the United Nations for their officials.

- Family Passports are passports that are not issued to individuals but to family units (parents and children).

Standards

In the past, there were no approved identities or standards for passports for the reason that they were not generally required for traveling abroad until the First World War. After the war the League of Nations Paris Conference on Passports & Customs Formalities and Through Tickets (1920) agreed the first set of standards that were expected of all passports issued by members of the League. The establishment of the International Civil Aviation Organisation (ICAO) in 1947 with 188 contracting states saw the conscientiousness for setting passport standards fall to that authority. Now, Passports have a standardized format with a serial number by the issuing authority. The cover of the passport identifies the issuing country, and then has a title page also naming the country. This is usually followed by pages giving information about the bearer and the issuing authority, (while some European Union member state passports provide this information on the inside back cover of the document).

Then, a number of blank pages are given for foreign countries to affix visas, or stamp the passport on entrance or exit. It is common for a passport to have a note, usually near the front of the booklet requesting and requiring help for its holder. Passports used to carry information (Surname, given names, date of birth, place of birth, nationality etc. In recent years, however, passports issued by many countries have become more complex due to the rise of terrorist activities in many parts of the world (especially in Muslim dominated areas.)

- Machine-readable passports are the standardized world-wide standard by the International Civil Aviation Organization (ICAO). They bear a zone where some of the information otherwise written in textual form is written as strings of alphanumeric characters, printed in a manner suitable for optical character recognition. This enables border controllers and other law enforcement agents to process such passports quickly, without having to input the information manually into a computer.
- Biometric passports with RFID chips will carry supplemental information about the bearer, in a digitized form. These passports have already been introduced many years ago in Malaysia and more recently in Australia, New Zealand, Japan,

Sweden, United Kingdom, the United States, Germany, the Republic of Ireland and Poland. These new passports were primarily introduced to prevent identity fraud. When technology improves, the embedded chips may also allow rapid clearance through immigration controls with quicker confirmation of identity. Facial Maps are popular for use in Biometric passports as the data (the distances between key facial features) can be gathered from the holder's passport photo without any other information. The irony is that although many countries now have biometric passports very few have introduced the equipment to read them at ports of entry and in the absence of an international standard it is not currently possible for one country to read the biometric information of another one.

Languages

In the year 1920, the International Conference on Passports, Customs Formalities and Through Tickets mandated that passports be issued in French and at least one other language. Now, many countries issue passports in English and the language of the issuing country.

- Belgium allows its citizens to choose which of its three official languages (Dutch, French, or German) should appear first in the individual's passport.
- The face page of the Hungarian passports ("Útlevél" in Hungarian, lit. "Roadletter") is in Hungarian only, though on the inside there is a second, Hungarian-English bilingual page mentioning "Passport" as well. The personal information page offers Hungarian, English and French explanation for the details. An additional page including the explanations in English, French, Chinese, Russian, Spanish and Arabic has been added in recent years.
- Passports issued by European Union member states bear all of the official languages of the European Union. These are not printed in each location, however. A number of languages (2 or 3) will be printed in the relevant point, followed by a number, which is used as a reference for a page on the passport dedicated to translations into all the remaining languages.
- United States passports, once issued in English and French only, are now issued in English, French, and Spanish since the second Clinton administration, due to the fact that they

are used in Spanish-speaking Puerto Rico.

- Soviet internal passports were only printed in Russian and the language of Republic of the USSR; foreign passports were printed bilingual Russian and English, though they used French transliteration for names. The same situation exists in the present-day Russia except that in the newest version of the passports, names are no-longer transliterated according to the French method.

Common designs

The member states of the European Union (EU) have a common format for their passports. EU member state passports have identical layouts and designs, although the photo page can be at the front or in the back of the booklet and small differences in design indicate which member state is the issuer. Ordinary EU member state passports are burgundy-red, with the words "European Union" written in the national language or languages (e.g. Dutch, French, Finnish, Maltese) on the front, below which is the official name of the country, the national seal, and the word for "passport", in the respective language(s), can be found at the bottom. Malta was the first country of the new EU states from Central Europe and the Mediterranean to issue EU format passports. Estonia and Slovakia began issuing EU format passports in 2005. Slovenia and Poland started issuing biometric EU format passports in 2006.

In Central America, the members of the CA-4 Treaty have adopted a common accepted design passport, also called the 'Central American Passport'. Although the design has been in use by Nicaragua and El Salvador since the mid-1990, it will be the norm for the CA-4 area effective January 2006. The main features are its navy blue cover with the words "America Central" and a map of Central America with the territory of the issuing country highlighted in gold. This effectively replaces the national seals of the different countries with one single element, the map. At the bottom of the cover, the name of the issuing country and the passport type is shown. Since 2006, the Nicaraguan passport is issued in Spanish, French and English. The passport has 89 security features, including bi-dimensional barcodes, unique holograms and watermarks, ranking it as one of the most secure passport models.

Recently, the Caribbean Community (CARICOM) started issuing passports to a common design, featuring CARICOM's symbol along with the national seal and official name of the member state in its official languages (i.e. English, French, and Dutch). The first member state to issue CARICOM passports was Suriname, and currently four other member states use the common design: St. Kitts and Nevis, Dominica, St. Vincent and the Grenadines and Antigua and Barbuda. These five countries are to be followed by the other countries in CARICOM. The declaration adopted in Cusco (Peru), establishing the South American Community of Nations gestured objective to adopt a common passport design. Already, some member states of regional sub-groupings such as Mercosur and the Andean Community of Nations issue passports that bear their official name and seal along with the name of their regional grouping. Examples include Paraguay and Ecuador. Member states of the Andean Community of Nations have agreed to phase in new Andean passports bearing the official name of the regional body in Spanish by January 2005, although previously issued national passports will be valid until their expiration.

Government Restrictions and Special Cases

There are many exceptions in recognizing the passports of different countries. Generally these exceptions are due to circumstances where one country does not recognize another territory's administration as a sovereign state. Some countries also decline to accept passports that do not afford the bearer the right to live in the issuing country. Most countries make its policy not to accept passports issued by authorities they do not recognize. Standing exceptions include passports issued by the Hong Kong and Macau Special Administrative Regions of China. In Brazil, citizens of such countries must apply for a Brazilian laissez-passer.

Passports are the property of the state. The state has the right to withdraw the passport at any point of time without producing any reason. In some countries the executive authorities may declare a passport void, although such cases may be subject to judicial review; judicial decision may be needed for other countries. For example, usually a person on bail must temporarily surrender their passport while awaiting trial if they pose a flight risk. It is common that most countries issue only one passport per head. Once the passport expires, the holder must surrender the expired passport, or have the issuing authority punch holes through the passport to invalidate it. Exceptionally, in growing countries like the United Kingdom and the United States, citizens are allowed to use more than one passport per head because it may be useful for a person who travels frequently to many countries while one passport is used to obtain a visa, the person may travel abroad with another passport. Some countries issue passports and exit visas only to those who meet particular political and ideological requirements.

China (PRC and ROC) and colonial passports in Hong Kong and Macau

Hong Kong and Macau SARs have the authority to issue passports, to contract agreements, to abolish visa requirements with other countries, and to exercise immigration control on foreign nationals under the auspices of their Basic Laws. Passports issued by the respective SAR government states that the bearer is a Chinese national with a right of abode in the issuing SAR. The National People's Congress has also delegated powers to the Hong Kong and Macau governments to administer Chinese nationality laws in their respective regions. The Republic of China (ROC) is not recognized by the PRC as a sovereign state and considers Taiwan a part of its territory. The ROC based in Taiwan since 1949 has not renounced claims to mainland China. Despite presence of mutual immigration control, neither side of the Taiwan Strait considers travelling to and from the mainland and Taiwan international travel. The PRC and the ROC never stamp passports issued from the other side.

If a Taiwan citizen wants to enter into the mainland of China, he or she needs a special permit issued by mainland public security authorities and usually collects this permit in Hong Kong or Macau, which must usually be used as a point of transfer. The ROC government once required all Taiwan residents who planned to go to mainland China to obtain official approval beforehand. However, often unable to ascertain if someone has broken this rule as the PRC would never stamp ROC passports, the authorities practically could not enforce the requirement except on those who had lost their travel documents in the mainland. Except for officials of the administration, it has been completely abolished.

The Public Security Bureau of the Guangdong province has been issuing a special permit (dubbed Home Return Permit) for Hong Kong residents who are Chinese nationals to enter and exit the mainland before and after the handover. Although it has been proposed that the HKSAR passport should supplant this permit, the proposal has been dismissed. While many Chinese hold British National (Overseas) passports (and British citizen passports issued under the auspices of a programme instituted by the UK in 1990), the PRC Government considers them its nationals, and does not recognise these passports they hold while the PRC does not recognize dual nationality. Since past, these people have been using the Home Return Permit to enter mainland China. Although a Hong Kong resident may not use British National (Overseas) or HKSAR passports in its own right for entering Taiwan, these passports must be used in conjunction with a special travel permit issued by Taiwan's administration. First-time travelers must apply beforehand but most other travelers can collect this permit upon arrival, subject to certain restrictions. British Citizen passports obtained in Hong Kong can be used in its own right to enter the Republic of China on Taiwan. On the other hand, Taiwan residents traveling to Hong Kong apply for entry permits and collect them at specified airlines. Repeated travelers satisfying certain conditions may apply online.

Cyprus

The (TRNC), Turkish Republic of Northern Cyprus hands out passports, but only Turkey recognizes the statehood of Northern Cyprus. TRNC passports are not accepted for entry into the Republic of Cyprus. Until 2003, the Republic of Turkey did not accept passports of the Republic of Cyprus, because it did not recognize that government. Turkey now accepts Republic of Cyprus passports, but does not stamp them; rather, Turkish immigration officials stamp a separate visa issued by the Turkish state.The Republic of Cyprus also refuses entry to holders of Yugoslavian passports "bearing a renewal stamp with the name 'Macedonia'.

Israel

Several Arab and Muslim countries restricts entries to people with evidence of visits to Israel or used or unused Israeli visas in their passports, since the existence of the state of Israel is not recognized by these countries. To help foreigners circumvent these restrictions, Israel does not require visitors to have their passports stamped upon entry or advanced visas, making it difficult for those countries to tell if a citizen or tourist went there. Many of these nations are aware of the exit stamps placed in passports by Egypt and Jordan at their land borders with Israel and may obstruct entry based on these stamps. For instance, a traveler may be denied entry to certain countries because of the presence of an Egyptian exit stamp indicating the person left Egypt at Taba, at the Israeli border. Some nations will void old passports and reissue new passports to their nationals based on the presence of evidence of a visit to Israel, recognizing the passport's function is compromised. The United

Kingdom and the United States Department of State may allow a passport holder to have two valid passports to circumvent the restrictions concerning Israel if the applicant can agreeably explain the reason for his need of second passport, while applying.

The Arab and Muslim countries that do not accept Israeli passports are Afghanistan, Algeria, Bangladesh, Comoros, Djibouti, Indonesia, Iran, Iraq, Kuwait, Lebanon, Libya, Malaysia (except with written permission from the Malaysian government), Maldives, Oman, Pakistan, Qatar, Saudi Arabia, Somalia, Sudan, Syria, Tunisia, United Arab Emirates, and Yemen. The Muslim countries that accept Israeli passports include Bahrain, Egypt, Jordan, Mauritania, Morocco, Turkey, and former Soviet republics with Muslim majority: Azerbaijan, Kazakhstan, Kyrgyzstan, Tajikistan, Turkmenistan and Uzbekistan. And the only non-Arab and non-Muslim countries that do not accept Israeli passports are Cuba and North Korea due to these nations' enduring alliance with the Palestine Liberation Organization.

Koreas

The Republic of Korea's constitution considers the North as part of its territory, although under different administration. In other words, the South does not view going to and from as breaking the continuity of a person's stay, as long as the traveler does not land on a third territory. The privilege of a passport in North Korea is limited to a select few. Membership of the Korean Workers' Party is essentially a requisite.

Pakistan

The Government of Pakistan imposes three requirements on its Muslim citizens when they apply for a passport, requiring them to agree to the following:

(1) I am a Muslim and believe in the absolute and unqualified finality of the Prophethood of Hazrat Muhammad (peace be upon him) the last of the Prophets.

(2) I do not recognize any who claims to be a prophet in any sense of the word or any description whatsoever, after Hazrat Muhammad (peace be upon him) or recognize such a claimant as a prophet or a religious reformer as Muslim.

(3) I consider Mirza Ghulam Ahmad Qadiani to be an impostor nabi and also consider his followers whether belonging to the Lahori, Qadiani or Mirzai groups, to be non-Muslims.

The above declaration would have been made unnecessary with the issuance of the new biometric passport in 2005. However, this decision was recently reversed by the Pakistan Government on religious parties' resistance. After much debate, the column has come back. New passports will carry religion columns on Page 3; passports already printed will bear a rubber stamp mark declaring the holder's religion.

Saudi Arabia

The Government of Saudi Arabia does not officially recognize dual nationality for its citizens. Citizens who have dual nationality generally keep this confidential when in Saudi Arabia. If a second passport is discovered, it will be confiscated and the bearer may be arrested.

Spain and Gibraltar

The Government of Spain does not accept British passports issued in Gibraltar, on the reason that the territory's government is not authorized for issuing such documents. Consequently some Gibraltarians have been refused entry to Spain when traveling on these documents. However, the word "Gibraltar" now appears beneath the words "United Kingdom of Great Britain and Northern Ireland", as appears in passports of other British colonies and dependencies.

Tonga

Some countries decline to accept Tongan Protected Person passports, though they do accept standard passports issued to Tongan citizens.

Republic of Ireland and Northern Ireland

The Citizenship of the Republic of Ireland is entitled to only those who are born in the island of Ireland (from 2005 all those with parents legally resident) regardless of what side of border with Northern Ireland (which is a part of the United Kingdom). This was due to the Irish state's territorial claim to Northern Ireland and the situation was formalized by the Good Friday Agreement in 1998 with the United Kingdom government and the political parties in Northern Ireland.

Irish Citizenship can be claimed by grandchildren of Irish born people, meaning approximately 5 million people in Britain can obtain Irish passports. In the Republic of Ireland a significant number are entitled to UK passports. Those born before 6 December 1922 were born when Ireland was in the UK (their children can also claim UK passports). Furthermore those born before 1949 can also obtain UK passports as British subjects.

International Travel Without Passports

According to some circumstances, travel between countries may be done without showing a passport. These include:

Reciprocal Agreements

Some countries have a reciprocal agreement such that a visa is not needed under certain conditions, e.g. when the visit is for tourism and for a relatively short period. A few countries have agreements allowing for cross-border travel without passports (but generally with identification). Examples include :

- The United Kingdom and the Republic of Ireland: Citizens of the UK and Ireland do not require a passport to travel between the two countries. Other EEA nationals must show a national ID card or Passport. All other nationals require a passport. Many nationals also require visas for both countries.
- The CA-4 countries: Citizens of Guatemala, El Salvador, Honduras, and Nicaragua do not require a passport to travel between any of the four countries. A National ID card (Cédula) is sufficient for entry. In addition, the CA-4 agreement implemented the Central American Single Visa (Visa Única Centroamericana) for citizens of all other countries, eliminating the need for separate entry visas for each of the countries. Persons entering the region on Type "B" visas can enter the area through any Port of Entry. Persons entering on Type "C" visas (issued through prior consultation with the Ministry of Foreign Affairs) must enter through a Port of Entry in the country that issued the visa. Once a person has been admitted, they may travel onto any of the other countries and are allowed to stay through the date authorized at the original Port of Entry.
- The NAFTA countries: the United States, Canada, and Mexico, although after an announcement on September 02, 2005 (Western Hemisphere Travel Initiative), all persons entering the United States, including U.S. citizens, will be required to have a passport, even from Canada and Mexico, starting January 8, 2007 for air and sea travel. On December 31, 2007, the passport requirement will also be extended to all land border crossings.

In response to this, the Canadian Government stated that, very soon U.S. citizens will be required to have a passport to enter Canada. A passport is not generally required to enter Mexico. As of December 31, 2007 (January 8, 2007 for air or sea travel), citizens of the United States will not need a passport to enter into Mexico, but will be required to show their passport when leaving Mexico and re-entering the United States.

- Since 1952, the Nordic countries, Denmark, Finland, Iceland, Norway and Sweden, including Faroe Islands and Greenland. (Called the Nordic Passport Union, this area joined the larger Schengen treaty region in 1997.)
- Lebanese citizens entering Syria do not require a passport if carrying their Lebanese IDs. Similarly, Syrian nationals do not require a passport to enter Lebanon either, if carrying their Syrian IDs.
- Indian, Nepalese and Bhutanese citizens do not require a passport to travel between the three countries. However some identification is needed to cross the borders.
- Croatia does not require a passport for citizens of Bosnia and Herzegovina who have a Bosnian ID card. Likewise Bosnia and Herzegovina, Italy, Slovenia and Hungary do not require Croatian citizens to have a passport, only a Croatian ID.
- Serbia does not require a passport for citizens of Bosnia and Herzegovina who have a Bosnian ID card. Likewise Bosnia and Herzegovina does not require Serbian citizens to have a passport, only a Serbian ID.
- Russia and some former Soviet Union Republics: the participating countries may only require the equivalent of the national ID card (which is called Internal passport, as opposed to an "international" passport that a former Soviet citizen would be required to produce to enter other foreign countries.

Latin American nationals can freely travel within their respective regional economic zones, such as Mercosur (Argentina, Brazil, Paraguay, Uruguay and Venezuela) and the Andean Community of Nations (Bolivia, Peru, Ecuador, Colombia, Venezuela) or on a bilateral basis (e.g. between Chile and Peru) without passports, presenting instead their national identification cards or voter registration cards for a limited period. Often, this travel must be done overland rather than by air. There are plans to extend these rights to all of South America under the new South American Community of Nations.

- Turkey does not require a passport for citizens of Greece that hold a new ID card (the one including the bearer's details in both the Greek and the Latin alphabets.) Greece still requires a Schengen visa for Turkish nationals to enter Greece.

EU, EEA, and the Schengen treaty

The citizens of the European Economic Area are free to travel and work in any European Union country without a VISA, although transitory dispositions may restrict the rights of citizens of new members to work in other countries. The same rights are also accorded to citizens of Switzerland although they remain separate from the EEA. Furthermore, countries that have signed and applied the Schengen treaty (a subset of the EEA) do not implement passport controls between each other. The Schengen Treaty does not affect the Customs controls. Most of the balance of EU countries, plus Switzerland, have signed the Schengen treaty, but not applied it yet. The main reason is, that, according to EU laws, the member states which had joined the EU in 2004 would have to meet strict criteria with respect to their efforts protect EU external borders before intra-EU border controls between the old member states and such new member states may be lifted. To adopt national databases to those of the EU, Switzerland requires some time.

Refugees and stateless persons

Those persons who do not hold National Passports may be issued a Travel Document by the Country in which they live. Holders of these documents generally require visas for international travel and will not be entitled to Consular Protection in the event that they run into trouble while traveling. Exceptions to this include persons holding 1951 Convention Documents who may benefit from some visa free travel as a result of the convention and those persons who reside within the areas of a passport union such as the Schengen system or the Nordic Passport Union. Holders of UK and Irish Travel Documents do not, however, benefit from visa free travel within the Common Travel Area.

The Vatican

The Vatican has no monitoring cell nor strict control over immigration, as the only entrance to the tiny country is overland from Italy, the de-facto immigration requirements of the Vatican are the same as those of Italy. However, having crossed the border into the Vatican, visitors are subject to Vatican law, not Italian; the Vatican retains its authority as a separate state. The Vatican, however, does issue its own passports to certain Vatican officials born in foreign countries who need to be permanently based at the Vatican or in other Vatican offices. The pope is always given the privilege of 'Passport No.1', which is reissued with the same number for every successive pontiff.

The British Monarch

As British passports are issued in her name, the British monarch does not have a passport. In Commonwealth countries, where the

British monarch is also the head of state, passports are issued in the name of the Governor General of that state, except in Canada where passports are issued on behald of the Minister of Foreign Affairs.

Immigration stamps in passports

Immigration stamps are usually placed in passports while crossing the border by the Immigration authorities as part of monitoring and controlling immigration. This endorsement can serve many different purposes. In the United Kingdom the immigration stamp in the passport includes the formal "leave to enter" granted to a person subject to control when they enter the country. Alternatively the stamp activates and acknowledges the continuing leave conferred in the individual's entry clearance. Other authorities, such as the Schengen system, simply stamp a passport with a date stamp that does not indicate any duration and this stamp is taken to mean either that the person is deemed to have permission to remain for 3 months or an alternative period as shown on their visa. In both the cases, it is not allowed to stamp the passports of persons not subject to Immigration Control, for example citizens of that country (or other EU nationals within the European Union).

This is because the stamping of the passport imposes a control that the person is not subject to. This does not apply in other countries where the stamp in a passport simply acknowledges the entry and exit of a person - for example in Australia, Russia or China. Most countries have different stamps for arrivals and departures to make it easier for officers to quickly identify the movements of the person concerned.

Camouflage passports

A camouflage passport is a kind of passport which is issued in the name of a non-existent country. It is manufactured by private businesses and sold openly, usually by mail order or over the internet. These are marketed to security-conscious international travelers and tacitly as novelties. The motive or purpose is to allow a person to conceal their nationality in event of a terrorist hijacking, riot or some similar situation where their identity may single him out as a crime victim. To this end, the passports are also often sold with a package of matching documents, including an international driver's license and similar supporting identity papers. As of 2006, prices tend to range between $400 and $1000. These passports are not regarded to be counterfeit documents because they are not purporting to be internationally recognized passports. Nevertheless, some national authorities have expressed concern over the use of camouflage passports in criminal activities, e.g. taking advantage of under trained personnel to open a fraudulent bank account.

Travel Documents for Tourists

Travel documents usually assure other governments that the bearer or bearers may return to the issuing country and are issued in booklet form to allow other governments to place visas as well as entry and exit stamps in them. One of the most common travel documents is a passport, which usually identifies the bearer as a citizen or national of the issuing country.

Types of Travel Documents

- 1951 Convention travel documents are passport-like booklets issued by national governments to refugees under the 1951 Convention relating to the Status of Refugees.
- 1954 Convention travel documents are similar documents issued to stateless persons under the 1954 Convention Relating to the Status of Stateless Persons.
- Alien's passports and certificates of identity are passport-like booklets issued by national governments to resident foreigners, other than those issued under the 1951 and 1954 conventions mentioned above. However, some governments issue certificates of identity to their own nationals as emergency passports.
- Laissez-passers are issued by national governments and international treaty organizations for various purposes.

International Travel Documents

Visa

A visa is a document issued by a country giving a certain individual permission to formally request entrance to the country during a given period of time and for certain purposes. As a legal condition of entry for foreigners, most countries require possession of a VISA. Visas are typically stamped or attached into the recipient's passport, or are sometimes issued as separate pieces of paper. Visas are associated with the request for permission to enter (or exit) a country, and are thus, for some countries, distinct from actual formal permission for an alien to enter and remain in the country. While in the European Schengen area, a visa constitutes the formal permission to enter, according to the conditions; in other cases a visa does not guarantee admission into the country for which the alien has the visa. This formal permission is typically granted by stamping the visa and, in some cases, by providing an additional document as proof of status, such as the United States' I-94. The common phrase "he has to leave because his visa has expired" is thus, strictly speaking.

Some countries, such as some states of the former Soviet Union, require that their citizens, and sometimes foreign travelers, obtain an exit visa in order to be allowed to leave the country. Until 2004, foreign students in Russia were issued only an entry visa on being accepted to University there, and had to obtain an exit visa to return home. This policy has since been changed, and foreign students are now issued multiple entry (and exit) visas. Citizens of the People's Republic of China who are residents of the mainland are required to apply for special permits in order to enter the Special Administrative Regions of Hong Kong and Macao (and SAR residents require a Home Return Permit to visit the mainland).

Conditions of issue

Some visas can be allotted on arrival, usually only to citizens of countries enjoying good relations with the issuing country, or by prior application at the country's embassy or consulate, or sometimes a specialized travel agency with permission from the issuing country. If there is no embassy or consulate in one's home country, then one would have to travel to a third country (or apply by post) and try to get a visa issued there. The need or absence of need of a visa generally depends on the citizenship of the applicant, the intended duration of the stay, and the activities that the applicant may wish to undertake in the country he visits; these may delineate different formal categories of visas, with different issue conditions.

Some countries have reciprocal visa regimes, for instance, if Country A requires citizens of Country B to have a visa to travel there, then Country B may apply reciprocity and require a visa from citizens of Country A. Likewise, if A allows B's citizens to enter without a visa, B may allow A's citizens to enter without a visa.

Examples of such reciprocal visa regimes are between:

- Algeria and Canada, excluding for entry to Algeria citizens of certain Arab and Muslim countries and for Canada most Western countries.
- most CIS member states and African countries
- Brazil and Canada/CIS member states
- Armenia and most non-CIS member states

As a formality, payment may be charged for issuing a visa; these are typically also reciprocal, so if country A charges country B's citizens 50 USD for a visa, country B will often also charge the same amount for country A's visitors. The fee charged may also be at the discretion of each embassy and can be increased to discourage unserious applicants. A similar reciprocity often applies to the duration of the visa (the period in which one is permitted to request entry of the country) and the amount of entries one can attempt with the visa. In some countries, additional charges are taken in case of expedited processing of the visa application.

The issuing authority and typically consular officers may request appropriate documentation from the applicant. This may include proof that the applicant is able to support himself in the host country (lodging, food), proof that the person hosting the applicant in his or her home really exists and has sufficient room for hosting the applicant, proof that the applicant has obtained health and evacuation insurance, etc. Some countries ask for proof of health status, especially for long-term visas; some countries deny such visas to sufferers of certain illnesses, such as AIDS. The exact conditions depend on the country and the category of visas. Notable examples of countries requiring HIV tests of long-term residents are Russia and Uzbekistan.

Some developing countries commonly demand strong evidence or reason of the intent to return to the home country, if the visa is for a temporary stay. The issuing authority may also require applicants to attest that they have had no criminal convictions nor they are under judicial trial or they are not involved in certain activities like prostitution, smuggling and drug trafficking.

Types of visa

Some common types of visas are :

(1) *Transit visa*: Transit visas are usually valid for 3 days or less, for passing through the country to a third destination.

(2) *Tourist visa:* Tourist visas are for a limited period of leisure travel, no business activities allowed. Some countries (e.g., Kuwait) do not issue tourist visas. Saudi Arabia introduced tourist visas only in 2004 although it did (and still does) issue pilgrimage visas for Hajj pilgrims.

(3) *Business visa:* Business visas are meant for engaging in commerce in the country. These visas generally preclude permanent employment, for which a work visa would be required.

(4) *Temporary worker visa* : Temporary worker visas are meant for approved employment in the host country. These are generally more difficult to obtain but valid for longer periods of time than a business visa. Examples of these are the United States' E-3, H-1B and L-1 visas.

(5) *On-arrival visa* : On-arrival visas are granted immediately prior to entering the country, e.g. at an airport or border control post. This is distinct from not requiring a visa at all, as the visitor must still obtain the visa before they can even try to pass through immigration. The on-arrival visa usually is nothing more than an entrance fee, though the visitors can still be denied entry even with a visa.

Some less common visas include:

- *Student visa* : Student visas allow its holder to study at an institution of higher learning in the issuing country. However, students studying in Algeria are issued tourist visas.
- *Working holiday visa* : Working holiday visas are meant for individuals traveling between nations offering a working holiday programme, allowing young people to undertake temporary work while traveling.
- *Diplomatic visa* : Diplomatic visas confer diplomatic status on its holder and are normally only available to bearers of diplomatic passports.
- *Journalist visa* : Journalist visas are granted to peoples in that occupation when traveling for their respective news organizations. Countries which insist on this include Cuba, Iran, North Korea, Saudi Arabia, the United States (I-visa) and Zimbabwe.
- *Fiancée visa* : Fiancée visa is granted for a limited period prior to intended marriage based on a proven relationship with a citizen of the destination country: for example, a German woman who wishes to marry an American man would obtain a Fiancee Visa (also known as a K-1 visa) to allow her to enter the United States.
- *Immigrant visa* : Immigrant visa are granted for those intending to immigrate to the issuing country. They usually are issued for a single journey as the holder will, depending on the country, later be issued a permanent resident identification card which will allow the traveller to enter to the issuing country an unlimited number of times.

Entry and Duration Period

Regarding about the validity and purpose of Visas, it can also serve as single-entry, which means the visa is invalid as soon as the holder of the visa leaves the country, double-entry, or multiple-entry, permitting multiple entries into the country with the same visa. Countries may also issue re-entry permits that allow temporarily leaving the country without invalidating the visa. Even a business visa will normally not allow the holder to work in the host country without an additional work permit. If once issued, in general, a visa will have to be used within a certain period of time allotted. The validity of a visa is not the same as the authorized period of stay in the issuing country. The visa validity usually indicates when the foreigner can apply for entry to the country. Once in the country, the validity period of a visa or authorized stay can often be extended for a fee at the discretion of immigration authorities. Overstaying a period of authorized stay given by the immigration officers is considered illegal immigration even if the visa validity period isn't over and a form of being "out of status" and the offender may be fined, prosecuted, deported, or even blacklisted from entering the country again.

Traveling in a country without a valid visa or visa exemption may lead to detention and deportation from the country. Undertaking activities that are not authorized by the status of entry can result in the individual being deemed removable, in common speech an illegal alien. Such violation is not a violation of a visa, however despite the common misuse of the phrase, but a violation of status hence the term "out of status." Even having a visa does not guarantee entry to the host country. The border crossing authorities make the final determination to allow entry, and may even cancel a visa at the border if the alien cannot demonstrate to their satisfaction that they will abide by the status their visa grants them. Visa and immigration laws may vary among countries according to the laws of the land. As such, aliens are advised to check with immigration lawyers for visa and immigration laws governing the countries they wish to enter and eligibility to receive visas or other immigration benefits.

Visa extensions

Different countries have different mechanism to allow the holder of a visa to apply to stay longer in that country. For example, in Denmark a visa holder can apply to the Danish Immigration Service for a Residence Permit after they have arrived in the Country. In the United Kingdom applications can be made to the Immigration and

Nationality Directorate. In certain circumstances, it is not possible for the holder of the visa to do this, either because the country does not have a mechanism to prolong visas or, most likely, because the holder of the visa is using a short stay visa to live in a country.

Visa refusal

Visa may be denied for many unavoidable reasons reasons, for example (not limited) :

- If the applicant has committed fraud or misrepresentation in their application;
- If the applicant is felt to be intending to stay permanently or finding a job while applying for a temporary visa;
- If the applicant does not have a legitimate reason for their journey;
- If the applicant is asking for a resident visa and has no visible means of sustenance;
- If the applicant has a criminal record or has criminal charges pending;
- If the applicant does not have a good moral character;
- If the applicant is considered to be a security risk;
- If the applicant is a citizen of a country with whom the host country has poor or non-existent relations.

References

1. Tourism and the Countryside: Richard Sharpley (Northumbria University).
2. Mobility, Tourism, and Second Homes: Dieter K. Muller (University Sweden).
3. *Linking Tourism, the Environment, and Sustainability*. McCool, Stephen F., and Alan E. Watson, comps. 1995. Ogden, Utah: Intermountain Research Station, U.S. Department of Agriculture. Report No. INT-GTR-323.
4. *Sustainable Tourism: A Marketing Perspective*. Middleton, Victor T. C., and Rebecca Hawkins. 1998. Woburn, Massachusetts: Butterworth-Heinemann.
5. *Tourism and Sustainability: Principles to Practice*. Stabler, Michael J., ed. 1997. New York: CAB International.

11

Travel Bookings Using the Internet

The advent of the Internet has greatly changed tourism market scenario. One of the several impacts of the advent of this technology on tourism industry is the birth and growth of the marketing of travel on the Internet and travel e-commerce. Unfortunately, the research information to date on people searching for travel information online and booking travel through the Internet has lacked depth and sophistication. Therefore, this study developed and tested predictive models for the likelihood of booking travel online and for being a repeat booker of travel online. Using an interactive survey method, the respondents were asked to provide information on their sociodemographic characteristics, travel-related behaviours, Internet usage patterns, perceptions of the Internet, and last trips booked online. Stepwise logistic regression analysis was then applied to develop the two predictive models. A conceptual model was suggested and it depicted process of booking travel of the Internet.

Like many great changes known to human beings along their path to the present civilization, Internet marketing and e-commerce are irreversible trends. By using the Web and Internet as marketing tools, tourism organizations have gained some distinct advantages in cost reduction, revenue growth, marketing research and database development, and customer retention. All the leading hotel chains, car rental and airline companies now have their own Web sites. Many smaller tourism organizations are also beginning to use the Internet as a marketing tool. No marketing programs in the future will be successful without an Internet strategy. The number of travelers who turn to the Internet for browsing it to explore and choose destinations and book for the same is growing rapidly. Almost all Internet users in 1998 were also travelers. Half of them got information on travel products via the Internet ("Internet travel lookers"). More Internet travel lookers (hereafter referred as to "lookers") are booking online and becoming "Internet travel bookers" (hereafter referred as to "bookers").

In 1999, the number of Americans booking travel online increased by more than 80% to 11 million. Some 31% of the lookers who visited online airline sites in 1999 made reservations through the Web, compared with 21% in 1998. The percentage that booked rooms through hotel Web sites grew from 21% to 28% from 1998 to 1999, according to The NPD Group, Inc., and the percentage that booked vehicles through car rental Web sites rose from 19% to 28% in the same time span. Furthermore, the potential for online travel is enormous. Eight million American travelers are poised to make their first online purchase. Online travel retailers target at this rapidly growing population. They are always poised to identity possible customers (bookers) for their success depends on their ability to identify them. Repeat booker segment has to be paid specific attention which has several advantages. Building repeat patronage is a means by which suppliers can increase revenues and decrease costs by reducing reliance on the much more difficult task of attracting new bookers.

Repeat patrons also have the potential to be employed as a marketing resource, providing referrals and promoting positive images of online booking, which can expand the retailer's customer base. Identifying repeat bookers could be important because appealing to the repeat bookers may be the most practical and cost-effective way of developing a business. But not any research aimed at determining the characteristics of repeat bookers has so far been conducted. The primary purpose of this study was to model lookers' probability of being bookers in terms of demographic characteristics, travel-related behaviour, Internet usage patterns, Internet perception variables, and variables about the last trip booked online in the past 12 months. The second purpose was to model bookers' probability of being repeat bookers in terms of the same five categories of variables. It was expected that the results of this study would help online travel retailers to develop more effective marketing strategies.

While marketing costs are reduced, their sales efficiency and their speed are reduced by online travel retailers. They also increase access to large numbers of people at identifying potential bookers and repeat bookers. Besides this, online travel retailers can also increase their revenues improving marketing strategies and providing better service to attract and retain more bookers if they know which factors significantly increase or decrease the probability of booking online.

Internet Marketing in Tourism

Before 1990, organizations could not apply for Internet membership without providing valid reasons for connectivity, and it were hard to get connectivity even the so-called valid reasons were provided. During the last 10 years, the Internet has revolutionized the whole business world and transformed corporate strategies, including marketing strategy. The Internet represents a potentially powerful communication and distribution tool for tourism organizations. It is becoming a major force in building new relationships between customers and organizations.

Tourism organizations can eliminate the obstacles created by geography, time zones, and locations by utilizing the Internet because it enables them to communicate directly with customers. It has also been made possible by Internet marketing to significantly reduce distribution and reservation through lower agent commissions (who dominated the scenario before the advent of the Internet) thereby increasing savings of reservations staff time and costs. The use of the Web and e-mail is the dominant mode of Internet marketing. A Web site is a powerful medium offering unique marketing, advertising, product and service information, and communication opportunities between an organization and existing and potential customers. The contents of Web pages vary ac- cording to the type and size of organization, but usually a reservations function is available at the Web sites of larger organizations. Though Web pages for smaller organizations generally serve just as a tool for information dissemination, they can still provide online reservations through Internet travel services like Travelocity.com.

The most commonly used feature of the internet is e-mail. Its major advantages over other communication means, such as telephone and fax, include its instantaneousness, inexpensiveness. E-mail provides tourism organizations with enormous marketing power and is playing a more important role in tourism. It can be used to communicate with customers directly through personalized messages realizing one-to-one relation- ship marketing. Internet travel retailers use e-mail to inform potential customers about limited-time offers, as well as last-minute promotions. Previous buying behaviours are recorded in databases. Internet travel retailers can send confirmation mails promptly to the online booker by e-mail just after they have made online reservations. The Internet, for the point of view of the travelers, is a tool for gathering information and marketing reservations. Based on the WWW user survey conducted by the Graphics, Visualization, and Usability (GVU) Centre in October 1997, Weber and Roehl stated that online information represented the most popular source for making travel arrangements.

Moreover, the attraction of Internet marketing to businesses is the fact that people are making intensive use of the Internet and the numbers of Internet users and travel lookers are growing quickly. Travel is one of the most popular e-commerce purchase types, with 45% of online buyers saying they had purchased travel online. Only books outpaced this, and it was at 54%.

Internet travelers' profiles

Any sophisticated analysis of lookers and bookers, at this time, is not available. However, this section re-views the important factors used in previous comparisons of lookers and nonlookers, lookers and bookers, and bookers and offline bookers. Most previous studies analyzed these factors using frequencies and group differences were tested by chi-square analysis.

Demographic characteristics

Bookers, lookers and other Internet users are found to be of different academic level, age groups, age and occupation classes. Weber and Roehl (1999) found that, compared with people who searched for travel information offline, lookers were more likely to be 26 to 35 years of age and to have completed 4 years of college or to have professional or postgraduate degrees. Bonn, Furr, and Susskind found that lookers were more likely to be under 45 years of age. The more likely lookers are management, professional or computer-related occupations with household incomes of at least US $50,000.

The difference of age, education and income among Internet travel bookers and people booking offline was also found by Weber and Roehl. People between 26 and 55 years of age were more likely to book online. Respondents with 4-year college degrees or postgraduate degrees were more likely to purchase travel online than were people with less education. As for searching for travel information online, those who purchased travel online and those who did not, have the same patterns of occupation and income. Research into the travel-related behaviours of Internet travelers has so far been very limited. Bonn et al. (1999) found that those using the Internet to search for travel information were more likely to stay in commercial lodging establishments, and spend more money each day while traveling. Xu (1999) tested the differences between people who purchased travel products online and those who did not using a sample of students at a major US university. She found a significant difference in travel expenditures, with bookers tending to spend more on travel than nonbookers.

Kang's study (1998) showed that there was an association between lookers and nonlookers in the self-arrangement of travel. Planning trips in advance affected Internet travel lookers' buying behaviour. It was also pointed out by another study that those who looked around online before buying airline tickets accounted for 65% of the online traveler population.

Internet usage patterns

Years of Internet use, time spent online per week and attitudes toward Internet use were also found to differ between travel bookers and those booking travel offline. Weber and Roehl found that Internet bookers were more likely to have used the Internet for four years. Other researchers have confirmed that Internet travel bookers spend more time online per week than those booking offline. Kang arrived at the same result when comparing lookers and non lookers. At the same time, while Internet bookers were more likely to use free sources to access Web pages, those booking travel offline were more likely to say that they personally paid for Internet access.

Weber and Roehl analyzed the primary reasons for using the Web and wrote that bookers were more likely to use the Web for 'communication with others' and 'wasting time' while those booking offline were more likely to use the Web for 'entertainment'. The two groups did not differ significantly in using the Web for "education," "shop- ping/gathering product information," "work," and "gathering information for personal needs." When comparing travel prices, travelers usually search the Web sites of online travel services instead of the pages of travel suppliers.

Internet perception variables

While some lookers book online, others find it convenient for them to approach travel agents or call the toll-free numbers of travel suppliers after getting travel information online. The perception of the Internet as an information and reservations tool contributes to explaining this phenomenon. Kang, quoting from Ostlund's work, stated that product perception variables had great predictive power when related to purchase probability. She created a Web perception scale to predict if business travelers would adopt or reject the Web for hotel information and reservations. She demonstrated that business travelers' Web adoption behaviour was positively affected by the perceived relative advantage of the Web and the perceived room rate advantage. Roehl defined the relative advantage as 'the degree to which an innovation is perceived as being better than the idea it supersedes'. Kang also found that the other perceptions of complexity, perceived risk, and ambiguity were negatively related to Web adoption. Complexity was defined as "the degree to which an innovation is perceived as being relatively difficult to understand and use". Perceived risk was the expected probability of economic, personal, or social problems resulting from adoption. Ambiguity represented "the degree to which a respondent felt that hotel information and reservations, and room rates on the Web are clear". There are other online reports available to explain why lookers do not book online. Many researchers agree that the main reason for this is the concern for at a major US university.

The qualification for par credit card security and pricing. According to the 1998 Travel e- Commerce Survey by PhoCusWright, the other reasons for not booking travel online were that customers were used to contacting travel agents or corporate agencies; there were no financial incentives; customers' knowledge about booking online was limited; and online booking was time consuming. The NPD Group, Inc. discovered other reasons including the need for human contact and assurances that reservations were correct. Not many studies have addressed the factors attacking lookers to book online. BizRate.com found that discounts motivated lookers to make travel reservations online. Earning frequent flyer miles or points may also be a strong influence for lookers to book travel online. Frequent flyer incentives were more likely to attract online travel purchases from buyers with higher household incomes. Thus, prices and incentives were the key to attracting lookers to book online.

Among the 1998 bookers, 83% bought airline tickets, 40% reserved a hotel room, 32% rented a car, and only 3% bought a vacation or tour. Thus, lookers in booking online seem to be affected by the type and nature of the travel products. What all the evidence we have so far discussed above suggests is that travel e-commerce will incessantly grow and that traditional travel 'shopping' habits will change in due course of time. In the new millennium, a fuller understanding of online travel bookers will be needed if travel e-commerce sellers are to succeed. Knowing the differences between repeat and one-time bookers, online travel retailers can more effectively identify repeat bookers and build greater loyalty among these customers. However, scientific research on bookers is still in its infancy, and no research is available that analyzes re- peat bookers. Thus, distinguishing Internet travel bookers and lookers was the first goal of the study while identifying the differences between repeat bookers and one-time bookers was its second goal.

Methods

Sampling and data collection

A convenience group was chosen as the sample to represent Internet travel lookers. They were graduate students and the participation was based on the response of "yes" or "no" to the question: "Have you ever used the Internet for travel-related information?" A questionnaire was constructed based on previous research and online reports. The questionnaire was modified based on the results of a pilot survey to 20 graduate students at the university. Data were collected using an interactive survey method combining the Web and e-mail. The Universal Resource Locator (URL) of the questionnaire Web site was given to respondents in a personalized e-mail message. The respondent answers were submitted online and a data file was automatically generated.

Compared with a mail survey, the interactive method had four distinct advantages. They are: (i) less expensive because no paper or postage was involved; (ii) data collection time was shorter; (iii) time was saved in data entry because the data file was automatically generated; and (iv) it was easier to communicate with respondents by e-mail if they had concerns. It normally takes several weeks to collect data by mail questionnaires. However, in this study respondents submitted their answers in about one week. This method was more effective in getting qualified respondents and therefore it also had another advantage for this particular study. A total of 1184 e-mails were sent out to randomly selected respondents; 85 of them could not be delivered due to inaccurate or inactive e-mail addresses.

The total number of e-mails that the researchers sent randomly out to selected respondents was 1099. Some 416 responses were received, for a response rate of 37.9%. No incentives were used in this study to achieve this response rate. Thirty-six responses (8.7%) were disqualified, as the respondents did not use the Internet for travel information. Therefore, 380 responses were used for the analysis. There were 132 respondents who just used the Internet for travel information (lookers) and 248 respondents who booked travel online (bookers). 176 persons among the bookers were also found to have booked more than once in the last 12 months.

Model specification and variables

A first-order multiple logistic regression model with five sets of independent variables was developed and it was based on the study goals and the specific research context. For the first research goal, the dependent variable (B) was the lookers' probability of being bookers. For the second research goal, the dependent variable (Y) was the bookers' probability of being repeat bookers. A represented the vector of independent variables including sociodemographic characteristics, travel-related behaviours, Internet usage patterns, and Internet perception variables. The other independent variables were about the last trip booked online.

Data analysis

In order to provide background information on the respondents such as sociodemographic characteristics, travel-related behaviours, Internet usage patterns, and last trip booked online, descriptive statistics were used. Specifically, frequencies and percentages were calculated for categorical variables, and means and standard deviations were calculated for continuous variables. In order to examine the underlying patterns or relationships among 22 Internet perception statements, factor analysis was employed. This analysis was also used to group these variables into smaller sets of factors. Before proceeding to factor analysis, a Kaiser's Measure of Sampling Adequacy (MSA) was used to quantify the appropriateness of factor analysis.

The number of factors retained was determined based on a scree plot and the Schwarz's Bayesian Criterion (SBC). The SBC is used to determine the best number of factors and the number of factors that yields the smallest SBC value is considered best. Bartlett's chi-square significance test and Akaike's Information Criterion (AIC) are inclined to include some trivial factors and therefore they were not used to estimate the best number of factors. In order to represent 22 perception statements in the subsequent stepwise logistic regression analysis, the factors obtained were used as independent variables. Stepwise logistic regression analysis was employed to shed light on the two important research goals related to online booking behaviours: (1) Which variables significantly affected respondents' probability of being bookers? (2) Which variables significantly affected respondents' probability of being repeat bookers? The answers to these questions should provide valuable information for Internet travel retailers. It was after developing the logistic regression models by stepwise selection method that classification tables were created in order to determine how well the models predicted.

This study did not use discriminant analysis because it was considered inappropriate here. If the distribution within each group (bookers and lookers) was assumed to be multivariate normal, then a parametric method could be used to develop a discriminant function. The discriminant function, also known as a classification criterion, is determined by a measure of generalized squared distance. However, in this study most of the variables were of the 0-1 variety or with restricted ranges. In these situations, multivariate normality is not a realistic assumption. Thus, logistic regression was found more appropriate.

Bookers vs. Lookers

Results of factor analysis

A Kaiser's Measure of Sampling Adequacy (MSA) was calculated before performing the factor analysis and the overall MSA found was 0.87. It indicated that the 22 perception statement variable met the fundamental requirements of sampling adequacy for factor analysis. Maximum likelihood factor analysis with the Varimax Rotation method was performed to group the 22 Internet perception variables. Four factors were retained based on a scree plot and the Schwarz's Bayesian Criterion (SBC) (n = 4, SBC = -606; n = 5, SBC = -576). The Tucker and Lewis's Reliability Coefficient for these four factors was 0.92, which results of the Varimax Rotation method showed a clear pattern except for four of the perception statements (items 3, 16, 17, and 18). These four variables were eliminated from further analysis because their lodgings were very low.

Factor I was identified as the 'disadvantage' of booking online, because it has the ambiguity of reservations procedures, uncertainty of reservations and cancellations, security and the difficulty of making reservations online. Factor II included the "nonfinancial benefits" of the Internet as a planning and booking tool, encompassing convenience, ease of use, and satisfaction with travel planning online. Factor III reflected the "financial benefits" of booking online and the expectation of using the Internet more in the future. Factor IV was labeled as "communicability" and included two statements, which related to the influence of friends and others. The stepwise logistic regression analysis used these four factors.

Logistic regression analysis

A total of 343 cases were used in the stepwise logistic regression analysis because of some missing values for the household income variable. A total of 343 cases were used in the stepwise logistic regression analysis because of some missing values for the household income variable. The sample size was still adequate based on the rule of at least 10 observations per parameter in the logistic model. Before performing the logistic regression analysis, multi collinearity was checked by calculating the values of the Variance Inflation Factor (VIF). All the VIF values were less than 3, which indicated that there was no serious multicollinearity. Three outliers were identified that had a large influence on the regression estimate, and so they were removed from further analysis. Initially, 20 variables were used for the stepwise logistic regression analysis. Both the significance levels for entry and staying in the model were set at an alpha of 0.30. Finally, eight variables were retained in the selected model. The 2 Log Likelihood statistic was 301.646 for the selected model, and the chi-square statistic for this test was 184 (df = 14, p = 0.0001).

This indicated that the overall fit of the model was very good and at least some of the explanatory variables' coefficients were not zero at alpha = 0.05. The results of the analysis of Maximum Likelihood Estimates (MLE) for the selected predicted probabilities for a discrete change in an independent variable is an alternative to the marginal effect that Long found more effective for interpreting a Binary Regression Model. 'Discrete changes' were calculated for the eight significant independent variables in the following interpretation. Although sociodemographic variables were important in distinguishing bookers and lookers in some previous studies, except for education they were not significant in this model. The study also found that respondents with Master's or Doctoral degrees, compared with those with just Bachelor's degrees, were more likely to book online. In other words, the more education the respondents had, the more likely they were to use the Internet for booking travel.

Specifically, the probability of booking online for a Master's degree holder was 0.16 greater than for those with a Bachelor's degree only, holding all other variables at their means. For those with Doctoral degrees, the probability of booking online was 0.27 greater than for those with a Bachelor's degree only, holding all other variables constant. The type of travel Web sites respondents visited most often also affected the probability of booking online. The study also found that those who visited the Web sites of online travel services most often, compared with those who most often visited the Web sites of travel suppliers, travel agencies, tour operators and travel guidebooks, were more likely to reserve travel online. The first group of people's probability of being a booker was 0.13 higher than those who visited the Web sites of travel suppliers and 0.17 higher than those who visited other travel Web sites, holding all other variables constant.

People who had traveled to other countries in the past 12 months were more likely to be bookers than those who did not. For those who had traveled to another country once in the past 12 months, the probability of being a booker was 0.08 higher than those who had not traveled internationally. So far as those traveling to other countries twice in the last twelve months are concerned, their probability of being a booker was 0.07 higher than those who had just one international trip, holding all other variables constant.

Factor analysis

Again factor analysis was used to group the Internet perception variables. And this was done using the sample of 248 bookers. The same procedures were followed as in the comparison of bookers and lookers. First, the Kaiser's Measure of Sampling Adequacy (MSA) was checked, and the overall MSA was 0.799, indicating that the 22 perception variables met the fundamental requirements of sampling adequacy for factor analysis. Four factors were retained based on a scree plot and the Schwarz's Bayesian Criterion (n = 4: SBC = -590). The Tucker and Lewis's Reliability Coefficient for these four factors was excellent at 0.90. The results were found to be slightly different from those obtained in the analysis of bookers and lookers.

Stepwise logistic regression analysis

In order to find a model for predicting bookers' probably of being repeat bookers, stepwise logistic regression analysis was also conducted. In total, 225 responses were used in this model selection procedure due to some missing values for household incomes. There were 157 re- peat and 68 one-time bookers. Initially, 25 variables were used in the stepwise logistic regression analysis. It was at 0.30 that both the entry alpha and stay alpha levels were set.

It was not surprising to find that the significant variables in the final model were different from those in the logistic model for bookers and lookers. For distinguishing repeat and one-time bookers, twelve independent variables were retained in the model. Six of these variables were significant when using a Type I error probability alpha of 0.05 [travel products booked online last time, amount of use of the Internet per week, membership of frequent flyer programs (FFPs), number of domestic trips, communicability, and age].

It was only one Internet perception variable, communicability of booking online that significantly affected both the probabilities of being bookers and of being repeat bookers in a positive way. The probability of being a repeat booker was closely related to the amount of time per week spent online. The longer respondents spent online per week, the more likely they were to be repeat bookers.

For those respondents spending 5 to 9.9 hours a week online, the probability of being repeat bookers was 8.8% higher than those who only spent 4.9 hours or less online per week, holding other variables constant. Membership in an FFP was another significant independent variable. It has contributed significantly to predicting the probability of being a booker.

Correct incorrect

Compared with that of nonmembers, the probability of FFPs' being repeat booker was 16.2% higher, holding all other variables at their means. The age of respondents positively affected their probability of being repeat bookers. A classification table was developed to assess how well the model fit the data. The selected logistic model predicted 73.3% of the responses correctly. The sensitivity was 82.2%, showing that 82.2% of the event (being repeat bookers) responses were correctly predicted to be events. The specificity value was 52.9%, with 52.9% of the non-event responses correctly predicted to be non-events. The false-positive rate indicated that 19.9% of the predicted events were actually non-events, while the false-negative rate showed that 43.8% of the predicted non-events were events. Overall, the selected model could identify potential online travel bookers – a good performance.

Implications

As the growth of e-commerce in travel retailing continues incessantly, in future it will become even more important than ever in better understanding and identifying online bookers and repeat bookers. The goals of this study were to distinguish Internet travel bookers and lookers and to differentiate repeat and one-time bookers. A model with eight variables was produced through stepwise logistic model selection for predicting lookers' probability of being bookers.

The significant variables in the model were education, number of international trips, travel Web sites visited most often, Factor I (disadvantages), Factor III (financial benefits), and Factor IV (communicability). To speak for marketing standpoint, while some variables can be useful in identifying potential bookers, others can be of some help in improving Internet marketing strategy and service.

The study also pointed out that the frequency and number of booking travel online is directly proportional to people's education level. About 65% of respondents in this study purchased travel online, compared with only 26% for the general population of lookers. In other words, once graduate students searched for travel information online, they were more likely to book through the Web. This suggests that graduate students could be a good target market for Internet travel marketing in terms of increasing the ratio of bookers to lookers. After graduation, these people are well educated and are likely to be frequent business travelers with higher income levels. They have a greater probability of being high spenders for tour- ism businesses. It can be concluded that Internet marketers should make it a point to further educate this group to accept the Internet as a tool for travel reservation and build loyalty among them when they are still attending university.

Some larger airlines refuse to pays full rates of commission to both traditional travel agencies and online travel services. Nevertheless, some smaller travel suppliers rely on online travel services to obtain online bookings. The Internet perception variables contributed greatly to predicting respondents' probabilities of booking online. This information can help marketers to modify Internet marketing and increase online bookings. In particular, it is especially important to generate more favourable perceptions of booking travel online, as well as eliminating the unfavourable perceptions. Lookers hesitated to book travel online because of Factor I (perceived disadvantages). The same result was obtained in previous studies on bookers and lookers. The perceptions of the ambiguity of reservations procedures, uncertainty of reservations and cancellations, doubts about online security, and difficulty of making reservations online were included.

However, something arguable here is that fact of there being no warranty of the respondents' perception of the lack of online security. A way to ease lookers' anxieties about security is for online travel retailers to develop alliances with credit card companies, so lookers will feel more comfortable with online booking when they know that a credit card company is backing it up. Quicker confirmations and responses are necessary to relieve lookers' uncertainties about reservations and cancellations. Educating lookers to properly use the Internet for travel reservations is critical for converting them into bookers. One respondent talked about the insecurity of online reservation. He said that once he reserved a room online and he thought that it was done, but when he arrived at the hotel the receptionist told him that they had not received his reservation.

While the probability of booking online is closely, significantly and positively related to Factor III (financial benefits), Factor II (nonfinancial benefits) was not significant in the model. The nonfinancial benefits included convenience, ease of use, and self-satisfaction with using the Internet for travel planning and booking. That respondents tended to book online to eigher get lower prices or other financial benefits is what this implied. A recent PhoCusWright survey of 500 online travelers found that price, above convenience peat bookers who provide referrals to other people and ease-of-use, was the motivating factor for purchasing airline tickets online. In this survey, the sample consisted of American online travellers who had flown on a commercial air carrier in 1999 and visited Web sites in the past month.

The study suggested using lower prices or other financial benefits to attract new online bookers. It confirmed that price was the best means to entice new customers, and no other benefits (saving time, taking control, obtaining better information) could compete with the power of price. But online travel retailers should be cautious not to ignite price wars. Instead of simply cutting prices, they can avoid this by providing special offers or limited-time discounts. This suggests that people are more likely to book online and to frequently book online if they know that it is not only them who are booking online, many other people are doing the same. This implies that the population of bookers could grow steadily and a huge potential market for online travel retailers could emerge. This demonstrates the power of "word of mouth" in marketing and suggests that online travel retailers should take advantage of the effectiveness of word-of-mouth communications among lookers. That word of mouth is the most important source in making purchase decisions has also been pointed out by other studies.

When most travel purchase and use decisions are made, referrals and informal communications from previous users are relied upon. Some researchers have found that there is a relationship between the characteristics of travelers and reliance on word-of-mouth communications. Repeat bookers usually have positive feelings about online booking. Additionally, repeat bookers not only represent a stable source of revenues, they can also be information channels informally bringing friends, relatives, and other potential bookers to Internet travel retailers. Therefore, repeat bookers could be an effective conduit of word-of-mouth communications, by promoting greater awareness of online travel service and encouraging others to become bookers and then repeat bookers. They might be encouraged by online travel retailers to influence potential bookers to book online by using incentives.

The variables for predicting bookers and lookers on the one hand and repeat and one-time bookers on the other are different from one another. The significant variables in the repeat booking model were other travel products booked online last time, amount of use of the Internet per week, membership of FFPs, number of domestic trips, communicability, and respondent's age. The Internet perception variables were not as important as they were for predicting bookers, with only communicability being significant. One reason for this may be that because respondents were more comfortable with Internet travel reservations after booking online once. Those respondents who have booked travel products including rental cars and vacation packages were more likely to be repeat bookers. Normally the first travel product respondents booked online was an airline ticket or a hotel room, and most of the respondents who bought other products online were repeat bookers. Airline ticket sales represented 73% of all online travel bookings in 1999. This may be attributed to the airline companies providing special discounts and bonus miles or flights to attract new online bookers. Once people have become comfortable with purchasing online, they may be more receptive to buying other travel products online. This implies that there is an online purchasing sequence for most lookers: airline tickets or hotel rooms first followed by other travel products. It also suggests that it is difficult to attract new bookers to purchase travel products other than airline tickets or hotel rooms. Those who have booked airline tickets or hotel rooms online, however, represent a lucrative potential customer group for booking other travel products online.

This is believed to be the first occasion in which FFP membership was first tested in travel e-commerce research. This variable was very important in explaining the probability of being repeat bookers, even though it was not significantly related to the probability of being bookers. If respondents were FFP members, they were not significantly more likely to be bookers than other respondents. However, once they had booked online, they were more likely to book online again. This finding makes an important contribution to the travel e-commerce literature and has a practical implication for online travel retailers. It was airlines that FFPs were initially created in the early 1980s. They created FFPs so that they could encourage customer loyalty from frequently traveling passengers. Free flights or gifts were given to members of these programs. They were also upgraded from business to first-class by converting a certain number of 'air miles' accrued every time flights were taken with the same airline. Most business travelers are now members of FFPs. By offering bonus miles or points to FFP members if they book online, airline companies could attract more repeat bookers and enhance the marketing power of FFPs. As FFP members are potential bookers and are easy to target, FFP member databases could be a great marketing tool for online travel retailers.

Conceptual model

A conceptual model was developed by using previous research coupled with this study's results. This model should assist online travel retailers to better understand how people become online travel bookers and then to develop effective Internet marketing strategies. Internet travelers are all the people who have access to the Internet. When Internet travelers are planning trips, some use the Internet for travel information (lookers) and some do not (nonlookers). After making travel decisions, some lookers use the Internet to book travel products (bookers) and some go to travel agents or call toll- free numbers of travel suppliers (offline bookers).

Most bookers are likely to reserve airline tickets or hotel rooms online for their first online travel purchase (ticket or room bookers). If they have become comfortable with online booking, the great probability is that they may then book other travel products online. Current customers, main potential bookers, and potential lookers are also specified by the conceptual model. By doing so, it suggest a general marketing strategy for online travel retailers. All Internet travelers could be potential bookers, but the main potential bookers are the lookers-only. To increase the customer base, online travel retailers will benefit more from targeting this group. The lookers-only are more likely to first purchase airline tickets or hotel rooms online before any other travel products. Retailers could pro- vide special offers on airline tickets or hotel rooms to attract them to make the first online travel booking. The retailers, if they want to increase the number of bookers of other travel products including vacation and cruise packages, should target at the ticket or room bookers.

Limitations of study

This analysis may be effective, but the study's findings are limited because to the limited nature of the sample (graduate students at a major US university). Great care is needed in applying the findings of the research to other populations. The response rate (37.9%) was acceptable for this study because the sample of graduate students was quite homogeneous. For other general population samples, and in order to avoid a potential non-response bias, a higher response rate would be desirable. Incentives and follow-up reminders may be helpful in achieving this goal. Though the Internet is an innovative and fast-growing distribution tool born just recently, scientific research in this area is still in its infancy. Most previous research studies have focused on providing demographic profile information on Internet travelers and their Internet usage patterns. More comprehensive and creative scientific research is needed to better comprehend the travel e-commerce trend. A replication of this study is recommended using the general population of Internet travel lookers. This will provide a test of the reliability of this study's findings. Such different results for the sociodemographic variables as occupation, age and marital status are expected. Further research is necessary for identifying online booking behaviours and testing the proposed conceptual model of online purchasing procedures

The potential variables for this research could include first travel product booked online, date of first online travel purchase, first travel Web site used for purchasing travel products, favourite travel Web site for booking, and total number of travel products booked online. This research would help online travel retailers to better understand and retain bookers. More research is needed on repeat bookers and it is especially important to identify the reasons for repeat bookings. E-commerce retailers will be helped by these future research findings in retaining bookers with greater efficiency.

Travel Modeling

The use for analyzing tourism and travel can complement and extend the current research with Tourism Satellite Accounts (TSAs). The TPF model consists of an innovative integration of tourism and travel analysis within a computable general equilibrium (CGE) modeling framework, to assist the formation of government policies relating to tourism and travel. These models are formal economic models that extend, rather than replace, TSAs. Indeed, the increasing implementation of TSAs is a stimulus to the use of TPF models because they provide data that is ideal for implementing a TPF model. While the full potential of the detailed data contained within TSAs to be realized, these models also facilitate :

- the assessment of tourism's overall economic impact,
- the analysis of tourism policy,
- tourism forecasting, predicting long-term trends in tourist numbers and expenditures.

Tourism Satellite Accounts and TPF Models

Countries across the world are formulating TSAs. They formulate these so that they can provide accurate measures of the size of tourism sectors, the nature of demand for tourism, the nature of supply in tourism sectors and the direct contribution of tourism to GDP and employment. This makes an invaluable contribution to our knowledge of the tourism sector. When measuring the economic impact of tourism, input-output (IO) models have often been used in the past. While these models successfully capture some of the economic impact of tourism, they do not capture all of the economic impact, leading to estimates of the economic impact of tourism that are not only unreliable but heavily biased. Computable general equilibrium (CGE) models have their historical origins in input-output methodology, but were developed to overcome the many shortcomings of IO models.

In particular, CGE models allow prices to vary and resources to be reallocated between production sectors. This framework is what Tourism Policy and Forecasting (TPF) models are based upon, and these models include tourism data from TSAs to provide a consistent means of modeling tourism in the entire economy. One of the most flexible and innovative economic techniques developed in recent time is the computable general equilibrium modeling. It has been used extensively by such international Organizations as the World Bank, the World Trade Organization and the OECD as well as in academia. Diverse fields such as international trade, economic development, agricultural economics and environmental economics have been using this model.

It is input-output (IO) modeling that tourism impact models have traditionally relied on. More recently, there have been initial applications of CGE models in the tourism field. The use of CGE models uses the latest methodology and gives more accurate predictions than techniques such as IO modeling. CGE models are formulated in a way that is radically different from input-output modeling, macroeconomic modeling, partial equilibrium modeling or, indeed, any other form of numerical simulation. Then, a CGE model is solved simultaneously for all markets, production sectors and economic agents. This gives CGE models a significant advantage in flexibility over other forms of modeling, because other forms of modeling can only trace the effects of specific initial stimuli, and do so in a one-way deterministic system.

In a CGE model, the initial stimulus can originate anywhere in the economy, and can be literally anything that can occur in an economic framework, ranging from changes in taxes and subsidies, to technological change, population growth, shifts in demand and regulatory changes. CGE models are not deterministic in the same way that other simulation approaches are. The initial stimulus affects markets, production sectors and economic agents who react to the stimulus and provide further changes to the economy. These changes working in multiple way directions, the effects can feed back to where the stimulus started. The construction of a CGE model, to speak roughly, is a process of setting up a chain of markets, and production sectors and demand groups. Each market, sector and household has its own set of economic rules that determine how it reacts to external changes. Typically, markets for goods and services are market clearing, so that if demand exceeds supply, the price of the good or service will increase until the market clears. If the price of the good that a production sector produces increases, the output of the sector will increase. Consequently its use of factors of production will increase and the supply of the good will increase. Ultimately, these demand and supply changes will, owing to the demand-supply correcting behaviour of prices in markets, increase production factor prices but reduce the price of the output good, until it is no longer profitable to increase output any further.

A CGE model sets up the economic conditions where each market, sector and household reacts to changes in the economy and thus it can model a variety of possible scenarios. In other forms of numerical simulation, models are set up whereby the simulation follows a direct causal relationship from one effect to the next. CGE models by their very nature allow interactions between markets, and between sectors, that may be very complex. IO models stand on an input-output table for data, and at the same time they trace the intermediate demands for goods and services needed to satisfy final demands by consumers, the government, investment and exports. Hence, they calculate the indirect effects of final demand. The earnings of income (by private consumers and the government) can also be included to calculate the induced effects, which are similar to Keynesian multipliers. CGE models include other effects through factor markets and foreign currency. While doing so, the model includes both the indirect effects and the induced effects.

Tourism Policy and Forecasting models extend the CGE framework to incorporate tourism and travel, with data on tourism demand and the supply of tourism industries, and frameworks for modeling tourism and travel. It is its four basic characteristics that distinguish Nottingham TPF models from IO models of tourism and travel. The characteristics are:

- Prices and wages are flexible in a TPF model. This enables factors of production, such as labour and capital, and foreign exchange markets to be modeled.
- Income-expenditure consistency must be maintained for all private households, the government, firms and any other economic agents that are modeled.
- Consumers' responses to changes in prices and income levels

are taken into account by behavioural assumptions.

- Substitution between intermediate inputs and factors of production, as prices and wages change, is taken into account by production assumptions.

A TPF model has the following types of equation :

- Equilibrium conditions for each market ensure that supply is equal to demand for each good, service, factor of production and for foreign exchange.
- Income-expenditure identities keep the economic model a closed system. All earnings must be accounted for through expenditure or savings. These conditions apply to all private households, the government, firms and any other economic agents that are modeled.
- Behavioural relationships show the mode economic agents' reacting to changing prices and income levels. These then determine consumers' demand levels for each good and service.
- The quantity of production for any given level of factor employment is determined by production functions. With assumptions regarding market structure, these determine what levels of labour employment, capital usage and intermediate input usage are required to satisfy a given level of output for a set of prices.

Flexibility is one of the strengths of the TPF models. The TPF models usually contain certain core components of the model structure, and can be expanded by extending the scope of the model to suit the circumstances of the tourist origin/destination country or region. The components of the model structure are:

- Market competition. Various forms of market competition can be included, from perfect competition to monopoly.
- Labour markets can be modeled in various forms, with the possibility of allowing for unemployment.
- Foreign trade can be treated in several different ways, to enable the modeling of small and large countries.
- Dynamics can be incorporated to show how the economy moves through time, with economic agents' expectations about future events incorporated into their decision- making processes.

In addition, extensions to the model scope can be made, such as:

- Income distribution can be modeled by incorporating many

household groups. The distributional effects of tourism or tourism policies could then be examined.

- Inter-regional effects could be modeled by modeling distinct regions within a country.
- International effects can show how tourism's effects are spread between countries.
- The environment can be incorporated to show the effects of tourism and tourism policy on environmental issues.

Tourism impact modeling

In fact TSAs have contributed a lot in the measurement of the economic size of tourism. In spite of this, they do not assess the total impact of tourism. Estimating the impact of tourism has the advantage of showing the desirability of tourism, in addition to measurement of size. It can also show what impact tourism has on different sectors, regions or on income distribution, depending on the specification of the model. One problem with any attempt to measure the size of a sector such as tourism is that it is usually measured from the demand-side and it is difficult to compare results with sectors such as mining, agriculture or manufacturing that are usually measured from the supply- side. Though the direct impact of tourism is comparable to the greatest extent with supply-side sectors on the surface, it is problematic in defining.

Suppose an aircraft is owned by an airline, the direct measurement of tourism will consider a proportion (according to the proportion of airline services tourists consume) of the aircraft. If, however, the airline rents the aircraft from another company, the value of the rental service will be attributed as an intermediate input into tourism, and the corresponding returns to investment will not be included in tourism value added. In an attempt to rectify this situation, various countries have included indirect effects through input-output (IO) models as an alternative in their TSAs. While this solves problems relating to definitions of intermediates, it goes beyond the measurement of the size of tourism in an accounting sense and loses direct comparability with supply-side sectors. IO models include some intermediate purchases (such as food and fuel, for example) that should clearly be thought of as intermediate purchases and not as being within the tourism sector itself. To be brief, the IO models do something beyond measuring the size of the sector to measuring its economic impact. However, the full impact of tourism is not measured by IO models. These models make various assumptions that evidently exclude some of the economic effects that a sector has. Therefore the measurement of indirect impacts through IO models gives only a partial picture of the full impact of tourism. While IO results are more misleading due to their incorporating only some of the impact of tourism, the TPF results, in fact, are more comprehensive.

Tourism policy analysis

The TPF models can also be made use of in providing other forms of economic analysis. Policy analysis is an important way in which the potential of TPF models can be further demonstrated. The TPF models can also perform "what-if" simulations:

- Examine the economic effects of existing policies on tourism or of proposed alternatives. For example, they can show the net effective taxation of tourism that exists or provide a quantitative assessment of policy alternatives.
- Provide a theoretical viewpoint or an applied quantitative estimate.
- Examine purely taxation issues, or other policy instruments such as investment incentives and planning regulations.
- Examine the effects of tourism policy, or the effects that other policies have on tourism.

What these examples show is the fact that the scope for tourism policy analysis with the TPF models is large. Cases of particular relevance include:

- Examination of the current levels of tourism taxation, i.e. whether tourism is taxed at too low or too high rates relative to the rest of the economy.
- Quantitative estimates of tourism policy alternatives, such as planned tax changes or tourism development plans.
- Quantitative estimates of the effects of other policies on tourism, such as trade liberalization or general taxation changes.

Tourism forecasting

TPF models can effectively be used to forecast the trends of future tourism industry. Such forecasting models show how changes in the world economy will feed through to tourism. The three main factors that trigger changes are:

- Factor accumulation, including capital accumulation through investment, labour growth through population growth, and changes to the skills of labour through education and training.

- Technological change, through technical progress.
- Policy changes, which may be foreseeable.

Both income growth on the demand side and production costs on the supply side are influenced by both these factors. As each factor may be changing at different rates in different sectors and in different countries, forecasting their total effect requires a TPF model. Relative prices strike a balance between the demand and supply side factors so that equilibrium in each market can be achieved. For example, growing increases in overall skill and education levels will bring about high growth rates in sectors using highly skilled and highly educated labour. How this affects tourism depends very much on the skill and education levels in tourism characteristic sectors, and on the intermediate relationships between tourism characteristic sectors and the rest of the economy. Differential growth rates between tourist source countries will affect international tourism growth rates in different destination markets. Tourism growth will, in general, be highly responsive to increases in income levels in source countries, and will depend on the relative prices for tourism and other goods and services. The TPF models give the opportunity to access not only the potential long-term growth of tourism in response to changes in the economy (such as population growth and changing education levels) that are highly predictable, but also the short-term impact of macroeconomic changes including currency market crises and natural disasters.

Tourism impact

The Effect of a 10% Increase in Foreign Tourist Expenditures

A 10% increase in foreign tourist expenditures in simulated in order to measure the impact of foreign tourism. This 10% increase is \$9.6bn. Economic welfare, as measured by equivalent variation rises by \$5.8bn, just under 0.1% of GDP. These comparative illustrate that just over half of the expenditure is captured as an increase in welfare, as markets adjust to reallocate resources, imports increase, and other exports are crowded out.

The impact of this expenditure is captured by GDP, in terms of

(i) direct expenditure impact,

(ii) input-output estimates, and

(iii) general equilibrium estimates with the TPF model. While the direct impact of the \$9.6bn extra expenditures is \$4.5bn and the input-output estimate is $9.4bn, the TPF estimate is $6.0bn.

This indicates that:

- A large proportion of the expenditures leads directly to purchases of intermediate inputs, hence the low figure for the direct expenditure impact.
- Almost all of the expenditure leads to increased GDP in the input-output estimate. The IO estimate has no crowding-out, and there is very little import leakage.
- The TPF estimate includes significant levels of crowding-out and resource reallocation.
- Some tourism and travel sectors have significantly higher increases in GDP in the TPF model than the IO model suggests. Here, the initial stimulus of foreign tourism expenditures is reinforced by domestic expenditures as firms benefiting from the initial expenditures increase there own expenditures on business tourism, and private households which have increases in income spend more on domestic tourism.
- Others tourism and travel sectors, such as water and rail transport, have a lower GDP increase than the IO model suggests. These are sectors that sell products that are relatively small proportions of the foreign tourist's expenditures. Resources are reallocated to other sectors that are able to pay higher wages. These reallocation effects outweigh the induced effects that these sectors experience from higher incomes.
- Non-tourism industries (here, 'all other commodities') have a decline in sector GDP that the IO model completely misses, because it does not include price crowding-out effects and resource allocation. Here, there is no direct stimulus from the foreign tourism expenditures. Indirect (intermediate demands, as captured through the IO model) and induced effects are positive, but are outweighed by resource allocation effects.

The General equilibrium effects of indirect taxation

The levels of effective protection that the structure of taxation gives to industries are exposed by the overall effect of indirect taxation. The same also shows how distortions that indirect taxes introduce lead to economic loses. As such, it is an important indicator as to how economically efficient taxes are in each sector. The results therefore remove arguments about the motives for taxation because the total level of taxation is maintained. Overall, replacement of all indirect taxes with non-distorting direct taxes results in an improvement to GDP of $528.4bn, which was 2.1% of GDP in 1997. This therefore is the measure of the total distortionary impact of the indirect taxation system. This improvement to GDP comes about through an increase in the GDP contribution of labour and capital ($1,033.8bn) outweighing the loss in indirect taxation revenue ($-505.4bn). With some exceptions, tourism and travel sectors have a lower GDP increase than the national average of 2.1%.

Non-tourism sectors ('all other commodities' is a much larger sector than 'gasoline and oil' or the wholesale sector) have a larger GDP effect than the national average. This implies that the tourism sectors have levels of effective taxation that are higher than the national average because tourism sectors do not expand by the national average when indirect taxation is removed. We can briefly say that the results of these seventeen separate simulations are the welfare effects of removing the individual taxes. Taxes in a range of sectors such as auto and truck rental, recreation and entertainment and retail margins, impose distortions on the economy that lead to a higher welfare loss than the tax revenue that they raise. Some sectors, such as water transport, air transport and hotels and lodging places, have much lower distortionary impact when compared to the tax revenue. The reasons of sectors' having different distortionary impacts include:

- The distortionary impact of tax rates are often more than proportional to the tax revenue raised, so that higher tax rates lead to a higher distortion/revenue ratio.
- The distortionary impacts are related to other sectors through intermediate demands, and substitution in final demand. Sectors that have high distortions can effectively pass some of these distortions to related sectors.
- The distortionary impacts are related to how readily supply and demand change in response to price changes, in other words to the elasticities of supply and demand. Sectors with inelastic supply and demand (i.e. low levels of supply and demand response to prices) tend to have lower distortionary impacts from taxation. In a general equilibrium framework, the responsiveness of supply and demand depends on many factors, such as who purchases the product (a product mainly purchased by firms will often have a lower demand elasticity than one purchased by households) and the structure of production (an industry that relies heavily on one type of input

will tend to have a lower supply elasticity than other industries).

TPF model is flexible enough to be used in analyzing other types of issues. 'What-if' scenarios can simulate the effects of anything from productivity growth, changes to competition (anti-trust) legislation and environmental controls. The total general equilibrium effects of such diverse issues can be a complex product of many different changes. Here, we show the results of a productivity improvement in air transport. The $20.6bn increase in GDP that results is spread across industries, with air transport itself increasing in size to account for an extra $2bn in GDP, industries that use air transport such as 'all other commodities' also increasing. Other transport industries compete with air transport and such sectors have a reduced GDP contribution.

Tourism is applied by the Nottingham Tourism, Policy and Forecasting models within a general equilibrium setting. They are an innovative and significant means of combining tourism satellite accounts, input-output tables and economic modeling. They expand on the TSA's measurement of tourism's economic size to provide estimates of tourism's economic impact, including many effects that are not captured in input-output models. TPF models also provide an important tool for policy analysis, enabling the complex interactions in the economy that result from policy actions to be traced through a general equilibrium framework and assessed. The ability to have quantitative estimates of the effects of policy is of vital importance to policy makers. Forecasting the levels and expenditures of tourists, taking relatively stable and predictable long-term trends in tourism, source and destination countries (to providing a method of robust long-term forecasting) use the TPF models as a basis. An example of the TPF model's capabilities is provided by the results presented here for the USA Tourism, Policy and Forecasting model.

The impact of tourism when including induced income effects and resource reallocation effects is dramatically different to the standard input-output results. In particular, the IO models overestimate the total GDP effect, underestimate the total effect on tourism sectors and completely miss the negative effects on non-tourism sectors. The results of the policy analysis using the TPF model are that most tourism sectors are effectively taxed at higher than the national average level. In sectors such as hotels and transport sectors indirect taxation imposes lower welfare losses on the economy than in other sectors.

This implies that the most urgent sectors for tax reductions (i.e. those where welfare distortions are disproportionately high relative to tax revenues) are auto and truck rental, retail, eating and drinking, recreation and entertainment, participant sports, and parking, automotive repair and highway tolls. We also report the results of a 'what-if' scenario that shows the effect of improved productivity in the air transport sector. The results show that increases in GDP are spread across the economy in sectors that use air transport. As a result, competing transport sectors may contras.

It is an indication of the potential applications which TPF modeling has that the USA TPF model is intended to give. While the sector classification for this model is small to match the U.S. TSA as closely as possible, a full 494-sector model is also in operation. For the U.S., the model can be extended in various directions: tourism demand data on domestic tourism by state would enable the TPF model to include state effects.

Otherwise, the model can be expanded to include different skill categories of labour and different households groups according to geographical location, income category, or other classification. This would be able to show how these different household groups are affected by both an expansion in tourism and by policies. Other possible ways of expanding this model are to incorporate similar data from other countries: a model of North America would, for example, include Canada and Mexico. In order to assess the effects that a tax on a tourism sector in the US has on economies of Canada and Mexico, this would incorporate cross-border effects.

As well as these extensions the U.S. TPF model, it is of course possible to build similar models for any country where a TSA and input-output table exist, and these can also incorporate regional differences, household distributions and different types of labour as well as incorporating more than one country. The underlying methodology of TPF models find the most appropriate applicability to developing countries which have so long used computable general equilibrium modeling.

References

1. Elite Clubs of India / Bhageria, Purshottam & Malhotra, Pavan – 2005.
2. Into the Untravelled Himalaya: Travels, Treks and Climbs/ Kapadia, Harish – 2005.

3. "Illinois Rural Tourism: Do Rural Areas Benefit from Increases in Travel Expenditures," *Small Town*, Bowling, M. 1992. Vol. 22, No. 4: pp. 19-26.

4. "Bibliography of Economic Impacts of Parks, Recreation and Tourism." Chang, Wen-Huei. 2000.

5. "Economics and Tourism," Eadington, William R., and Milton Redman. 1991. *Annals of Tourism Research*, Vol. 18, No. 1: pp. 41-56.

6. *Impact of Visitor Expenditures on Local Revenues*.Goldman, George, and Anthony Nakazawa. 1994. Corvallis, Oregon: Western Rural Development Center, Oregon State University. Report No. 145.

7. *Cost-Benefit Analysis of Local Tourism Development*.Goldman, George, Anthony Nakazawa, and David Taylor. 1994a. Corvallis, Oregon: Western Rural Development Center, Oregon State University. Report No. 147.

8. *Estimating Community Visitor Days*. Goldman, George, Anthony Nakazawa, and David Taylor. 1994b. Corvallis, Oregon: Western Rural Development Center, Oregon State University. Report No. 146.

12

Air Travel and Ticketing Processes

Air travel is a form of travel using an airplane. The comfort experienced when traveling by air depends on several factors starting with the airport, the choice of the airline and the travel class. Travel class on an airplane is usually split into a two or four class model. National flights usually have two classes: economy Class cabin and business class cabin, whereas long haul flights usually have four classes: an economy class cabin, a premium economy cabin, a business class or a club class cabin and finally, a first class cabin. The differences between premium economy and economy are quite significant, but the cost is not greatly altered by purchasing a premium Economy ticket. The price difference between an economy class ticket and a first class ticket, however, are often extreme, with prices for a first class ticket being at least $1700 (£850) more expensive. The difference between Economy and First Class when travelling by rail is often not as much, but an uplift of $1200 (£600) more expensive is not uncommon. Most air travel starts and ends at a commercial airport. The typical procedure is check-in, border control, airport security baggage and passenger check before entering the gate, boarding, flying and pick-up of luggage and - limited to international flights - another border control at the host country's border.

International Carrier

International Carrier Responsibilities

The relationship between governments and carriers is complex and has potential for misunderstanding and conflict. A number of issues must be addressed in order to develop an effective relationship. These include: the role of the industry; how to deal with improperly documented travellers; the denial of boarding to potential asylum-seekers; and arrangements in regard to inadmissible passengers who are in transit. The legal responsibilities of carriers are found in the migration laws and regulations of the State that grants them landing rights. International carriers must therefore be familiar with, and comply with, a wide range of legislation and regulations. A balance between an enforcement approach and a cooperative approach is the most effective way to build a partnership with carriers. The partnership between the carrier and the government should be managed at both the executive and local levels to ensure carrier compliance with State expectations for migration management. This is essential for a successful programme. Transportation companies engaged in the carriage of travellers by land, sea, or air.

Compliance mechanisms

Institutional and administrative arrangements that encourage and ensure compliance with established requirements

Control authorities

The administrative and organizational units within a national government those are responsible for managing the orderly movement of regular migrants, and for control of irregular and illegal migration

IATA

The International Air Transport Association, established in 1919 as the trade association for the airline industry

IATA/CAWG

The International Air Transport Association/Control Authorities Working Group (IATA/CAWG) brings together airlines and immigration control authorities from 19 countries to develop and pursue a cooperative programme for the facilitation and processing of air passengers, while ensuring effective action against illegitimate traffic.

ICAO

The International Civil Aviation Organization, established in 1947 to give expression to the terms of the International Convention on Civil Aviation (The Chicago Convention)

IMO

The International Maritime Organization, established in 1958 as the United Nations' specialized agency responsible for improving maritime safety and preventing pollution from ships.

Domestic Carrier

Persons of Indian origin spiring to hold 100 per cent stake in private Indian carriers will have to wait for some more time before they can make their move. This is because the Directorate-General of Civil Aviation issued a notification on July 27, reiterating the existing guidelines that restrict PIO holdings to 49 per cent. Existing policies allow non-resident Indians to hold 100 per cent in a domestic carrier, but cap investments by all other foreign entities, including PIOs, at 49 per cent. The latest notification by the DGCA, which is a part of the civil aviation ministry, comes less than a month after the department of economic affairs and department of industrial policy and promotion ruled that investments by PIOs be treated at par with investments by NRIs.

The notification by DGCA says that the investment guidelines have been issued after a communication from the civil aviation ministry to this effect on July 11. But sources in the civil aviation ministry said a Cabinet note will be moved soon on the issue of treating investments by PIOs at par with that of NRIs soon. "We expect the Cabinet to take a final view on the status of investments by PIOs in the domestic aviation sector," said a ministry official. What status PIOs will be accorded is a question that has driven a wedge between government departments concerned with the matter. The DEA and the civil aviation ministry had said PIO investments should be treated as foreign direct investment, while the DIPP had favoured equal status for PIOs and NRIs. This decision of the civil aviation ministry has put in limbo the application of Nira Radia, a PIO, to start a domestic carrier owned 60 per cent by her.

The application of Radia, who holds 60 per cent of Magic Air's equity, had been blocked due to the stand taken by the DEA and the civil aviation ministry. The commerce ministry has, from the beginning, held that PIOs should be treated at par with NRIs. The finance ministry, in June this year, took the view that PIOs, who have been granted dual citizenship, are a subset of NRIs. The ministry has so far taken the stand that FDI in Magic Air has breached the regulatory ceiling of 49 per cent. The government had raised the FDI cap in domestic aviation from 40 per cent to 49 per cent in November 2004, when the Cabinet also allowed 100 per cent investment by NRIs in Indian carriers. But the Cabinet had not taken a call on the status of PIO investments. While considering FDI norms proposed by the civil aviation ministry in November last year, the Cabinet had observed that the issue of PIOs being accorded parity with NRIs in case of FDI should be examined in a time-bound manner. The Cabinet had asked the DEA for its views on this issue.

Air Transport Regulation

Regulate Air Transport Affairs

CAA is responsible for the negotiation and maintenance of bilateral air transport and bilateral search-and-rescue agreements. Air transport agreements are vital instruments to ensure proper regulation of scheduled air services between the RSA and various other States. Search-and-rescue agreements facilitate rescue operations through cooperation and coordination of facilities and equipment within the region. The Directorate further controls and manages South Africa's obligations in terms of ratified aviation conventions with multilateral organisations. Obligations in terms of the conventions and protocols must be fulfilled to ensure that South Africa maintains international aviation standards. South Africa's relationships with African regional organisations and ICAO must be managed optimally to ensure that South Africa gains maximum benefit from these organisations. CAA renders secretariat services to the Air Service Licensing Council and the International Air Services Council, the Search and Rescue Executive Committee, the Regulating Committee and the Regulations Committee. CAA furthermore facilitates the coordination of the activities of certain organisations and manages assets to provide South Africa with a national and international search and rescue capability.

Airport Handling Procedure

The IATA Ground Handling Council (IGHC) reports to the Airport Services Committee. It is the principle forum of organisations involved in world-wide airline ground handling services. The IGHC brings together IATA and non-IATA airlines, independent ground handling companies, airports, participants in the IATA Strategic Partnerships and other parties. The IGHC meets on an annual basis usually in May. At this meeting more than 650 executives meet to discuss issues of mutual concern and of special interest to the ground handling community. The trade show, seminar held in conjunction with the annual meeting provide an ideal opportunity to meet new business contacts, maintain and establish new ones and learn about the latest products and services available to the ground handling industry.

Working group activities for the AGSA, RAMPSG and ASG are scheduled twice during a given year and provide the forum in which new industry standards are developed and agreed prior to being published in the IATA AHM.

Reservation Practices of Air Travel

To avoid any possible inconvenience to our customers, it is important certain items are packed in your checked in baggage. Should a customer try to carry these types of items in their cabin baggage or on their person, the airport screening services will remove them and regrettably such items will not be able to be returned to the customer.

The new measures are:

- All liquids, aerosols or gels such as drinks, creams, perfumes, sprays, gels, toothpaste, lip gloss and mascaras must be in individual containers not greater than 100ml in volume
- All containers must be carried in a re-sealable transparent plastic bag no larger than one litre (approximately 20cm x 20cm or 8 inches x 8 inches)
- Only one bag is permitted per passenger
- The plastic bag must be sealed and presented separately from all other carry-on baggage at the screening point
- Liquids in containers of more than 100mls can be packed in your checked in baggage.

There are exemptions for personal medications, baby products and dietary supplements in liquid, aerosol or gel form. The new security regulation is consistent with that already in place in the USA, European Community and Canada. It is also consistent with the security regulation being introduced in Australia from 31 March 2007. To assist you in understanding the nature of other restricted items prohibited within your carry on luggage, Airport authorities advises the following:

- Sharp objects or cutting implements include but are not limited to: knives, box cutters, letter openers, scissors, tradesman's tools, screwdrivers, darts and knitting needles.
- Sporting goods or club like items include but are not limited to: Baseball bats, pool cues, golf clubs, lacrosse sticks, ski poles, brass knuckles and hammers.
- In order to comply with Transportation Security Administration (TSA) effective 14 April 2005, passengers

travelling to, from or via the US are prohibited from carrying any lighters on their person or in cabin baggage in the sterile areas of airports or onboard an airplane. This includes butane, absorbed-fuel (Zippo-type), electric/battery-powered and novelty lighters.

In respect of any medication a customer may be carrying in their cabin baggage or on their person, it is important that the medication has a professionally printed label identifying the medication or manufacturers name or pharmaceutical label affixed. Diabetes related supplies/equipment may be carried, however they will be inspected to ensure prohibited items are not concealed. Customers are advised to carry a letter from their Doctor verifying the need for any medical items to be carried, as some countries require such a letter to be presented. Traveling with someone who is disabled or traveling with a companion with special needs might be a little intimidating. However, if you put a little time and effort into the planning process, flying with the disabled companion can be an enjoyable experience for you both. Here are some helpful suggestions for planning your flight.

- Post a Comment
- Add to Favorites
- Email
- Print Article

Step1

Bring a physician letter when traveling. This should include a general description of the disability and standard means of treatment along with any prescription information.

Step2

Check with your airline carrier for any requirements on flying with medical equipment. Most airlines are not allowed to transport medical oxygen or other hazardous materials in carry-on or cargo.

Portable, battery operated options are allowed, but additional restrictions apply such as the person is required to sit in a window seat.

Step3

Request any additional assistance that may be needed upon arrival. If a wheelchair or attendant will be needed, they can note this on the reservation to ensure airport staff is adequate.

Step4

Consider travel times when booking a reservation. If your travel plans are flexible, consider traveling during the middle of the day or mid-week when the airport is generally less crowded.

Step5

Pack a light carry-on bag that contains a snack, a bottle of water and a two to three day supply of medication. Airlines don't offer the meal options they used to, but special meals may be ordered at the time of reservation when meals are available for longer flights.

Step6

Allow yourself plenty of time for the arrival and check-in process. Security is no less or no more strict based on a disability. If you beep going through the monitors, additional screening will be required.

Step7

Notify check-in clerks and attendants if assistance is needed in boarding or during any layovers when dealing with connecting flights. The boarding process usually begins 30 minutes prior to scheduled take-off. Most airlines will allow a passenger needing any special assistance to board the plane first regardless of ticket class or seating.

Step8

Communicate your needs to the flight attendants and personnel at the gate, as they have been trained to assist people with disabilities. Wheelchair storage is available, but space is limited and on a first come first serve basis. Most airplanes are equipped with a service wheelchair for mobility around the cabin.

Step9

Communicate any needs your passenger has if deaf or hard of hearing at the check-in counter so the flight attendants are aware of the passenger's disability. Communication cards are pre-printed and available on most airplanes.

Step10

Trained assistance animals are also accepted on flights. They are allowed in the passenger cabin on the floor in front of or next to the passenger with disabilities. If the animal is too large to be kept in the cabin, you must provide a portable carrier so the animal can be transported in the cargo area.

Standby Travel

Flying standby used to be one of the cheapest ways to travel. The idea was that an empty seat doesn't earn the airline any money. So some airlines would sell special fare "standby tickets". Using such a ticket you were NOT guaranteed a seat on a particular flight, but on the next flight with empty seats. You'd be enplaned on a flight subject to the availability of space at departure time. This was only after all passengers with reservations for the flight have been boarded. Passengers from a previous flight who were bumped also had priority. No stopovers were permitted on standby fares. Since advance reservations were not accepted, you had to get to the gate early to put yourself down on the standby list. If it was a busy day and the flights are full, you would have to wait several hours to get a seat, or maybe not get a seat at all. A standby ticket didn't guarantee you a seat, but if you did not absolutely, positively have to be there tomorrow, you could get some good deals.

But the days when students could hang out at the airport and fly standby for dirt cheap prices are long gone. The term "standby" is still used, but doesn't mean what it used to:

- Most airlines no longer sell standby tickets at a special fare, but will sell you a standby ticket at regular fare. In other words, if they have space on the flight, the gate agent or ticket agent will sell you a ticket for the flight on the spot. All this means is you can buy a full fare ticket on the spur of the moment.
- Nonrefundable, nonchangeable tickets can often be used for standby travel on the same or similar route (sometimes with a slight surcharge). This most often comes up if you missed your flight (e.g., you arrive at the gate after the plane has left, and catch another flight to the same destination later that day), but you may be able to use unused flight coupons in this manner. For example, if you bought a ticket but didn't go for some reason (a reason that didn't entitle you to a refund), the ticket may still be usable for standby travel on the same airline. (Your best bet with such a ticket, however, is to have your travel agent or airline credit it towards your next ticket. You'll probably have to pay a fee, but it's better than throwing away the ticket.) All this is often at the whim of the gate agent, and is based on the notion that a ticket is often designated as being good for travel on the airline for one year from the date of issue. Your luck will vary by airline and gate agent.
- If you're on a later flight but get to the airport early, check with the attendant at the gate. You may be able to get on the earlier flight is there's space available (but this may result

in your getting no "snack" or losing your special meal). This works even for "non-changeable" tickets.

Airlines stopped the practice of selling standby tickets for a variety of reasons:

- Even if a seat isn't taken, putting somebody in the seat still costs the airline some money (e.g., fuel).
- Standby travel played havoc with airline load management programs. Airlines were sometimes faced with having to unload fuel to change the weight distribution of the aircraft because of a sudden appearance of several standby passengers.
- Some people would "ensure" the availability of standby seats by making a large number of regular reservations, and then an hour before the flight release the block of seats, virtually ensuring that standby passengers will get aboard at cheap standby fares. This caused airlines to overbook flights, and eliminated their ability to schedule their flights accurately. Since the elimination of standby tickets, overbooking errors have dropped significantly. (Another result of this practice is the automatic cancellation of unpaid reservations after 24 hours.)
- Airlines felt that they were losing regular business to standby travel. Flying standby, however, may be making a comeback. In 1993, some airlines had special one-day fares for folks traveling on Christmas and New Years. These holidays are the nadir of the travel season, so by offering these fares, the airlines were able to increase their business on flights they had to fly anyway. (Yes, airlines still have to fly the routes, even with empty planes, because scheduling is so complex. For example, the plane in Atlanta might need to fly to Boston so that it can be used on the Boston-Washington route later in the next day.)

Now these holiday fares weren't true standby fares, but the concept was similar. Since most flights these days fly at 85-95% of capacity, one of these days an airline is going to get the bright idea of reinstating standby fares in one variation or another. For example, some airlines now sell discount flight coupon booklets to senior citizens; the coupons may be used for standby travel. And of course, US Air Force personnel can fly standby on some US Air Force planes on a space available basis for dirt cheap prices, but with no amenities (and maybe no real seat either, but strapped to webbing on the wall). Some foreign airlines still provide standby fares, sometimes limited to youth.

If you are flying standby one way or another, here's some advice:

- Make sure you get to the gate EARLY. If several people are flying standby, you want to make sure that your name is first on the list. Note that connecting passengers, bumped passengers, etc., get priority over local boarding standbys.
- Days which are bad for getting bumped are usually good days for standby seats. Don't fly standby on the day before Thanksgiving or the Sunday after, you won't get a seat. On Thanksgiving day itself, you're likely to find a seat.
- On really busy days it might pay to show up early for the *first* flight of the day, since standbys who don't make it can "roll over" to the next flight.

Some airlines will only allow "same day" standby travel (i.e., you overslept and missed your flight, and will take a flight on the same route later that day). Others will not allow you to fly standby on a flight if all the seats in your fare class have sold out, even if there are empty seats available. If the agent at the check-in counter gives you trouble, go directly to the gate and see what happens. Agents at the check-in counter are under more pressure to enforce the rules than gate agents, who have some discretionary power. If you can avoid dealing with the agents at the check-in counter, (e.g., no checked baggage), so much the better. If you want to try flying standby on one airline using another airline's ticket, bypass the check-in agent and go directly to the gate. Most airline employees (and their spouses and dependents) can fly standby on that airline for cheap or free (as "representatives" of the airline). Crew who must reach their destination for work purposes have priority over all non-revenue passengers. Active employees have priority over retired employees and dependents of an employee. There is a pretty strict dress code suit and ties for men, and similar requirements for women so you can't fly wearing a jogging suit.

Passenger Check-In

Passenger Check In Officer

Passenger check in officers book in airline passengers and their luggage. At the check in desk, officers:

- greet passengers and deal with their enquiries

- check passengers' tickets and passports, allocate seats and issue boarding cards
- weigh passengers' luggage, check it in and ask passengers security questions
- direct passengers to the boarding gate.

Officers may also work at the boarding gate, announcing when a plane is ready to board and checking passengers' boarding passes. They may also escort passengers to the waiting plane. Check in officers work variable shifts to cover all the times that an airport is open. This can include early mornings, evenings, nights, weekends and bank holidays. Part-time work is possible. Most of check in officers' work takes place indoors. Salaries range from around £11,300 to £20,000 a year.

A passenger check in officer should:

- have a pleasant, helpful, confident manner and excellent customer service skills
- have good communications skills, both spoken and written
- enjoy working with the public
- like working in an airport.

Officers are employed at airports throughout the UK, although around two thirds of air passenger transport is concentrated at the larger airports. Some check in officers work for large airlines, but most are employed by ground handling companies that work on behalf of airlines. The number of check in officers is growing, but entry is still competitive. Anyone seeking this work must live near an airport and be able to travel to and from work at times that fit in with their shifts. Most employers prefer entrants with three to five GCSEs/S grades (A-C/1-3), including English and maths, and some previous experience of customer service work.

Minimum age on entry varies from 16 to 20 years old. A relevant qualification in travel and tourism or customer service can be helpful. Some young people enter this work as apprentices. There is no upper age limit for entry to this work and employers often prefer adult entrants for their experience and maturity. Check in officer's train on the job under the supervision of experienced staff and may work towards qualifications in passenger handling. Check in officers may progress to team leader, passenger services supervisor or other ground-based airline operational work, such as flight dispatcher. Some use check in work as a step towards work as cabin crew. It may possible to work abroad.

Cancellation and Delay

Your flight has been canceled. You are stranded at the airport. You are wondering if there is anything you can do about it. When it is the airline's fault that you are stuck at the airport you may have an option — Rule 240. There is a certain mystique that exists around Rule 240 and how (sometimes if) it guarantees you certain rights as a passenger. It is important to note before delving into the particulars of Rule 240, that Rule 240 was originally established in the United States.

Rule 240

Rule 240 deals with the obligations that an airline has to a passenger when his/her flights cancel or delay, or connecting flights are missed due to the actions of the airline. It does not include flight delays or cancellations that result from inclement weather or other factors that are outside of an airline's control. Rule 240 was a U.S. federal requirement prior to airline deregulation in 1978. It was one of the many stipulations that existed prior to deregulation - the U.S. government obligated airlines to abide by a set of rules regarding the transport of passengers and the rights of passengers. Rule 240 has remained in existence because after deregulation most airlines continued to respect the 'old rules'.

Checked Baggage

The Free Baggage Allowance Weight Concept

For Travel starting from India to Europe/Far East/Middle East a passenger is allowed Free Baggage allowance by the airlines that are based on the class of travel. A child gets the equivalent allowance as an adult. Infant are not allowed any free baggage allowance, except for items like Strollers or Infant's utility bag. Normally, the following entitlement is allowed based on the class of travel:-

- First Class: 40 Kg
- Business Class: 30 Kg
- Economy Class: 20 Kg

Piece Concept

International Air Transport Association (IATA) has formed certain guidelines and rules for smooth processing of various aspects of travel. The rules framed by IATA are enforced by all member airlines to avoid any ambiguity and ensure service/quality standards..

Countries where the piece system applies

- between USA/US Territories and all countries.
- between Canada and Europe, Middle East, Southern Africa, South Asian Subcontinent, the Far East except Guam and South West Pacific, Argentina, Bolivia, Brazil, Chile, Mexico, Panama, Paraguay, Peru, Uruguay.
- between the Far East and Argentina, Bolivia, Brazil, Chile, Panama, Paraguay, Peru, Uruguay, Mexico, USA.
- between Guam/Saipan and Japan, Okinawa, Hong Kong, Korea Republic, China, Taiwan, Philippines, Thailand, Indonesia, Malaysia, Singapore, India.
- between Pago Pago and South West Pacific.

The normal Free Baggage Allowance

First and business class passengers

2 pieces of free checked baggage upto a maximum weight of 70 lbs (32 Kg) each, where the total of the three dimensions does not exceed 157cm (62 inches) for each bag.

Economy class passengers

2 pieces of free checked baggage upto a maximum weight of 50 lbs (23 Kg) each, where the total of the three dimensions for any one bag does not exceed 157 cm (62 inches) for each bag. Maximum weight of any one bag is 32 kg (70 lb) except within North America where it is 23 kg (50 lb). (Note: domestic airlines within USA may apply a Free Baggage Allowance based on a weight or piece system. Children are entitled to the same free baggage allowance as adult passengers. Infants not entitled to a seat are allowed one checked bag of which the total of the three dimensions should not exceed 115 cm (45 inches) plus one fully collapsible stroller or pushchair.

Articles considered as a single piece of baggage

The following articles, irrespective of their actual dimensions, may be considered as a piece of baggage at 135 cm (53 inches):

- one sleeping bag or bedroll.
- one rucksack/knapsack/backpack.

- one pair of snow skis with one pair of ski poles and one pair of ski boots.
- one golf bag, golf clubs and pair of golf shoes.
- one duffle-type bag of B-4 type bag.
- one suitably packed bicycle.
- one pair of standard water skis or one slalom water ski.
- suitably packed fishing equipment comprising not more than two rods, one reel, one landing net, one pair of fishing boots and one fishing tackle box.
- certain sporting firearms (subject to each airlines conditions of carriage).
- any portable musical instrument not exceeding 100 cm (39 inches) in length.

Cabin Baggage Allowance

With ever growing emphasis on security and to avoid over crowding of Inside Cabin luggage overhead bins, airlines are now enforcing the principle of one cabin baggage in all parts of the world. Coats, Canes, umbrellas, reading material, small purses/camera cases don't usually count against your carry-on allowance. Backpacks, laptops, large purses or briefcases may be counted especially on crowded flights. Most of the cabin /check-in baggage restrictions are based on linear inches that can be described in layman terms as total of length + width + height. One small bag or one garment bag whose three dimensions should not exceed 115cm/45in and the maximum weight should be 10kgs.

Excess Baggage Charges

The Excess Baggage Charge levied on baggage in excess of the free allowance is determined by a number of factors: the city or country of departure; city or country of arrival; and, in a number of instances, by the airline of travel. Each combination of factors has a standard Excess Baggage Fee. Each bag in excess of the number permitted which does not exceed the dimensions/weight limits is charged at the standard fee. If within the baggage allowance a bag exceeds the dimensions limit for free carriage but does not exceed 203 cm (80 inches) and is within the weight limit, the standard fee is still applied. However, any bag both in excess of the number and dimensions, but where the sum of the three dimensions does not exceed 203 cm (80 inches) and is within the weight limit, twice the standard fee is charged. Any piece of baggage in excess of 203 cm (80 inches) or in excess of the 32 kg (70 lb) or, within North America 23 kg (50 lb), weight limit will not be carried unless prior handling arrangements are made with the airline. If accepted for carriage, such bags are weighed and charged at three times the standard fee for each additional 10 kg (22 lb) or fraction thereof.

Special Charges

Special charges apply for the carriage of:-

- bulky or fragile items as hand baggage warranting the use of one or more additional seats. To/from the USA the normal piece system excess charges apply but the minimum charge will be 75% of the full one-way adult fare for the class used by the passenger. Elsewhere, a standard excess charge of 75% of the full one-way adult fare for the class used by the passenger applies.
- accompanied pets. The animal and container cannot be allowed in the passenger's free allowance. To/from USA the normal excess baggage fee is charged. Elsewhere, the charge is twice the standard fee.
- snow skiing and golf equipment. If in excess of the normal free allowance, one set of skis/ski poles/ski boots will be carried at 25% of the standard excess baggage fee and one golf bag/ golf shoes at 50% of the standard fee. Additional sets are charged at the full standard fee.

Incidents of Lost Baggage/Delay/Damaged Baggage

Even though airlines try to ensure that the checked-in baggage arrive at the destination in safe condition and at the same time as the passenger, there are cases of Lost or Damaged baggage due to in-flight/airport/ transit mishandling of the baggage by the airline staff. Again IATA helps the passenger to claim his loss based on certain rules and regulations.

Lost Baggage

If the baggage on arrival is found to be missing, passenger must file a complaint with the concerned airline immediately. In most of the developed countries the process of retrieving the baggage is quick and delivery process smooth, with airlines delivering the luggage at the doorstep of passenger. However in India the process is not as smooth. Once the baggage is reported lost by the passenger, he must take Property Irregularity Report (PIR) that is issued by all airlines. In India, passenger must get this PIR endorsed by Customs before leaving Airport premises, as failure to do so will result in customs charging Duty on the goods being claimed. Once you take the PIR for customs endorsement, they would value the Duty Free allowance being claimed and balance due so that when passenger comes to the airport for retrieval of his/her lost baggage the same is given to him. If the airline is unable to retrieve your lost baggage and declares it lost and unrecoverable, then the compensation process is activated.

As per IATA guidelines, passenger is entitled for claim with maximum liability of the airline being limited to USD 20 per Kg or a maximum of USD 635 per piece of checked-in baggage. For items checked-in with Limited Liability baggage tags, different compensation rules apply this amount can be higher if the lost/ damaged bag was insured.

Damaged Baggage

Damage to the checked-in baggage are governed by various rules, that primarily regulates the type of damage. An airline will not be liable for normal wear and tear/scratches, manufacturers defect etc. Any damage to the baggage should be reported to the concerned airline immediately, within 24 hrs of arrival at the airport. In case of the travel being made through a combination of various airline alliance partners, the delivering carrier is held responsible.

Ensure Your Baggage Safety

To avoid the possibility of losing your baggage either due to airline's fault or a fellow passenger's fault because of identical appearance of the baggage - Label all your baggage with **Name Label**, that gives your address, destination port, telephone number etc. Lock all bags and remove old destination and identification tags before checking baggage. Never put Cash, Jewellery, Electronic equipment, computers in the checked-in baggage, as airlines will not be liable for any loss/damage.

Pet Transport Policy

Air Travel for Your Pet

Pets, mostly dogs and cats, can and do travel safely aboard commer aircraft. This document is designed to provide general guidelines t customers with safely transporting their pets by air. Please ke that not all airlines accept pets for travel, either in the cabi Those carriers that do accept pets for travel have transportation policy. Customers need to contact their airline directly when making travel plans for their pet. Most airline Web sites will provide detailed information on pet transportation policies. Also, different rules apply for service animals. The Animal and Plant Health Inspection Service (APHIS) of the U.S. Department of Agriculture (USDA) sets and enforces regulations for the transportation of live animals. These regulations apply to customers and their pets, as well as to the airlines. If you transport your pet by air, you must comply with the applicable laws, which are designed to ensure pet safety and comfort.

There are a number of ways to transport your pet by air. First, some airlines will allow you to travel with a small pet in the cabin of the plane if your pet will fit in a carry-on kennel or approved carrier under a passenger seat. For animals other than dogs or cats, contact your airline for its acceptance policy. Note that carriers have very specific rules. For example, a pet cannot have an offensive odor, nor will it be allowed to disturb other onboard travelers and must adhere to FAA rules. Also, the pet must remain in the carrying case throughout the entire flight. A second option offered by many airlines is "accompanied baggage," where your pet travels in the cargo hold alongside your checked luggage. What's important to know is that the airlines allow you to transport your pet as accompanied baggage only when you are a passenger traveling on the same flight as your pet.

A third option available through most airlines is to transport your pet as a "live animal" cargo shipment. In the cargo system, your pet travels either through regular cargo channels or special expedited delivery services that many airlines have developed. Pets in the cargo system are transported in the same pressurized holds as those in the checked-baggage system. Many airline cargo departments employ pet transportation specialists who can assist you with answers to questions. These methods are safe and humane ways to transport your pet. Contact your airline directly to determine the best option for you and your pet. APHIS requires your pet to be at least eight weeks old and fully weaned before traveling by air. Whenever possible, book a direct, nonstop flight and avoid holiday or weekend travel. Consider schedules that minimize temperature extremes. For example, try to avoid travel during excessively hot or cold periods. Morning or evening flights are preferable during the summer. In the cargo system, it is possible to reserve space on a specific flight by paying for either priority or special expedited delivery service. Note that carriers reserve the right to embargo pet travel during extreme conditions. Check with a veterinarian to be sure that your pet is fit to travel. Some species – for example, pug-nosed dogs (e.g., Boxers and Boston Terriers) – simply do not fly well because they may have difficulty breathing even under normal conditions. You will need a health certificate, provided by your veterinarian, in order to comply with the rules of most airlines, as well as state and federal rules. To be valid for your trip on most airlines, the certificate should be issued no more than seven to 10 days prior to departure. Be sure to check with your airline to get the exact amount of time they require before your pet's trip.

Most veterinarians advise against sedating your pet since the effects of tranquilizers on animals at higher altitudes are unpredictable. The decision to prescribe a tranquilizer for your pet should be made by you and your veterinarian. If you believe that some form of sedation might be helpful, be sure to obtain and follow a veterinarian's advice. You and the airlines must follow APHIS regulations on the size of kennel for your pet. The kennel must be sturdy, properly ventilated and large enough for your pet to freely be able to stand, turn around and lie down. The kennel must close securely with a mechanism that requires no special tools to operate. APHIS regulations require that the kennel have projecting rims or spacers to ensure that the kennel's ventilation slats cannot be blocked by adjoining kennels or cargo. Appropriate kennels are available at pet stores and from most airlines. Remember to check with your airline because airline policies can vary. As far in advance of the trip as possible, let your pet get to know the travel kennel. Veterinarians recommend leaving it opens in the house with an old sock or other familiar object inside, so that your pet will spend time in the kennel. It is important for your dog or cat to be as relaxed as possible during the flight. At the time of travel, be aware that most airlines do ***not*** permit pet toys in the kennel during transport in the cargo hold.

When your pet travels, the kennel should

- Clearly display your name and address
- Use arrows or other marking to indicate the top of the kennel
- Include food and water dishes (both empty), which are secured inside the kennel and accessible from outside
- Show a food and water schedule and, if any food is necessary, include an ample supply in a bag attached to the outside of the kennel
- Contain no more than one adult dog (or puppy between eight weeks and six months old that weighs more than 20 lbs.) or one cat per kennel. (Two puppies or kittens that are between the ages of eight weeks and six months old and under 20 lbs. Each may share the same kennel if they are personal pets of comparable size and are socially compatible with one another)
- A general rule of thumb is that your pet must be able to stand comfortably in the kennel and be able to turn around while standing in the kennel
- Contain absorbent material or bedding, such as newspaper

- Display labels on top and on at least one side with the words LIVE ANIMALS printed in 1-inch-high letters

At the time you book a trip on which you plan to transport your pet, advise the airline directly that you will be traveling with a pet either in the cabin with you, as accompanied baggage in the cargo hold on your flight, or as cargo. Be sure to contact your airline again 24-48 hours prior to departure to reconfirm your pet's transportation plans. This is important since airlines will transport only a limited number of pets on each airplane. Please note that advance arrangements do not guarantee that your pet will travel on a specific flight. Airlines reserve the right to refuse to transport a pet for reasons such as illness, poor kenneling or extreme temperatures at origin, transfer or destination airports. If you are flying to a foreign country or Hawaii, be sure to find out whether there are quarantine or other health requirements at the destination. For example, rules in the United Kingdom are very strict. It is essential to comply with such requirements.

A full-service travel agency or pet travel service should be able to assist you with this information. You should also contact the appropriate embassy or consulate at least four weeks before the trip to verify these requirements; most countries have Web sites that can provide information about pet travel requirements, or you can find them through the APHIS Web site. You are ultimately responsible for the required documentation that will allow your pet to complete its trip. An airline cannot guarantee that it will accept a pet that it has not seen. Since an airline cannot transport a pet that is violent or dangerous, important considerations for acceptance of pets include the pet's health and disposition. A health certificate will help to address any concerns. An airline must also determine that all paperwork is in order and that the kennel meets all requirements. USDA requires that you offer your pet food and water within four hours before check-in with the airline. Do not overfeed your pet at this time.

A full stomach is not good for a traveling pet. When you check in with the airline, you must sign a certification of the time when you last offered food and water to your pet. (Do not leave food or water in the dish in the kennel. It will spill and make travel unpleasant for your pet.) Get to the airport with plenty of time to spare so that there will be no rush. If your pet is traveling as unaccompanied baggage or by special expedited delivery service, check-in will usually be at the passenger terminal. If your pet will be traveling through the cargo system, you may need to go to the air freight terminal, which typically is located in a separate part of the airport. Be sure to check with your airline for the acceptance cutoff time for your flight, and the location from which you can retrieve your pet at the destination airport. You may not give your pet to the airline more than four hours before flight time (six hours by special arrangement). Finally, airlines are required to must make sure that the facilities at the airports of transfer or final destination are able to handle pets. APHIS has set clear guidelines on allowable temperature limits for animal holding areas, which airlines must obey.

Security Screening of your Pet

Transportation Security Administration (TSA) regulations require physical screening of all pets and their kennels whether transported in the passenger cabin, as accompanied baggage or air cargo.

- If your pet is traveling with you in the passenger cabin or as unaccompanied baggage, TSA will likely require your pet to accompany you through the passenger screening equipment at the security checkpoint. You will usually need to remove your pet from its kennel to allow for TSA screening of the kennel or pet carrier. In most cases, the kennel will be subject to the same security procedures as your carry-on luggage or checked bags.
- For pets transported as cargo, the airline may require you to remove your pet from its kennel to allow for security screening of the kennel before your pet can be accepted for transport.

Interline Transfer of Pets

When your pet travels as accompanied baggage, most airlines cannot transfer your pet from their own systems to a final destination served by another airline. Each airline must inspect your pet at the time it accepts your pet for transport. On a trip involving more than one airline, therefore, you may need to claim your pet at the connecting stop or stops where you change airlines and check in your pet with the agents at the new airline. Be sure to plan adequate time for this transfer. A good rule of thumb is: if you booked your trip through separate airlines or through a travel agent, you will likely need to retrieve and re-check your pet when making connections. If you booked the entire trip though one airline, verify with them whether you will need to re-check your pet when transferring from one airline to another. However, when your pet travels in the cargo system, airlines can transfer your pet from one airline to another. Adequate time for transfers between airlines will be necessary, so be sure to consult the airlines involved, since you will need to make advance arrangements with the connecting airline. The minimum transfer times will vary by airport and sometimes by airline.

Helpful Tips

- It is a good idea to carry a leash or cat harness with you on a trip so that you may walk your pet before check-in and after arrival, and so that you can secure your pet during security screening. (Do not keep the leash with your pet, either inside or attached to the outside of the kennel.)

- Do not take your pet out of its kennel inside the airport unless TSA personnel ask you to do so. In keeping with airport regulations and out of courtesy for other passengers, you should let your pet out of the kennel only after you leave the terminal building. Some airports offer special pet relief areas. Check with your airline or the airport information desk when you arrive at the terminal.
- You should clearly mark the kennel with your pet's name.
- In addition to showing your name and address as required by APHIS, you must mark the kennel with the telephone number of a person at the destination who can be contacted about your pet. This is especially important if you are sending your pet unaccompanied through the cargo system, because you will not be at the airport to claim your pet upon arrival. It may be helpful to contact a pet travel service to handle an unaccompanied pet, since these services manage pick-up and delivery and can advise on quarantine requirements for international travel.
- If your pet is traveling in the cargo system, remember that there is a processing period for cargo after arrival, which may vary depending on the airline, the airport, and whether your pet is arriving from a domestic or international location.
- If you have questions, be sure to contact your airline.
- Remember: Even under the best conditions, air travel can be stressful on your pet. Be sure to talk to your veterinarian before transporting your pet by air to make sure that your pet is sufficiently healthy to withstand the stresses associated

Special Meals

Special Meals is the common term used by airlines to represent a wide variety of meal types. In order to address the various dietary needs of its customers, and to promote passenger loyalty, many airlines offer a vast array of meals that answer virtually any dietary requirements. An hour or two of grumbling stomachs may not be of great concern to airlines. On longer flights however, passenger comfort includes providing meals for all by taking into account that not everyone can eat the standard inflight meal. Certainly, when in doubt the best adage is bring your own food if you have specific dietary needs.

This may work easily enough on flights of let's say less than four hours, but when it moves beyond that time frame it becomes fairly difficult to plan and pack what you might need. There is the problem of refrigeration, or heating of meals. On long, full flights, a request to have meals that you have brought with you to be heated or refrigerated may sadly fall by the wayside and be forgotten. If you are bringing your own food, the most practical method is packing food that does not require refrigeration or reheating. By doing so, you ensure that you will eat when you need to. For longer flights it is not unreasonable to expect that special dietary needs are taken into consideration.

Although it is not a restaurant in the sky, with enough advance planning you can request meal service that will at least satisfy most dietary concerns. The operating word is advance - special meals do take more time to prepare, and they involve the paper work of linking your name and seat number to the request. Therefore it really is best to make requests sooner rather than later. Most airlines have some sort of program for accommodating special meal requests. Many of these airlines will advise you to request special meals at least 12 to 18 hours prior to departure. To be on the safe side, special meal requests should really be made as soon as possible. Although special meals are never 100 percent guaranteed, you will most likely receive your requested meal.

Airport Taxes

An Airport Improvement Fee or Embarkation Fee or Airport Tax or Service charge or Service fee is an additional fee charged to departing and connecting passengers at an airport. It is levied by government or an airport management corporation and the proceeds are usually intended for funding of major airport improvements or expansion or airport service. Some airports do not levy these fees upon connecting passengers who do not leave the airport or whose connecting flight is within a specific timeframe after they arrive. In the United States, the federal Passenger Facility Charge (PFC) Program allows the collection of PFC fees up to $4.50 for every enplaned passenger at commercial airports controlled by public agencies. Airports use these fees to fund FAA-approved projects that enhance safety, security, or capacity; reduce noise; or increase air carrier competition. Federal law limits use of PFC funds strictly to the above categories. Depending on the location, the Airport Improvement Fee is included in the cost of traveller's airline ticket, in which case the airline will forward the fee to proper agency. However, in some locations the fee must be paid at the point of embarkation.

This often creates difficulties for departing passengers who are unfamiliar with this type of procedure, or for departing international passengers who have already exchanged all their local currency. The amount varies usually between US$10 and US$30. In some instances, the fee continues to be charged long after construction has been completed (i.e. Ottawa Macdonald-

Cartier International Airport). A legitimate reason for this is that the airport must finance the cost of the improvement and then pays off these costs over an extended period of time.

Airports currently collecting an explicit airport improvement fee include:

- Jorge Chavez International Airport Lima, Peru
- Ministro Pistarini International Airport (Ezeiza), Buenos Aires, Argentina
- Ngurah Rai Airport (Denpasar), Bali, Indonesia
- Soekarno-Hatta International Airport Jakarta, Indonesia
- Auckland International Airport, Auckland, New Zealand
- Carrasco International Airport, Montevideo, Uruguay
- Chiang Mai International Airport, Chiang Mai, Thailand
- Norwich International Airport, Norwich, United Kingdom
- Almost all Canadian international airports
- Almost all Brazilian airports administered by Infraero

References

1. Financial Management of Travel and Tourism / B.S. Badan.
2. Tourism: Conceptualizations, Institutions, and Issues: C. Michael Hall, Allan M. Williams, and Alan A. Lew (University of Otago; University of Exeter; Northern Arizona University).
3. Transport and Tourism: Stephen Page (University of Stirling).
4. *The Economic Impact of Visitors to Your Community*. Goldman, George, Anthony Nakazawa, and David Taylor. 1994c. Corvallis, Oregon: Western Rural Development Center, Oregon State University. Report No. 144.
5. *Touring Historic Places: A Manual for Group Tour Operators and Managers of Historic and Cultural Attractions*. Baker, Priscilla. 1995. Washington, DC: National Trust for Historic Preservation. Washington, DC: National Trust for Historic Preservation.
6. "Once Upon a Time, Happily Ever After," Baldwin, Fred. 1994*Appalachia*, Vol. 27, No. 4: pp. 38-44.
7. *Views from the Road: A Community Guide for Assessing Rural Historic Landscapes*. Copps, David H. 1995. Washington, DC: Island Press.
8. *A Heritage Tourism Tool: National Register of Historic Places*. Curtis,

Mary E. 1993. Radnor, Pennsylvania: Northeastern Forest Experiment Station. General Technical Report No. 176.

9. "Railroads, Tourism, and Native Americans in the Greater Southwest," Tisdale, Shelby J. 1996. *Journal of the Southwest*, Vol. 38, No. 4: pp. 433-462.

10. *Profiles of Travelers Who Participate in Historic and Cultural Activities: Results from the TravelScope Survey*. Travel Industry Association of America. 1997.

Bibliography

1. Aaron Tornell, "Real vs. Financial Investment", Vol. 32, Journal of Development Economics, North-Holland: E.lsewier Science Publisher B.V. 419-444 (April 1990).
2. Adams, J. 1972. Why the American Tourist Abroad is Cheated: A Price Theoretical Analysis. Journal of Political Economics 80:203-207.
3. Adams, Kathleen M. 1997a Ethnic Tourism and the Renegotiation of Tradition in Tana Toraja (Sulawesi, Indonesia). Ethnology 36:309-320.
4. Back, Roy C. 1978. Boundary Maintenance Revisited: Tourist Experience in an Old Order Amish Community. Rural Sociology 43:221—.
5. Backstrand, G. 1976. Changing the Use of Resources by the Rich. International Development Review 18(2):14-16.
6. Barker, Mary L. 1982. Traditional Landscape and Mass Tourism in the Alps. Geographical Review 72:395-415.
7. Broederlijk Delen, "A Tax on Financial Speculation Background Paper", (Bart Bode) Brussels, (March 2000).
8. Brogan, E. 1994. Human Resource Development in Tourism: The Scottish Perspective. In Tourism: The State of the Art. A. V. Seaton, ed. Pp. 552-562. Chichester, England: Wiley.
9. Brown, Bryan J. H. 1985. Personal Perception and Community Speculation: A British Resort in the 19th Century. Annals of Tourism Research 12:355-369.
10. Brown, Carolyn Henning. 1984. Tourism and Ethnic Competition in a Ritual Form: The Firewalkers of Fiji. Oceania 54:223-244.

11. Brown, Donna. 1995. Inventing New England: Regional Tourism in the Nineteenth Century. Washington, D.C.: Smithsonian Institution Press.

12. Brown, G., and R. Giles. 1994. Coping with Tourism: An Examination of Resident Responses to the Social Impact of Tourism. In Tourism: The State of the Art. A. V. Seaton, ed. Pp. 755-764. Chichester, England: Wiley.

13. Canadian Centre for Policy Alternatives, "The Tobin Tax on International Monetary Transactions", (Interview with Dr. James Tobin) (September 1995).

14. CAFOD, "Capital Punishment: Making International Finance Work for the World's Poor", (Written by Duncan Green) 1-39 (September 1999).

15. CIDSE, Report of a Consultation held by CIDSE in collaboration with the University of Antwerp, "A Tax on Foreign-Exchange Transactions" (Anthony Clunies) 1-16. Antwerp, Belgium (March, 2000).

16. Caribbean Tourism Research Centre. 1983. Cultural Patrimony and the Tourism Product: Towards a Mutually Beneficial Relationship. Washington, D.C.: International Trade and Tourism Division, Department of Economic Affairs, Organization of American States.

17. Caribbean Tourism Research Centre. 1988. Caribbean Cruise Ship Study. Washington, D.C.: General Secretariat, Organization of American States.

18. Carpenter, Edmund. 1972. Oh, What a Blow That Phantom Gave Me. New York: Holt, Rinehart and Winston.

19. Carroll, John. 1980. Skeptical Sociology. Boston: Routledge and Paul.

20. Casson, Jean. 1967. From Travel to Tourism. Communications 10:24-34.

21. Chambers, Erve, ed. 1997. Tourism and Culture: An Applied Perspective. Albany: State University of New York Press.

22. Chambers, Erve. 2000. Native Tours: The Anthropology of Travel and Tourism. Prospect Heights, Illinois: Waveland.

23. Chapin, Mac. 1990. The Silent Jungle: Ecotourism Among the Kuna Indians of Panama. Cultural Survival Quarterly 14(1):42-45.

24. Cohen, Eric. 1996. Hunter-Gather Tourism in Thailand. In Tourism and Indigenous Peoples. Pp.??-??. Richard Butler and Thomas Hinch, eds. London: International Thompson Business Press.

25. Cohen, Erik, and Robert L. Cooper. 1986. Language and Tourism. Annals of Tourism Research 13:533-563.

26. Cohen, Marvin. 1967. Saving Art for Tourism in One Tragic Lesson. Twentieth Century 176(1035):39-45.

27. Cohen, Yehudi. 1974. Comments. Current Anthropology 15:250-251.

28. Collins, Charles. 1979. Site and Situation Strategy in Tourism Planning: A Mexican Case Study. Annals of Tourism Research 6:351-366.

29. Dann, Graham M. S. 1977. Anomie, Ego-Enhancement and Tourism. Annals of Tourism Research 4:184-194

30. Dann, Graham M. S. 1992. Predisposition Toward Alternative Forms of Tourism Among Tourists Visiting Barbados: Some Preliminary Observations. In Tourism Alternatives: Potentials and Problems in the Development of Tourism. Valene L. Smith and William R. Eadington, eds. Pp. 158-179. Philadelphia: University of Pennsylvania Press.

31. Dumazedier, Joffre. 1974. Sociology of Leisure. New York: Elsevier.

32. Dumont, Jean-Paul. 1984. A Matter of Touristic "Indifférance." American Ethnologist 11:139-151.

33. Ebron, Paulla A. 2000. Tourists as Pilgrims: Commercial Fashioning of Transatlantic Politics. American Ethnologist 26:910-932.

34. Edgell, David L. 1990. International Tourism Policy. New York: Van Nostrand Reinhold.

35. Edgell, David L. 1993. World Tourism at the Millennium: An Agenda for Industry, Government, and Education. Washington, D.C.: Department of Commerce, United States Travel and Tourism Administration.

36. Elkan, Walter. 1975. The Relationship between Tourism and Employment in Kenya and Tanzania. Journal of Development Studies 11:123-130.

37. Ellis, Michael J. 1973. Why People Play. Englewood Cliffs, New Jersey: Prentice-Hall.

38. Fages, Jean, and Thomas B. McGrath. 1975. Tourism Development in Guam and Tahiti: A Comparison. In The Impact of Urban Centers in the Pacific. Roland W. Force and Brenda Bishop, eds. Pp. ??-??. Honolulu: Pacific Science Association.

39. Faché, W. 1994. Short Break Holidays. In Tourism: The State of the Art. A. V. Seaton, ed. Pp. 459-467. Chichester, England: Wiley.

40. Farrell, Byran H. 1974. The Tourist Ghettos of Hawaii. In Themes on Pacific Lands. Michael C. R. Edgell and Byran H. Farrell, eds. Pp. 181-221. Western Geographical Series, Vol. 10. Victoria, British Columbia: Department of Geography, University of Victoria.

41. Finance for Sustainable Development: The Road Ahead, (1997). United Nations Department for Policy Coordination and Sustainable Development, Division for Sustainable Development (Conference Proceedings of the Fourth Group Meeting on Finaccial Issues of Agenda 21, Santiago, Chile). New York: United Nations publication.

42. Gable, Eric, Richard Handler, and Anna Lawson. 1992. On the Uses of Relativism: Fact, Conjecture, and Black and White at Colonial Williamsburg. American Ethnologist 19:791-805.

43. Gearing, Charles E., William W. Swart, and Turgut Var, eds. 1976. Planning for Tourism Development: Quantitative Approaches. New York: Praeger.

44. Gewertz, D. B., and F. K. Errington. 1991. Twisted Histories, Altered Contexts: Representing the Chambri in a World System. Cambridge.

45. Glikson, Artur. 1956. Recreational Land Use. In Man's Role in Changing the Face of the Earth. William L. Thomas, Jr., ed. Pp. 896-914. Chicago: University of Chicago Press.

46. Globalization of Finance: A Citizens' Guide, (1999). Kavaljit Singh, Zed Books.

47. Global Public Goods: International Cooperation in the 21st Century, (1999). Inge Kaul, Isabelle Grunberg, and Marc A. Stern, New York: Oxford University Press.

48. Good Taxes: The case for taxing foreign currency exchange and other financial transactions, (1997). Alex C. Michalos,

New York: Duncan Press.

49. Henry, Paget. 1981. De-colonization, Tourism and Class/Race Structure in Antigua. In Contemporary Caribbean: A Sociological Reader, Vol. 1. Susan Craig, ed. Pp. 243-263. Maracas, Trinidad and Tobago: College.
50. Henry, Ralph, and Kim Johnson. 1985. Linking Tourism and Agriculture to Create Jobs and Reduce Migration in the Caribbean. In Migration and Development in the Caribbean: The Unexplored Connection. Robert A. Pastor, ed. Pp. 289-300. Boulder, Colorado: Westview.
51. Henshall, Brian D., and Rae Roberts. 1985. Comparative Assessment of Tourist Generating Markets for New Zealand. Annals of Tourism Research 12:219-238.
52. Herbin, Jackie. 1986. A Model Tourist Development: The Case of the Austrian Tirol. Society and Leisure 9:95-116.
53. Hervik, Peter. 1999. Mayan People Within and Beyond Boundaries: Social Categories and Lived Identity in Yucatan. New York: Harwood.
54. Hill, Carole. 1990. The Paradox of Tourism in Costa Rica. Cultural Survival Quarterly 14(1):14-19.
55. Hiller, Herbert L. 1974. Where Is Tourism Traveling? Journal of Interamerican Studies and World Affairs 16:508-515.
56. Hills, Theo L., and Jan Lundgren. 1977. The Impact of Tourism in the Caribbean: A Methodological Study. Annals of Tourism Research 4:248-267.
57. Hitchcock, Michael, Victor T. King, and Michael L. G. Parnwell, eds. 1993. Tourism in South-East Asia. London: Routledge.
58. Ichaporia, Niloufer. 1983. Tourism at Khajuraho: An Indian Enigma? Annals of Tourism Research 10:75-92.
59. International Public Finance, (1992). Ruben P. Mendez, New York: Oxford University Press.
60. Issues in Global Governance: Papers Written for the Commission on Global Governance, (1995). London: Kluwer Law International.
61. Jud, G. Donald, and Joseph Hyman. 1976. International Demand for Latin American Tourism. Growth and Change (January):25-31.

62. Jules-Rosette, B. 1984. The Messages of Tourist Art: An African Semiotic System in Comparative perspective. New York: Plenum.

63. Jud, G. Donald, and W. Krause. 1976. International Tourism and Economic Development. Texas Business Review 50:136-139.

64. Jules-Rosette, Bennetta. 1984. The Messages of Tourist Art: An African Semiotic System in Comparative Perspective. New York: Plenum.

65. Kahn, Joel S. 1997. Culturalizing Malaysia: Globalism, Tourism, heritage, and the City in Georgetown. In Tourism, Ethnicity, and the State in Asian and Pacific Societies. Robert E. Wood and Michel Picard, eds. Pp. 99-127. Honolulu: University of Hawai'i Press.

66. Kaiser, Charles, Jr., and Larry E. Helber. 1978. Tourism Planning and Development. Boston: CBI.

67. Kamarck, Andrew M. 1976. The Tropics and Economic Development: A Provocative Inquiry into the Poverty of Nations Baltimore: Johns Hopkins University Press.

68. Lawrence H. Summers and Victoria P. Summers, "The case for a securities transactions excise tax", Tax Notes 879-884 (August 13, 1990)

69. Lawrence H. Summers and Victoria P. Summers, "When financial markets work too well: A cautious case for a securities transactions tax", Vol. 3 Journal of Financial Services Research 261-286 (1989)

70. Market-Oriented Society, Democracy, Citizenship and Solidarity: an Area of Confrontation?, (1999). Conference Proceedings, 31 May-1 June 1999, Council of Europe Parliamentary Assembly, Strasbourg: Council of Europe Publishing.

71. Network Institute for Global Democratization (NIGD), "The Tobin Tax: How to Make it Real- Towards a Socially Responsible and Democratic System of Global Goverance. Ulkopoliittinen Instituutti (UPI) Working Paper No. 13 (1999).

72. Oxfam Great Britian, "Time for a Tobin Tax? Some practical and political arguments", Discussions Paper (Compiled by Heinz Stecher).

73. Our Global Neighborhood: The Report of the Commission on Global Governance, (1995). New York: Oxford University Press.

74. Panic Rules: Everything you need to know about the global economy, (1999). Robin Hahnel, Massachusetts: South End Press.

75. Paul Bernd Spahn, "International Financial Flows and Transactions Taxes: Survery and Options", International Monetary Fund Working Paper WP/95/60, (June 1995)

76. Paul Bernd Spahn, "The Tobin Tax and Exchange Rate Stability", Finance and Development, Vol. 33, No. 2, 24-27 (June 1996)

77. Rudiger Dornbusch and Jeffrey Frankel, "The Flexible Exchange Rate System: Experience and Alternatives", National Bureau of Economic Research, Working Paper No. 2464 (December 1987).

78. The Hague Report: Sustainable Development, from Concept to Action, (1992) Jan Pronk and Mahbub ul Haq, available through the United Nations Conference on Environment and Development (UNCED).

79. The Tobin Tax: Coping with Financial Volatility, (1996) Mahbub ul Haq, Inge Kaul, and Isabelle Grunberg, eds. New York, London: Oxford University Press.

80. Taming Global Financial Flows: A Citizen's Guide, (2000). Kavaljit Singh, New York: St Martin's Press, Inc.

81. The United Nations: Policy and Financing Alternatives: Innovative Proposals by Visionary Leaders, (1995) Harlan Cleveland, Hazel Henderson, and Inge Kaul. New York: Apex Press. (Also available in Futures, Vol. 27 No. 2, March 1995.)

82. United Nations Conference on Trade and Development, Andrew Cornford, "The Tobin Tax: Silver Bullet for Financial Volatility, Global Cash Cow or Both?", Geneva, Offprint UNCTAD Review 105-119 (1998).

83. United Nations Department of Economic and Social Affairs, Executive Committee on Economic and Social Affairs, "Towards a new international financial architecture", Task Force Report of the Executive Committee on Economic and Social Affairs of the United Nations.

84. United Nations General Assembly, "Report of the Ad Hoc Open-ended Working Group of the General Assembly on Financing for Development", 2-7, General Assembly Official Records Fifty-fourth Session Supplement No. 28 (A/54/28) New York: United Nations (1999).

85. United Nations General Assembly, "Global Financial Flows and Their Impact on the Developing Countries", Resolution Adopted as Fifty-second Session Agenda Item 95 (a) (January 4, 1998).

86. War on Want Campaign Against World Poverty, "The Global Gamblers: British Banks and the Foreign Exchange Game", London: Fenner Brockway House (Helen Hayward) (1999).

Index

M

N

O

P

Q